T0330790

'Organisations stand between the individual and the intense pressures of our global society. None of us can make sense of the world by ourselves; we need others and a shared task. This thoughtful book explores how organisations make collective work possible, make the irrational more manageable – and how they can fail us. "Containment" is a code word for all of this, and this wide-ranging exploration is essential reading for leaders, scholars, and the rest of us who are trying to make sense of the organisational worlds we are so desperately trying to improve'.

Edward R. Shapiro, MD, *author,* Finding a Place to Stand: Developing Self-Reflective Institutions, Leaders, and Citizens*, 2019*

'This is a bold, surprising and very well organised book. Written simply, but at the same time with great rigour and depth, it follows in the great tradition of the British school of psychoanalysis, which has inspired and enriched the learning of many clinicians and mental health researchers. It also has the merit of being an excellent manual of applied psychoanalysis. Bob Hinshelwood and Tiago Mendes integrate complex knowledge and, in an almost pedagogical way, show us how it is possible to extend clinical elaborations to very diverse fields of human behaviour and the dynamics of social organisations. Well framed historically and theoretically, this book allows the reader to follow the creative development of a long research endeavour, which is of interest to all those involved in the vast field of social science'.

Rui Aragão, *Psychoanalyst, former President of the Portugese Psychoanalytic Society*

'Having long appreciated the contribution Wilfred Bion has made to the understanding of individuals, groups and organisations, I have also sometimes struggled to grasp the full depth and breadth of his insights and contributions. Therefore, I found this book very helpful in increasing my understanding of and high regard for him and the profound influence he has had upon the psychodynamic understanding of people and organisations. In particular, this book sets out its explorations and explications from the ground of Bion's theory of containment and the evolution from which it enabled growth and extension into other fields. Contributors support readers to think and reflect upon these concepts and approaches that assist greater understandings and helpful interventions with individuals, groups, organisations and even beyond into communities. I commend this book to all with a curiosity and desire to strengthen positive interventions into the lives and work of people, groups, organisations and communities'.

Richard Rollinson, *former Director of the Mulberry Bush Therapeutic School in Oxfordshire and Trustee since 2014, consults government departments and organisations in the UK, Ireland and Portugal*

Containment, Organisations and the Working Task

With close attention to Wilfred Bion's influence on the literature about groups and organisations, this book explores how containment has been transposed from the clinical setting to enlighten the work being carried out by psychodynamic practitioners and researchers, especially within organisations.

In the first part, contributors explore the origins of containment, comparing and contrasting it with similar concepts such as holding. A second part is devoted to addressing the implications of utilising psychoanalytic ideas beyond the couch and bringing them to the social field of groups and organisations. The early days of such ideas, as well as the wide range of methods applied, are also addressed in this section with the aim of giving the reader a more comprehensive base for the application of psychoanalytic knowledge. Finally, the third part provides a detailed view of the different applications of containment in consulting, leadership, therapeutic communities and group relations.

Drawing on their own experiences, the authors highlight how psychoanalytic concepts impact their own practice, contributing to a collection that will prove essential for psychoanalysts, managers, policymakers, consultants and researchers in a wide range of professional and clinical settings.

Tiago Mendes is a Psychologist who holds an MBA (Rice University, US) and a PhD in Psychoanalytic Studies (University of Essex, UK).

R.D. Hinshelwood is a Fellow of the British Psychoanalytical Society, Fellow of the Royal College of Psychiatrists and Professor Emeritus, University of Essex, UK.

Containment, Organisations and the Working Task

Edited by Tiago Mendes and R.D. Hinshelwood

Routledge
Taylor & Francis Group

LONDON AND NEW YORK

Designed cover image: Orbon Alija © Getty Images.

First published 2025
by Routledge
4 Park Square, Milton Park, Abingdon, Oxon OX14 4RN

and by Routledge
605 Third Avenue, New York, NY 10158

Routledge is an imprint of the Taylor & Francis Group, an informa business

© 2025 selection and editorial matter, Tiago Mendes and R.D. Hinshelwood; individual chapters, the contributors

The right of Tiago Mendes and R.D. Hinshelwood to be identified as the authors of the editorial material, and of the authors for their individual chapters, has been asserted in accordance with sections 77 and 78 of the Copyright, Designs and Patents Act 1988.

British Library Cataloguing-in-Publication Data
A catalogue record for this book is available from the British Library

Names: Mendes, Tiago, 1978- editor. | Hinshelwood, R. D., editor.
Title: Containment, organisations and the working task / edited by Tiago Mendes and R.D. Hinshelwood.
Description: Abingdon, Oxon ; New York, NY : Routledge, 2024. | Includes bibliographical references and index.
Identifiers: LCCN 2024004067 (print) | LCCN 2024004068 (ebook) | ISBN 9781138505117 (hardback) | ISBN 9781138505131 (paperback) | ISBN 9781315146416 (ebook)
Subjects: LCSH: Organizational behavior. | Small groups--Psychological aspects. | Organizational sociology.
Classification: LCC HM791 .C66 2024 (print) | LCC HM791 (ebook) | DDC 302.3/5--dc23/eng/20240223
LC record available at https://lccn.loc.gov/2024004067
LC ebook record available at https://lccn.loc.gov/2024004068

ISBN: 9781138505117 (hbk)
ISBN: 9781138505131 (pbk)
ISBN: 9781315146416 (ebk)

DOI: 10.4324/9781315146416

Typeset in Times New Roman
by KnowledgeWorks Global Ltd.

To my wife and children, who make everything
possible – Tiago Mendes

Contents

Acknowledgements

We both want to acknowledge the easy-going nature of working with each other on the book, and previously on the research at Essex University, from which the book comes.

Notes on the Contributors

Louisa Diana Brunner, PhD, has been a leadership and organisational consultant and coach for about 30 years and also has longstanding managerial experience. She works with profit and non-profit organisations. She is Advance Practice Lead and Visiting Lecturer for the Professional Doctorate in Consultation and the Organisation at the Tavistock & Portmann NHS Foundation Trust. She is a Faculty Member of GEN (Global Education Network) of the Family Firm Institute. She has been a member of staff (Director or Consultant) of international Group Relations conferences (in person in Cyprus, England, Israel, Italy, Poland, The Netherlands and USA and for two online conferences). She is a founder and Board Member of PCCA (Partners for Confronting Collective Atrocities), an Honorary Member of the Nodo Group (Italy) and a Member of ISPSO and OPUS. She also works at Bocconi University Milano in graduate career orientation and the School of Management MBA in participant selection. Her work has been published and presented at international conferences.

John Diamond worked for 40 years in therapeutic communities for severely emotionally troubled and traumatised children, young people and their families. He retired in 2022 and is now an organisational consultant and practising artist.

Stanley Gold, Psychiatrist, Psychoanalyst and Organisational Consultant. Member and Past President ISPSO 2013. Distinguished Member 2019. Current Member Mental Health Tribunal Victoria Australia. Has published more than 35 scientific papers covering child development, research and behaviour, and racism and socio-dynamic analysis, and two books: *How to Bring Up Your Parents* (1990) and *Unthinkable Evil: Understanding Racism* (2021).

Susan Long is a Melbourne-based Organisational Consultant and Executive Coach. Susan is Professor and Co-Lead for the PhD programme at the National Institute for Organisation Dynamics Australia (NIODA). She has published several books and many articles in books and scholarly journals, is General Editor of the journal *Socioanalysis* and an Associate Editor with *Organisational and Social Dynamics* where she is editing a special edition. Susan is a distinguished member of ISPSO.

Richard Morgan-Jones, Organisational and Group Relations Consultant and Senior Psychoanalytic Psychotherapist with the British Psychotherapy Foundation

& British Psychoanalytic Council. Distinguished member of the International Society for the Psychoanalytic Study of Organizations. Has international experience of teaching, consulting and workshops with universities and organisations. Author of *The Body of the Organisation and its Health* (2010).

Avi Nutkevitch, PhD, Clinical Psychologist, Training Analyst in the Israel Psychoanalytic Society and Organizational Consultant. Co-Director of the Centre for Researching the Psychoanalytic-Systemic Approach, Teacher and Supervisor at the Program in Organizational Consultation and Development: Psychoanalytic-Systemic Approach. Teacher and Supervisor, Israel Psychoanalytic Institute. Member and past Chairperson, OFEK.

Kalina Stamenova, PhD, is an academic, researcher and Organisational Development Consultant working at the University of Essex, UK, a member of OPUS and a Fellow of the Higher Education Academy. She has co-edited a book with R.D. Hinshelwood, *Methods of Research into the Unconscious: Applying Psychoanalytic Ideas to Social Science* (2018). Her current research interests include the unconscious dynamics of hybrid and remote work, and she has recently contributed a chapter to *Leading with Depth* edited by Claudia Nagel on leading by the screen. Kalina is the book review editor for the *Journal of Organisational and Social Dynamics*.

Nuno Torres holds a PhD in Psychoanalytic Studies from the University of Essex, UK. He is editor of two books and has published more than 30 papers in national and international peer-reviewed journals. His academic work is centred on developing a biopsychosocial model integrating socio-emotional developmental and psychoanalytic models to understand the developmental pathways to psychopathology. Presently Nuno's main research interests are centred on the social development of children, adolescents and young adults. More specifically what is the role of Oxytocin in social behaviour, social bonds and problem behaviours. He has taught courses in England and Lisbon both at graduate and undergraduate levels in Developmental Psychology, Developmental Psychopathology, Statistics, Research Methods and Psychoanalysis. He has expertise in both quantitative analysis and qualitative methods including autobiographical in-depth interviews.

Gillian Walker followed a biology degree with research into Freuds' biophysiological model of instinct function. Whilst researching psychoanalytic concepts she became aware of the difficulty in establishing verifiable and reliable research methods. Her PhD thesis on masochism required the creation of an operationalised model of Bion's container-contained model.

Alice White, PhD, is a Digital Editor at Wellcome where she commissions and writes articles about health, science and history. Her research examines the history of psychology and psychiatry in the British military during World War II, and human relations in mid-twentieth century Britain.

Foreword

Louisa Diana Brunner

It was a completely unexpected surprise that Tiago Mendes and Bob Hinshelwood invited me to write this foreword. It is a real honour for me and I am extremely grateful to them for this opportunity. I asked myself, why me? Before reading the draft, I thought I am not a psychoanalyst, therefore what could I offer? Bob convinced me by arguing that they wanted somebody from the world of leadership and organisational consultancy and Group Relations.

This book was and is very much needed. For years I have wondered why so little had been written about containment in the system psychodynamic approach to organisations and Group Relations. It puzzled me because it is such an important and basic dimension to be explored, understood and developed.

This book is very impressive and very well written; it is very thorough conceptually and includes evidence from a variety of interesting practices. It revisits the history of the development of the idea of containment from many perspectives (clinical, organisational, group dynamics, practice, etc.), starting obviously from Bion, Jaques, Klein, Winnicott, Lewin and other authors and considering the institutions involved (i.e. Tavistock and Portman NHS Foundation Trust, Tavistock Institute, AKRI, etc.). Different approaches in the field – systems psycho-dynamic, psychoanalytic-systemic, socioanalysis, psychosocial studies, social psychology, Group Relations – are also presented.

The volume is all-inclusive and it made me think of a handbook about containment where, if one is looking for some definition or concept or source, one will always find references to it (students – you should not use it exclusively, though; you need also to go to the original source!).

How to contain and what has to be contained are questions that any leader, manager or consultant working with organisations is continuously confronted with – often at an intuitive level (or even unconsciously). In this book many authors rightly explore and deepen Bion's concept of container and the contained or, as Morgan-Jones suggests, the idea of contained and the container, or Nutkevich's the container and its containment. They show and highlight how mental states and content can be transformed and processed through different forms of containment so they can transition from destructive to constructive, supporting development and change at an individual, group and organisational level.

This book made me think immediately about what I have been struggling with for years about containment: the tension between structural and content containment. Personally, I am a passionate advocate of structure and design as a means of containment and a pre-condition for the possibility of addressing and working with dynamic processes and mental elements. I often have conversations with colleagues about this topic. Interestingly I have never found anyone to disagree about this in informal conversations. I have had some discussions about Bauman's (2000) idea of today's liquid modernity with colleagues who would argue that in this type of context organisational structure is falling to pieces. This is true, structures do not seem to perform the same function as in the past in containing social systems' anxiety and projections; nowadays everything is more fluid, fragmented and uncertain.

I have applied structural containment to my work as a consultant, in Group Relations conferences and other events. I can agree that it is much more complicated than in the past, because it is counter-cultural, the social forces inhibiting it are very strong, also due to the overarching digital dimension. Therefore, today containment needs much more effort, work and sometimes courage, and also different competences linked to digital working, in order to allow a less difficult, confused and traumatic work dynamic, and improved capacity to carry out the task that the organisation is called to perform. It also fosters an overall work group mentality, helping it to prevail over the regressive push of basic assumptions mentality (French and Simpson, 2010). These authors use the word mentality instead of Bion's (1961) "basic assumption group" or "work group", stating "that [Bion's original] basic assumption and work group definition" can generate confusion since in reality he describes "two group mentalities" (French and Simpson, 2010, p. 1861). A more detailed description of Bion's ideas about basic assumptions and work group can be found throughout the book.

When I started my journey in Group Relations I was very impressed by Eliott Jaques' work. It is not only his earlier ideas about defences against anxiety in groups and organisations, but his initial fundamental contribution to psychoanalytical thinking applied to organisations that has shaped many academics and practitioners in the field; I was intrigued by his ideas in the book *Requisite Organisation* (1989). Jaques revised his main research discovery of social defences against anxiety and advocated for the establishment of a strong structural approach as a container to prevent dysfunctional destructive paranoid anxieties and allow work to be carried out constructively. In a way he was suggesting that the social defences systems apply to failed containment. He also argued that this should be a universal feature that should be applied in any organisational context. This led to splits in the Group Relations and systems–psychodynamic community with some repudiating Jaques' new ideas.

My initial background is in organisational studies and later in life I became involved first in Group Relations and then in systems psychodynamic consultancy and psychosocial research. This imprinting leads me to look first of all at the organisation structure, design and systems and then to group dynamics and individuals. Therefore, Jaques' ideas in *Requisite Organisation* (1989) were not a surprise. His argument about "how to design organisations – or systems of roles – whose nature is such that they can be occupied by people who are enabled to collaborate in pursuing objectives for which the organisation has been established, and which provides a setting for those people to be able to relate to each other with mutual trust, personal dignity, and the opportunity to continue their lifelong working through of paranoid anxieties in a constructive working rather than acting out" (Jaques, 1995, pp. 359–360) makes sense to me. Jaques acknowledges that an organisation has complex tasks, including managing the human aspects of staff as well as efficiency, competitiveness and financial profit. Also Bion (1985) recalls the importance in the psychoanalytical setting of "a location in time and space" (p. 127) as the condition for psychoanalytical observation, exploration and interpretation, tasks to be carried out by the analyst. The organisational structure, design and systems can have some similarity to the therapeutic setting in a broader social, political and economic context.

There is an interesting question concerning whether social defence systems (following Jaques) coincide with containment (following Bion) or whether they are different models for thinking about the management of emotional tensions in organised work. While the concept of social defences was developed within organisational research and consultancy (Jaques, 1955; Menzies-Lyth, 1960), the idea of containment comes from the clinical setting. But with the establishment of systems psychodynamic consultancy and organisational work, especially at the Tavistock and Portman NHS Foundation Trust and the Tavistock Institute, nowadays it is quite often used by many professionals, also in business schools that offer this type of approach. Through its in-depth analysis of these two concepts, this volume seems to suggest that they are two different models for thinking: social defences against anxiety has more to do with symptoms arising from underlying unconscious dynamics, e.g. task resistance or work load demands, while containment is more concerned with the conditions for development.

Why was the requisite organisation felt to be so subversive? Is it because Jaques repudiated the psychoanalytical stance that it has been so difficult to acknowledge the value of the other part of his thinking? Required structure can go a long way to eradicating the needs for social defences. The point is that healthy containment by structure and clear lines of accountability contain the tensions which otherwise may interfere with efficiency and productivity.

For any leader, management or organisational consultant, not just in the domain of applied psychoanalysis, structure, design, task, authority, accountability, and boundaries are obvious parts of the container-contained dynamic and of containment, as also several authors in this book argue from different perspectives. Nevertheless, as French and Simpson rightly observed in 2010, the integration of organisational studies with more psychoanalytical thinking had not fully occurred.

But now, more than 30 years after Jaques' *Requisite Organisation* (1989) was published, it seems to me that the authors of this book have moved forwards by discussing containment from many angles and perspectives, including the more structural one, in a way seeking to repair or reconcile the spilt that was also created by Jaques himself. Although perhaps this is not always explicitly developed and referred to (the wound is still open), one can read it between the lines, especially in the last section about application (Long, Morgan-Jones, Gold, Diamond, Nutkevich).

Thank you Tiago and Bob and all the authors for providing so much food for thought and so many insights through their generous and passionate contributions to this book, which is an important development of the ideas about containment in the field of applied psychoanalysis to groups, organisations and also organisational studies, and will prove to be very helpful both for academics and practitioners.

References

Bauman, Z. (2000) *Liquid Modernity*. Cambridge: Polity Press.

Bion, W.R. (1961) *Experiences in Groups and Other Papers*. London: Routledge.

French, R. and Simpson, P. (2010) The "work group": Redressing the balance in Bion's experiences in groups. *Human Relations*, 63(12), pp. 1859–1878.

Jaques, E. (1955) Social systems as a defence against persecutory and depressive anxiety. In *New Directions in Psycho-Analysis*. London: Tavistock Publications; New York: Basic Books.

Jaques, E. (1989) *Requisite Organisation*. Arlington, VA: Cason Hall & Co.

Jaques, E. (1995) Reply to Dr. Gilles Amado. *Human Relations*, 48(4), pp. 359–365.

Menzies-Lyth, I. (1960) A case-study in the functioning of social systems as a defence against anxiety: A report on a study of the nursing service of a general hospital. *Human Relations*, 3(2), pp. 95–183.

Introduction

The psychoanalytic approach to groups and organisations has steadily developed as a semi-autonomous psychoanalytic tradition following the seminal work of Bion (1959, 1962, 1970), Jaques (1951, 1953), Isabel Menzies Lyth (1960), Eric Trist (1950 [1990]; Trist and Bamforth 1951) and A.K. Rice (1958), giving rise to important concepts such as Primary Task, Social Defence Systems and Basic Assumptions. Such conceptual development was continuously influenced by concepts and ideas stemming from the clinical practice of psychoanalysis as a source conceptualisation and inspiration. One idea that has decisively influenced the psychodynamic literature on organisations has been Bion's theory of containment (Gabriel 1999). In fact, several authors maintain that organisations should contain the anxiety of workers or discuss the role of containment in organisations, but far too often the concept has been used in a wide array of situations, eroding its meaning. This was the starting point for the present book: how can a psychoanalytic theory of emotional maturation be useful for those who study and work with groups and organisations. Such was not an easy task, given the growth that the concept has experienced in the past few decades. But we also saw such developments as proof that we were somehow on the right track and that interest in the topic would abound, and different authors might join this effort and contribute with their unique point of view.

But where to start such an endeavour. Clearly just highlighting every different way in which the concept was applied would not only be tedious, but also quite unhelpful. It has a history of almost 70 years, going back to Bion's early work with psychotic patients, and as it gained momentum became a hallmark of psychodynamic practice, at least for the more Kleinian inclined. We decided that the book should somehow reflect the reality, the journey of moving from a clinical concept to a group and organisation. In this way we could be truthful to reality while we accompanied the journey of the concept, as it were. This seemed a good starting point. So we decided to start a first part dedicated simply to the origins of containment and gathered different chapters to highlight what could be its main characteristics and what would set it apart from other similar concepts. This was easier said than done, but Part I provides the basis for our understanding of containment.

DOI: 10.4324/9781315146416-1

The second part of our journey starts with the strange route of cross-fertilisation. That is, of transposing psychoanalytic concepts and applying them to other fields, instead of the clinical setting. While this has been done successfully, criticisms of other disciplines are also relevant. So for this second part of the book, we collected chapters that would resonate with readers regarding the early efforts of working with organisations, the different methodologies used and even the links that can be established with other disciplines. We aimed for this part to build momentum towards the final part, while also arming practitioners with a set of ideas on how clinical concepts might be used to study different fields. A criticism might be made in the sense that this part does not study containment *per se*, but is rather an interlude for the third part.

What we aimed for in the final part was to show the breadth of applications of containment. Different authors provided their own views on topics ranging from leadership to consulting and therapeutic communities. We still attempted to provide a brief overview of the field, more as the basis for future development, but showing how the concept seems to have gained a life of its own, far beyond what Bion might expect. Of course, with greater use comes a greater need for conceptual clarity. And it hasn't always been the case, so this part also pledges that a common ground might be found that allows for conceptual unification.

Our own interest in this specific topic should also be noted. One of the editors (TM) first became interested in containment and organisations by a matter of pure chance. I had recently graduated as a Clinical Psychologist when I come across the paper 'A psychoanalytical perspective on social institutions' by Isabel Menzies Lyth (1990). I can still remember today my surprise as I read it at discovering how psychoanalytic knowledge could be effectively applied to improve organisational settings such as hospitals or coal mines. As my interest in the field grew, I decided to pursue a PhD at the Centre for Psychoanalytic Studies of the University of Essex, supervised by Bob Hinshelwood, addressing the links between Social Defence Systems (Jaques 1953; Menzies Lyth 1960) and Bion's concept of containment (1959, 1962, 1970). I (RDH) was very keen on Tiago Mendes' doctoral thesis exploring the function of containing in mental health. Nowhere is there a greater need for the containment of human suffering than in the institutions devoted to caring for those during their psychotic episodes. And yet such institutions do it so badly. I was shocked as a medical student in the early 1960s by the wretched zoo-like conditions those people were accommodated in. The capacity to contain them whilst preserving (and restoring their mental faculties) was failing. Institutionalisation was rife (Martin 1955) and represented a specifically rigid perversion of containment which stripped self-regulation abilities from the inmates. This ill-health of the institution was, in the UK, 'treated' by closing those institutions. The success of that solution is not altogether clear (Leff 1997; Chow 2016).

At the time such institutionalisation was becoming recognised in the 1950s and 1960s in the UK, psychoanalytic approaches were beginning to be applied to health care institutions and other working organisations. Jaques (1953) and Menzies Lyth (1960) revealed what came to be known as Social Defence Systems that developed as the group relations paradigm for working with organisations as consultants (Obholzer and Roberts 1994). This approach had emerged alongside the understanding of the interactive process of container-contained in the clinical practice of psychoanalysis itself (Bion 1959, 1962). Both Social Defence Systems and containment had a lot in common and they were descriptive models of the way the social contexts enable individuals to manage their own anxieties, either defensively or healthily. However there appear to be some important differences between the two approaches which Tiago's thesis explored with clarity in mental health institutions. That research therefore evolved into this obviously fruitful project which you the reader have in your hands. This book attempts to collect and to some extent compare different approaches to organisations that have been inspired by psychoanalysis.

Finally, this book has experienced a number of setbacks, not least of which a global pandemic that affected everyone and seems to have also required emotional containment. The writing process was also affected by the pandemic and it took longer than initially expected to be published. We acknowledge the efforts of all the authors involved and their patience with this longer process. As any task, this book is also the result of a transformation process and we expect that its output will enlighten and enliven any potential reader.

References

Bion, W.R. (1959) Attacks on linking. *International Journal of Psychoanalysis* 40: 308–315.

Bion, W. (1962) *Learning from Experience*. London: Tavistock Publications.

Bion, W. (1970) *Attention and Interpretation*. London: Karnac Books.

Chow, W.S. (2016) How has the extent of institutional mental healthcare changed in Western Europe? Analysis of data since 1990. http://bmjopen.bmj.com/content/6/4/e010188.long

Gabriel, Y. (1999) *Organizations in Depth*. London: Karnac Books.

Jaques, E. (1951) *The Changing Culture of a Factory*. London: Tavistock Publications.

Jaques (1953) On the dynamics of social structure: A contribution to the psychoanalytical study of social phenomena deriving from the views of Melanie Klein. In E. Trist and H. Murray (eds), *The Social Engagement of Social Science*, Vol. I. London: Free Association Books.

Leff, J. (1997) (ed.) *Care in the Community: Illusion or Reality*. Chichester: Wiley.

Martin, D. (1955) Institutionalisation. *Lancet* 2: 1188–1190.

Menzies Lyth, I. (1960) The functioning of social systems as a defence against anxiety. In I. Menzies Lyth (ed.) (1988), *Containing Anxiety in Institutions*. London: Free Association Books.

Menzies Lyth, I. (1990) A psychoanalytical perspective on social institutions. In E. Trist and H. Murray (eds), *The Social Engagement of Social Science*, Vol. I. London, Free Association Books.

Obholzer, A. and Roberts, V. (1994) *The Unconscious at Work*. London: Routledge.

Rice, A. K. (1958) *Productivity and Social Organization*. London: Tavistock Publications.

Trist, E. (1950) Culture as a psycho-social process. In E. Trist and H. Murray (eds) (1990), *The Social Engagement of Social Science*, Vol. I. London, Free Association Books.

Trist, E. and Bamforth, K. (1951) Some social and psychological consequences of the long-wall method of coal getting. *Human Relations* 4(2): 3–38.

Part I

Conceptual Origins and (Dis)Entanglements

Even Ideas Have Origins

A famous saying describes the breakthroughs in science as being done by dwarfs on the shoulders of giants. It is hard to find a more appropriate description regarding the progresses in psychoanalytic theory and practice, given the richness of its history and continuously growing literature. The endeavour of exploring the multiplicity of views in the application of a particular psychoanalytic concept which, despite its success, is clearly affiliated with a particular tradition can be seen in the light of this saying. In fact, what we propose in Part I is to contribute to the field by attempting to shed some light on the conceptual origins of *containment*, and then attempt to contrast and compare with other similar ideas. The three chapters that compose this part address Bion's concept from different angles, its origins, its links with emotional regulation, and its developmental and degrees of contact with Winnicott's *holding*. They also detail Bion's work, by resorting to different aspects and examples from Bion.

The first chapter ('The Antecedents and Development of Container-Contained' by R.D. Hinshelwood) addresses containment, from a historical point of view, detailing how the term was originally employed by Carl Jung to depict interpersonal exchanges. Although Bion himself never recognised the borrowing of the term, he did read and attend the lectures where Jung approached the matter. During the 50s the projection of parts of the self into the object was the focus of much attention and exploration by the Kleinian group, namely through the work of Money-Kirle and Elliott Jaques, where one can see the antecedents of the concept that Bion brought to a more mature form. The present chapter addresses the early work being done in this fertile period, namely the work of Money-Kyrle and his description of a session where a deep exchange of emotional states occurred. At the same time, analysts working at the Tavistock Institute were also experimenting with ideas of introjection and projection, albeit in an organisational context, such as a factory. The chapter expands this idea to settings such as hospitals and care homes, showing how they become part of organisational culture and become powerful forces deeply ingrained in the culture of organisations. The experience of projective-introjective exchanges drives the behaviour of employees in these settings, where attitudes towards the task at hand are shaped by unconscious anxiety. Pointing towards the future, a note of warning is given arguing that the evolution of Bion's concept

DOI: 10.4324/9781315146416-2

should not shy away from stress management in organisations and even the selection process of managers, who should be selected also by their ability to contain the anxieties of their subordinates. An important point, especially in present times where organisations focus mainly on productivity.

The second chapter ('Emotional Containment and Emotional Regulation' by Nuno Torres and Tiago Mendes) addresses containment in greater detail, focusing on emotional containment of raw affects and, based on the work of Bion (1962) and Hinshelwood (1988), highlighting that containment can have three fundamental forms: rigid, fragmented and flexible. In the first form the container rigidly crushes the content; in the second form the container is shattered by the content; finally, the flexible mode enables a mutually enriching relation that is beneficial for both. The different modes of containment, two of them mal-adaptive and one adaptive allow for a more complex view of the concept than the notion of 'containing'. Drawing on the work of several authors, a detailed view of the pre-verbal patterns of emotional interaction and the potential pitfalls where the process can break down are depicted. This allows the authors to attempt a formalisation of the process and connect it with another important concept, that of emotional regulation. This chapter makes the case that emotional regulation and containment can be seen as the same phenomena being looked at through different vertices.

Chapter 3 ('On Containment and Holding – A Short Introductory Note' by Tiago Mendes) picks up from the previous chapter and dives into the questions arising from the potential links and separations between Bion's *containment* and Winnicott's *holding*. Not an easy task, but given its current relevance in the literature, an important one. This chapter starts with an assertion that although both concepts originate in different branches of the psychoanalytic genealogical tree, nonetheless with the passing of time they appear ever more as interchangeable. This has been raised in the past few years by different analysts (Ogden 2004; Bott Spillius et al. 2011; Caldwell 2018) and has spilled over to the tradition of applying psychoanalytic knowledge to organisations. Certainly, a natural path one might consider, although one that should nonetheless be addressed given the concepts' different origins, traditions and possibly even meanings. In this sense, this chapter endeavours to address Bion's concept, detailing his description of a patient (Bion 1959) that serves as the basis for his model, highlighting its origins in his *psychotic period* and the key issues which arise from it, and briefly highlighting how Bion made different usages of the concept throughout his work. Winnicott, on the other hand, was very involved with evacuee children at the time, and studied the impact of a context of deprivation in such children. Both authors were concerned with the baby-mother relationship, but looked at it from different points of view, addressing different types of patients and, even more so, from different theoretical affiliations. Winnicott adhered to Freud's notion of primary narcissism, while Bion, a staunch Kleinian, supported the view that object relations were present from birth. This chapter ends with an attempt to highlight some of the differences between both ideas, while also exposing some of their similarities. More than casting a definitive light on the subject matter, this chapter attempts to raise questions regarding conceptual integration for practitioners of the systems psychodynamics field.

To finalise, these chapters raise different points and try to show how Bion himself seemed to have left us not with a clear-cut definition of a concept, but with an idea to which he kept returning throughout his work, through different points of view. Herein probably lies the great richness of the concept, but also its greatest pitfall. We hope this section may contribute to shed light on the concept, its evolution, but also its place and connection to the vast and rich ecosystem of psychoanalytical psychology.

References

Bion, W.R. (1959) Attacks on linking. *International Journal of Psychoanalysis*, 40, pp. 308–315.

Bion, W.R. (1962) *Learning from Experience*. London: Tavistock Publications.

Bott Spillius, E., Milton, J., Garvey, P., Couve, C., and Steiner, D. (2011) *The New Dictionary of Kleinian Thought*. Abingdon: Routledge.

Caldwell, L. (2018) A psychoanalysis of being: An approach to Donald Winnicott. *British Journal of Psychotherapy*, 34(2), pp. 221–239.

Hinshelwood, R.D. (1988) Models of demoralization. *British Journal of Psychotherapy*, 5, pp. 218–227.

Ogden, T. (2004) On holding and containing, being and dreaming. *International Journal of Psychoanalysis*, 85, pp. 1349–1364.

Chapter 1

The Antecedents and Development of Container-Contained

R.D. Hinshelwood

The understanding of the process of containing first emerged in psychoanalytic work with adult patients, and can be attributed to Bion's classic paper, 'Attacks on linking' (1959, and see later). A few remarks are necessary to describe how the conception of 'container-contained' arose and was developed as a model for the emotional side of organisational life, as well as the development of that thinking.

Interestingly the term came from an original interpersonal usage, when Jung (1925) used the term about a married couple. Bion had read Jung and went to his lectures at the Tavistock Clinic in the 1930s. Jung viewed a kind of mutual ex-change of personality traits as an innate part of intergender relations:

> It is an almost regular occurrence for a woman to be wholly contained, spiritu-ally, in her husband, and for a husband to be wholly contained, emotionally, in his wife. One could describe this as the problem of the 'contained' and the container.
>
> (Jung 1925, CW 17, para. 331C)

Bion never acknowledged this connection with his early interest. And in fact, it was almost incidental when he was investigating schizophrenic states in the 1950s. At that time he was experimenting with Klein's schizoid mechanisms, in particular projective identification. Bion's initial description is:

> When the patient strove to rid himself of fears of death which were felt to be too powerful for his personality to contain he split off his fears and put them into me, the idea apparently being that if they were allowed to repose there long enough they would undergo modification by my psyche and could then be safely reintrojected.
>
> (Bion 1959, p. 312)

Bion's contribution was to link the process of containing in the clinical setting of adult analysis with a major process of development at the beginning of life. The not-yet-verbal relationship between a mother and her baby involves the transmis-sion of powerful experiences and emotions. The baby's experiences will actually

DOI: 10.4324/9781315146416-3

enter its mother and she will literally feel for her baby. When a baby screams with increasing desperation as if he/she will die, a mother will in parallel begin to feel equally alarmed and she has to keep a presence of mind to convert the desperation into some reasonable understanding – shall we say, the baby needs a feed. Then she offers the nipple, and the baby takes the food, although in addition, begins to take something else – the understanding that the particular prompt for his desperation has a meaning – he needs feeding. This mother can supply some relevant mental functioning as well as the food, so that the baby can begin slowly to process its own experiences.

This is not merely a psychological defence against the intolerable anxiety – although it can be – but it is also an attempt at communicating with others who might be expected to help manage it. This form of projective identification has come to be called communicative and it implies a view of human interaction that suggests a penetrative quality. We are receptive to communications through feeling in empathic ways the actual feelings others put across to us.

The Social and Organisational

The passing of one's experiences into other people has been known for a long time by psychologists. For instance, Gustav LeBon (1895) used the term 'contagion' for the kind of infectious emotion in a group or crowd of people, such as football fans or at a pop concert. In fact, that word 'fan' is likely to have come from 'fanatic', which indicates intense and uncritical emotion. From the 1890s, Freud used the term 'projection' to describe this kind of attribution of some mental entity of one-self to another person. And his book on group psychology (Freud 1921) dwells at length on the emotional commitment people make to groups and organisations, including the small group of a couple in love, and also a hypnotist and his client.

It must be quite clear to us all how we can be affected emotionally by other people's emotions. In a pub, if there is a group of people laughing and enjoying a jokey conversation together, the feelings go around the members of the group freely. But anyone not part of the group will be much less likely to laugh even if they have heard the jokes. In fact, if someone outside the group does laugh, it is almost a request to join the group.

The impact of one person's feelings on another is not perhaps a prominent topic in social psychology, apart from psychoanalysis. But in fact, attributing certain feelings to others and certain aspects of personality to them is an everyday activity of everyone. We are all aware of others as that awareness is, simply, a part of being social. We are actively engaged in getting each other to feel and respond to things from within ourselves. And we are on the whole willingly open to other's feelings and experiences. This is quite normal, though it quickly extends into the less normal forms which psychoanalysts study. This makes the transmission, even contagion, of emotion an important aspect of understanding organisations. The prevalence of emotions in a working organisation can at times be regarded as an impediment in achieving the task. Or perhaps it is seen as so common it is easier to take the phenomenon for granted. Or some management teams seek to manipulate those emotions in order to improve commitment to, and motivation for, the organisation.

In technical terms the transmission of feelings and experiences between people is termed 'projection' and 'introjection', but may also involve the interchange of those psychological functions which produce the experiences that are projected. The example of the baby is a simple transfer of mother's function of understanding the hunger into a baby who can acquire that understanding for themselves. This kind of relating between people in which aspects of one personality – experiences, and functions – are transmitted is clearly fundamental for social psychology and therefore for organisational functioning and management. Psychoanalysts have called projection and introjection 'primitive' processes because it is apparent that they are a major form of communication in early life before the acquisition of language. As mentioned they imply a degree of instability of the personality as aspects may come and go. Technically this process of projecting a part of oneself depends on a splitting of the self into bits, or at least splitting off away from the self some bit that is painful, and anxiety-producing or conflicted. Freud (1927, 1938) had called it a 'splitting of the ego'. Although quite normal at the earliest stages of development, these primitive processes continue to be used unconsciously in various ways all through life, notably at times of stress.

The pattern of interpersonal transmission that we have been following was used, from the early 1950s, to understand aspects of social life. For instance, Elliott Jaques made observations on organisations, and described:

> Individuals may put their internal conflicts into persons in the external world, unconsciously follow the course of the conflict by means of projective identification, and re-internalize the course and outcome of the externally perceived conflict by means of introjective identification.
>
> (Jaques 1955, p. 497)

Thus one important feature of the unconscious dynamics of groups is that people will avoid the kind of conflicts they have in their own internal world and see it, as it were, in the external world. One very common example is the way people will see others as if they were a super-ego making a compelling demand to avoid certain behaviour. They thus see their internal conflict with their super-ego as if it were a strict demand from someone else. Even very ordinary behaviour is controlled from outside like this, for example almost everyone stops at traffic lights which control your behaviour in a car, for obvious advantage. A person can literally give up their own judgement in favour of an outside 'super-ego'. In a sense that person is not fully themselves. Perhaps we should not be so fully ourselves at moments (at a crossroads for instance) when we do not have the knowledge to judge responsibly. As far as the traffic is concerned, it is necessary that drivers give up a fragment of their autonomy to respect the need for traffic management.

It gets more serious if social forms begin to dictate behaviour (and supersede our own judgements) on a broader scale. Something of this sort takes place on a larger (even alarming) scale in more authoritarian and dictatorial cultures (Hinshelwood

1997). In cases of madness, assessment of an appropriate fitness to make realistic judgements is the work of psychiatrists. One can say that there is a splitting of the ego or of the personality. One part, the capacity for judgement in this instance, is separated off and it is then seen in some external object – the traffic light or a policeman or some other authority figure. We do not consciously experience these splitting and projection processes, but there is a sense of weakness and compliance that results. Melanie Klein when describing these primitive processes wrote: "As far as the ego is concerned the excessive splitting off and expelling into the outer world of parts of itself considerably weaken it" (Klein 1946, p. 8).

This kind of sharing out of mental capacities is an implicit or hidden feature of organisations. In fact, it can be a useful division of labour – some people have capacities for understanding IT, others for human resources, and so on. In organisations it is possible to make use of this propensity to share out mental capacities. It is like a team on a building site – different people have and develop different skills, the carpenter, the electrician, the plasterer and so on. To some extent this can be true of people specialising in different mental capacities.

In a strongly hierarchical organisation certain capacities are projected upwards and we see in the person of one's manager the capacity to make decisions and take responsibilities which we are, sometimes, relieved to give up. The capacity for making decisions and taking responsibility is not just implicit but quite explicit in a conscious sense when we adopt a specified role. What is implicit is when the relief of giving over responsibility is unrealistic. It is known that in healthcare organisations, the responsibility for making decisions about patients whose condition may deteriorate or who may die is very onerous, and the temptation is to offload some of the simplest decisions to a superordinate layer of authority (Menzies Lyth 1959, and see later). There is a kind of dumping process for relief, and it so often goes on without awareness, or in psychoanalytic terms, at an unconscious level.

Such unconscious activities within organisations are probably more prevalent than we anticipate, and are in fact ubiquitous. But it is likely that they are more prevalent in those organisations where there is a high level of stress, and the overall (primary) task is very onerous – like healthcare. The danger is that these primitive mechanisms – splitting and projection – can be exploited to avoid more responsible aspects of the work which are painful, conflicted or especially stressful. Responsibility can be painful if it threatens to result in guilt and blame, and so in certain situations it may be more comfortable to avoid it and leave someone else to take the responsibility. There is an important potential here to be aware of. By using projective opportunities individuals may avoid painful experiences.

Disturbed Containment

It is clear from what has been said so far that the containing of others' feelings and functions can be of important developmental value. And equally they can be a defensive process where responsibility conflict and other personally painful experiences are avoided with the risk of distorting organisational work.

The attempts at projection may not always achieve either the dumping result or the communicative result. As the analyst Hanna Segal said:

[A] great deal can go wrong in the projection. The relation between the container and the contained may be felt as mutually destructive or mutually emptying, as well as being mutually creative.

(Segal 1978, p. 317)

The forms of destructiveness that go on, and the forms of dumping, are numerous. Such mutually harming processes may go on between individuals and between groups within working organisations. The phenomenology of these unconscious processes is therefore useful to keep in mind when untoward occurrences take place in an organisation.

It is important to remember that the sharing out of the mental capacities across a team or organisation serves two possible functions. On one hand the important division of labour which has enabled extraordinary achievements of human civilisation, and on the other, projection outwards of certain mental functions can serve the purpose, unconsciously, of avoiding mental experiences and personal conflicts, with detrimental effects on the task. From the point of view of an organisation with a task in hand, the peace of mind of the individuals may come to interfere with achieving the task.

Some Examples

There are many and varied examples of the process of container-contained in the literature. Here, I shall start with the example of a process in an analytic setting because it is precisely where the whole idea came from, and also it is so well described by the analyst it is easily understandable and accessible. For the purposes of illustrating as simply as possible, the following is an instance of a case by the psychoanalyst Roger Money-Kyrle, published in 1956:

[A male patient arrived very anxious because] he had not been able to work in his office. He had also felt vague on the way as if he might get lost or run over; and he despised himself for being useless.

(p. 362)

He presented quite consciously the experience of feeling useless. At first, he used words, and the analyst made a link:

Remembering a similar occasion, on which he had felt depersonalized over a week-end and dreamed that he had left his 'radar' set in a shop and would be unable to get it before Monday, I thought he had, in phantasy, left parts of his 'good self' in me. But I was not very sure of this, or of other interpretations I began to give.

(p. 362)

The analyst himself began to feel unsure now – about his interpretations. Perhaps he is making premature interpretations, with a rather intellectual link. Perhaps he wanted to reassure himself, and so not have to feel the patient's uselessness:

> [The patient] soon began to reject them [the interpretations] all with a mounting degree of anger; and, at the same time, abused me for not helping. By the end of the session he was no longer depersonalized, but very angry and contemptuous instead. It was I who felt useless and bemused.
>
> (Money-Kyrle, 1956, pp. 362–363)

Perhaps it is understandable that the patient rejected the interpretation if the analyst did. But an interactive process between two minds is striking; first the patient came feeling vague and useless. And then by the end of the session, it had changed; the analyst felt useless.

This described a session of clinical psychoanalysis, but it is an intra-psychic process that manifested itself in an exchange between two minds. They interconnect in a deep way; one penetrated the other with the painful feelings.

Social and Organisational Psychology

This interactive process between the insides of two minds has developed the understanding of how the unconscious minds interact – outside the zone of awareness for either. They were taken up in the process of developing what might be called a social psychoanalysis. It is one that concerns the unconscious aspects of the mind, but it is parallel to a social psychology's interest in the conscious experiences of being social.

There follows now a couple of examples where this understanding of the way organisations are used to contain painful issues has been very explanatory.

A Nursing Culture

Working with Jaques' model, Isabel Menzies conducted a research project on a nursing service where the working practices appeared to have maladaptive results. She became interested in the way in which the practice, as conducted, had deleterious effects on aspects of the work. For instance, the anxiety arising from the responsibility for the care of people who might die, were frightened of serious or mutilating operations and so on, led to a particular psychological manoeuvre to reduce the sense of responsibility and potential guilt a nurse was constantly threatened by. One of the strategies was to project responsibility up the hierarchy, thus diminishing the personal responsibility. Moreover, the more senior members of the service did take on even elementary decision-making – introjecting the responsibility. This had the ultimate effect that senior people were making very mundane day-to-day decisions. This was detrimental as it hindered those managers from their own particular responsibilities in their senior positions. It also left junior nurses doing a job in a more routine mechanical manner with a less personal quality than they were professionally trained for. That led to a more distant relation with the patients who they cared for, and a diminished job satisfaction. As a result, many left the service.

This projective/introjective process occurred more or less without awareness and was carried in the implicit attitudes towards authority and responsibility in the culture of this service, and became embedded in the routines of the practice, as well as situated as defences within the unconscious minds of the nurses.

Care Homes

The understanding of Elliott Jaques (1955) was mentioned and quoted above concerning the projective-introjective interchange and its use to deal with internal conflicts which can be externalised. In a later study, Miller and Gwynne (1972) investigated a company that ran care homes for the permanently disabled. They found that under the stress of cases which provoked a good deal of sadness, the staff culture of the carers developed in ways not always helpful to the work and the long-term well-being of the inmates. In fact, there were two alternative trends in the cultural attitudes. One was that the inmates were permanently disabled and could expect to do nothing – which was not always the case and led to bleaker lives than necessary. The practice (in some of the homes) subsided into what was dubbed as a 'warehousing' approach, where inmates were merely fed and watered, with minimum attention or personal contact, which relieved staff of feeling responsible. The other attitude (in other homes), was the view that however disabled, everyone still had some abilities and talents which could be trained and developed so that everyone could live a near normal life. This was dubbed the 'horticultural' approach. The generalisation of normality could not apply to everyone, and many were pushed beyond their limits to their own disappointment and the disappointment of their carers.

Thus, two separate attitudes developed: one assumed an excessive helplessness; and the other denied real disability. Both were unhelpful to the residents but did help the carers as a defence against the sad in-between where severe disability was not necessarily a complete helplessness. That division in the culture led to the avoidance of real engagement to consider the actual capacities of each individual.

Evolution of Container-Contained: Issues and Questions

There have been many of these studies showing a cultural drift towards implicit attitudes which in the end hinder the work but provide a relief of conflicts and anxieties (see Trist and Murray 1990; Obholzer and Roberts 1994).

It is also important to be clear that there are two distinct versions of the projective-introjective strategy of containing. The first is, as indicated, to abolish from one's own mind a disturbing experience and leave it to someone else. Such a process is that of the junior nurse who avoids painful and risky responsibility by passing decisions upwards. It is a kind of 'dumping' into others. In contrast there is the communicative kind of strategy in which the intention is a kind of communication and plea for help.

Creative Cultures

Bion (1970) attempted to develop the containing idea as a theory of unconscious aspects of social life, creative and deleterious. He tended on the whole to see the individual as having the creative potential (the 'genius') and that individual is in a social context of a culture which can allow or stifle potential. He cites the Elizabethan era in England when the social culture allowed both the mushrooming of creative writers with literary masterpieces and the development of the language itself. This prompts organisations to consider the necessary creative conditions for performing its task.

Stress Management

Because high-stress tasks can so easily slip into cultural practices which deal unconsciously with the individual's distress rather than the task, examples here have been of health and social care. But there are many other high-stress occupations. Police and army personnel have acute peak stresses for instance. I have often wondered what it is like to work in an ammunitions factory, knowing what your product is going to do. This points to the need in many organisations to specifically consider a stress-management system just as carefully as a financial management system. It does of course require quite different capacities for thought. Numbers on a spreadsheet can also distract from painful gut responses which need to be contained.

Management Selection

Large organisations have HR departments. The kind of thinking in this book places some onus on the selection of managers who can help their staff to face stress, and to face it with them. Selection is not always done with this issue clearly in mind. How indeed might it be done?

Many or most organisations are organised in hierarchical levels with an unthinking assumption perhaps that more senior managers will contain anxiety from lower levels. This may be appropriate, but it may not. In some tasks, containing the stress may need to be shared rather than made the responsibility of a level above. The nursing service described above could be a good example. Or organisations where there is no selection, the monarchy for instance, may have to depend heavily on lower levels to support them emotionally – at times of a national war for instance.

Indeed, these kinds of issues may not be easily addressed. Part of the purpose of this book is to emphasise the need to address them more readily.

In Conclusion

Its implicit or truly unconscious quality has made it very hard to focus on the role of emotional containment in many management practices. However, there are instances where no amount of *conscious* effort to solve a problem has managed to achieve a resolution. That is the point when it is then worth having in one's arsenal a knowledge of how strategies and practices may develop *unconsciously* and elude those conscious strategies.

The recognition of primitive mechanisms, typically of the pre-verbal phase of early infancy, and its recurrence in later life, has alerted organisational consultants to the unconscious level of the need in organisations to contain high levels of stress. It is important to recognise the social containing function of certain behaviours and practices, but we need to understand when those social defences fail and evident anxiety comes to the fore and interferes with performance.

The early examples of container-contained in organisations imply that at times there are problems that cannot be explained with models that do not take account of the unconscious. This recognition, originally the profession of psychoanalysts, has expanded to include the widespread understanding of the unconscious level of interactions in small and large working organisations, and therefore the need for the specific management of stress in the organisation.

References

Bion, W.R. (1959) Attacks on linking. *International Journal of Psychoanalysis 40*: 308–315. Republished in Bion (1967) *Second Thoughts*: 93–109. London: Heinemann; in Elizabeth Bott Spillius (1988) *Melanie Klein, Today*, Volume 1. London: Routledge; in *The Complete Works of W.R. Bion*, Vol VI: 138–152. London: Karnac.

Bion, W.R. (1970) *Attention and Interpretation*. London: Tavistock. In *The Complete Works of W.R. Bion*, Vol VI: 211–347. London: Karnac.

Freud, S. (1921) *Group Psychology and the Analysis of the Ego*. In *The Standard Edition of the Complete Works of Sigmund Freud, Volume XVIII*: 67–143. London: Hogarth.

Freud, S. (1927) *Fetishism*. In *The Standard Edition of the Complete Psychological Works of Sigmund Freud, Volume XXI*: 147–158. London: Hogarth.

Freud, S. (1938) *Splitting of the Ego in the Process of Defence*. In *The Standard Edition of the Complete Psychological Works of Sigmund Freud, Volume XXIII*: 271–278. London: Hogarth.

Hinshelwood, R.D. (1997) *Therapy or Coercion: Does Psychoanalysis Differ from Brain-Washing?* London: Karnac Books.

Jaques, E. (1955) Social systems as a defence against persecutory and depressive anxiety. In M. Klein, P. Heimann & R. Money-Kyrle (eds) *New Directions in Psychoanalysis*: 478–498. London: Tavistock.

Jung, C.G. (1925) Marriage as a psychological relationship. *The Collected Works of Carl Jung* 17: 187–201. London: Routledge and Kegan Paul.

Klein, M. (1946) Notes on some schizoid mechanisms. *International Journal of Psycho-Analysis 27*: 99–110; republished in Melanie Klein, Paula Heimann, Susan Isaacs and Joan Riviere (1952) *Developments in Psycho-Analysis*: 292–320. London: Hogarth. Republished in 1975 in *The Writings of Melanie Klein, Volume 3*: 1–24. London: Hogarth.

LeBon, G. (1895) *Psychologie des foules*. Paris: Alcan. English translation, (1995) as *The Crowd*. Brunswick and London: Transaction Publishers.

Menzies Lyth, Isabel (1959) The functioning of social systems as a defence against anxiety: A report on a study of the nursing service of a general hospital. *Human Relations* 13: 95–121. Republished in Menzies (1988) *Containing Anxiety in Institutions*. London: Free Association Books; and in Trist and Murray (eds) (1990) *The Social Engagement of Social Science*. London: Free Association Books.

Miller, E. and Gwynne, G. (1972) *A Life Apart*. London: Tavistock.

Money-Kyrle, R. (1956) Normal counter-transference and some of its deviations. *International Journal of Psychoanalysis 37*: 360–366. Republished (1978) in *The Collected Papers of Roger Money-Kyrle*. Perthshire: Clunie Press. And republished in Elizabeth Spillius (1988) *Melanie Klein Today, Volume 2*. London: Routledge.

Obholzer, A. and Roberts, V. (eds.) (1994) *The Unconscious at Work*. London: Routledge.

Segal, H. (1978) On symbolism. *International Journal of Psychoanalysis 59*: 315–319.

Trist, E. and Murray, H. (1990) *The Social Engagement of Social Science: A Tavistock Anthology, Volume 1: The Socio-Psychological Perspective*. London: Free Association Books.

Chapter 2

Emotional Containment and Emotional Regulation

Nuno Torres and Tiago Mendes

Introduction

The model of emotional containment devised by Bion is a complex but inspiring one. Bion played with ideas and did not leave us with a complete formulation of his model. Nonetheless, it is possible to extrapolate some of its key features and shared complementarities with other ideas that go beyond psychoanalysis, such as emotional regulation. The present chapter addresses the model devised by Bion, arguing that it sustains different modes of dealing with emotional experience.

Emotional Containment of Raw Affects

We will address a theoretical framework about the strategies for dealing with emotions at a raw and pre-verbal stage; when an emotional experience at the bodily level becomes an inchoate mental experience, and when there are yet neither representations nor words available to express and signify the emotions. These states seem to be characteristic of the early stages of mental life, as well as of the adult when facing overwhelming emotional states that challenge his capacity to master them, give them meaning and communicate them to others using words. We will propose following Bion and Hinshelwood that – using a metaphorical model of *contents in a container* (sensory contents in a psychic container) – the modes of dealing with these states can be divided into three fundamental types a) *flexible*, b) *fragmented* or c) *rigid*.

As we understand this model, the main components are the following:

1) The sensory "contents" of an emotional experience, i.e. the signals from the *internal milieu*, have a dimension of *quantity* (excitation/arousal/salience).
2) The psychic "container" has a dimension of *quality* (goodness/badness originated from an *a priori* structure of survival-fitness values).
3) The integration of the sensory stimuli with the psychic-container results in psychological-experiential feelings and imagery: "ideograms" (Bion, 1959, p. 64), "dream-like visual images" (Bion, 1962, p. 7), "visual imagery" (Wisdom, 1959, pp. 137–138) or "imaged accounts"[1] (Damasio, 2000, p. 192).

DOI: 10.4324/9781315146416-4

4) These ideograms are initially simply "good" or "bad" objects (Imbasciati, 1989), and they structure the *mental* experiences and growth of the individual in context of their social field.
5) However, the sensory contents can be overwhelming, and the psychic container may be unable to accommodate them. This would lead to the *fragmented* and *rigid* types of emotional containment.

In this chapter we will incorporate the notions of *flexible, rigid* and *fragmented* modes of emotional containment with support from empirical research of other later and independent authors, from psychoanalytic, cognitive and psychometric schools of thought (Horowitz et al., 1979; Sundin and Horowitz, 2002; Pennebaker et al., 1990; Schumacher et al., 1999); we will argue that these three types of emotional containing can be seen at the same time as wide enough in their generality and specific enough in their classification to describe the principal features of most of the ways of dealing with raw emotional states. We will also argue that *rigid* and *fragmented* modes are both *deficient* forms of containing and regulating raw emotions that do not allow for the emergence of psychological and symbolic capacities. Hence, they fail to bring about mental adaptation and psychological learning from experiences, and the positive general state of health, which seem to be correlated with mental growth (e.g. Taylor, 1987; Vaillant, 1979).

Modes of Dealing with Pre-Verbal Emotional States

In trying to sum up the vast amount of theory and research available in this area (which includes a great part of the work of authors such as Klein, Bolwby, Winnicott, Bion, Fairbairn, Balint, Stern, Spitz, Main, Ainsworth Lichtenberg, Tronick and Gianino, and many others), it can be argued that the general pre-verbal patterns of emotional interaction can be described in the following meta-narrative:

a) The individual, normally a child or someone in a vulnerable position, is distressed by overwhelming psycho-physiological sensory stimuli (hunger, fear, pain, irritation, excitement, etc.), but is helpless to deal with the excitation.
b) They express distress by non-verbal somatic and emotionally charged signals, that have an experiential quality of "badness".
c) The other/caretaker receives the signals and gets emotionally aroused, and interprets them according to *a priori* survival-fitness values (hunger, fear, anger, lust, loneliness, etc.) and assigns meaning to the pre-verbal emotional communication of the individual and
d) Acts in order to solve the distress by fulfilling the needs of and/or soothing the distressed person, or tries instead to avoid the distress by some form of avoidance, alienation or abuse.
e) The vulnerable individual internalises and assimilates the strategies for dealing with the emotional distress, and by doing so "learns" to use them autonomously.

The outcomes of these containing/regulatory processes establish themselves as functions of the personality of the developing individual.

f) If the internalised strategies are successful ones, the individual is capable of reproducing the adequate response to emotional distress more autonomously; if they are unsuccessful and/or if the internalisation process is "faulty", there will be a sort of chronic incapacity of solving the distress and the need for a caretaker or of alternative ways of getting rid of emotional distress.

Note that although some of these processes are quasi-automatic and common to other mammals (namely a), b) and arguably c); see e.g. Panksepp, 2000), others seem to be highly influenced by cultural norms and beliefs about education, child rearing, values of the group, and other social elements and structures (Gergely and Watson, 1996; Leff, 1973).

Containment of the mounting excitation/distress and emotional rest can be brought about by a) the fulfilment of needs and restoration of the internal milieu and homeostasis, i.e. solace and soothing, or b) by the capacity to plan actions to fulfil needs, thereby achieving a sense of agency, mastery and control over the internal and external world (Lichtenberg, 1989, pp. 136–143). These two areas of emotional containment seem to correspond to different neural substrates: roughly speaking the subcortical emotional structures (such as the limbic system) and the neocortical action planning and conscious awareness structures (e.g. Lane and Garfield, 2005).

The Vital Importance of Interactive Emotional Containing/Regulation

We are focusing now mainly on a quantitative factor of affects. The capacity for emotional containment and regulation in which we are more interested in this work is the capacity to prevent emotional states reaching overwhelming levels, i.e. traumatic states and correlative somatic disruption. The idea of an *overwhelming level* of emotional states is to be placed in the context of Freud's original notions of *thresholds of stimulation* (e.g. Freud, 1895b, p. 138; Gediman, 1984) and *traumatic states*, and also of Cannon and Selye's notion of *stress*, as well as of later complementary elaborations such as by Krystal (1988) and Van der Kolk et al. (1996) that integrate psychodynamic and physiologic notions of traumatic stress. In the first chapter we saw, particularly as demonstrated in Walter Cannon's work on psychological shock, that containment/regulation of excessive emotional excitation is vital for actual physical survival. It seems that the lack of cortical mechanisms to inhibit emotional excitation leads to a cascade of autonomic reactions that totally exhausts various systems of the organism (Cannon, 1942; see also Sachar et al., 1970). It is quite well established that the process of containing emotions requires consistent emotional bonds and patterns of interaction with emotionally involved caretakers, and that interactive emotional regulation contributes greatly to the internal milieu's homeostasis and to the general state of health (e.g. Schmidt and Schulkin, 1999; Spitz and Wolf, 1946; Taylor, 1987).

In the following sections we will briefly describe the concept of emotional containment in the Bionian context, and take up again his notion of *alpha function*. We will compare it with some conceptions of *emotional regulation* and propose that the psychosocial processes described in the latter can be included in the notion of *emotional containment*. We will also review some independent studies that provide some empirical support to the containment notion and the three categories of containing modes (rigid, fragmented, flexible) at both the individual and interpersonal levels.

The Notion of Containing

The Post-Kleinian derived notion of "containing" (Hinshelwood, 1989a, pp. 246–253) denotes the process by which emotional states, experienced as "parts" of the person and as internal "things" that are felt as unbearable or "bad", are fantasised as being projected into an "object" in order to reduce the emotion's distressing power to the individual.[2] Bion proposed that these states are initially not experienced as mental "images" symbolically represented, but instead are experienced as sensations, as *things in themselves*, as concrete things that we can be rid of (e.g. Bion, 1962, p. 6). He described alpha function as a *mental* function with quantitative (i.e. energetic) and qualitative (i.e. cognitive) components: reducing anxiety ("detoxify" emotional experience) and attributing meaning to ideograms, or dream-like images.

Alpha Function and Failure of Alpha Function

The concept of alpha function proposes the idea that the person serving as a psychic container, if able to experience the elicited emotional state at a psychologically meaningful level, can identify the *feelings* that have been aroused, and in this way the emotional state emerges as psychosocial meaning out of the somatic-perceptive realm. From this stage it becomes possible to deal with the material in a *mental*, non-automatic way, through 1) intentional changes in the environment to solve the problem/need that had caused the emotional state in the first place, and 2) by representing it, *symbolising* it and making it available to storage and recall from memory.

Alternatively, the "projected" parts, remaining at a raw state of what Bion calls "beta" elements – quasi-automatic discharge action tendencies[3] and somatic alterations – can cause a distressing effect in the person serving as a container, and eventually spread to the larger interpersonal fields by further projection and evacuation (Hinshelwood, 1989b, pp. 75–78).

Internalisation and Assimilation into the Personality Structure

The Bionian model of containment also proposes that at the end of the containing process there is an assimilation and learning of the "process" of containment itself, as elaborated by the mechanism of *introjection* and *introjective identification* (Hinshelwood, 1989a). It becomes internalised as a function of the personality's structure, and will be active as privileged way of dealing with distress and emotions. Something of mother's mental ability has been introjected (mentally taken in) by the baby who can then use the understanding for themselves. Mother has in effect reprojected back into baby a modified form of what they projected into mother and which they then introjected with a resulting modification of their personality (Hinshelwood, 1987, p. 230)

An Attempt at Formalisation

Bion (1962, pp. 90–96) tried to develop a general abstract formal theory of the container-contained relations in the individual mind and the group.[4] In short, and what interests us most in this discussion, the sense impressions correlated with raw emotional experiences must be made coherent by being grouped (contained) into categories (containers); in other words, these sense impressions can be seen as efferent impulses from the internal milieu (Imbasciati, 1989, 2006) that must then be categorised according to *a priori* intrinsic values of the organism and of its social field (Damasio, 2000; Panksepp, 1998, 2005; Edelman, 1992) so that they have a meaning (i.e. goodness, badness, hunger, fear, pain, anger, etc.).

According to Bion, the ideational awareness of emotions can only develop when sense impressions, which are initially experienced as incoherent[5] (1962, p. 92), are *contained* by *pre-conceptions*. Preconceptions represent *a priori* innate states of expectation, at first "relatively simple undifferentiated preconceptions probably related to basic regulation of the organism (feeding, breathing and excretion)" (1962, p. 93). In other words, meaningful mental contents properly arise from the mating of very basic innate protomental structures (preconceptions) with sensorial data, which result in an internal "image-feeling" (Damasio, 2000). This is the basis of the *alpha function* and of an *apparatus for learning by experience* through thinking processes (Bion, 1962, p. 91).

Bion argued that the container-contained relations are seen as homologous intra and extra psychically, i.e. in the individual, the pair and in the group (e.g. Bion, 1970, p. 16). This idea is clearly formulated in the following quote:

> The activity that I have here described as shared by two individuals becomes introjected by the infant so that the [container-contained] apparatus becomes installed in the infant as part of the apparatus of alpha function.
>
> (Bion, 1962, p. 91)

Conceptions and Words

The result of the mating of container and contained is a *conception*, an initial abstraction (idea), which can include the formation of words.[6] The use of symbolic words is important to communicate and to modulate emotional states. We stress the importance of words as containers of meaning, instead of being at the service of action-discharge by sound, or of rigid alienation of emotional awareness (action discharge and rigid alienation both at a beta element state). Bion is particularly clear on words and containing in the following passage:

> These words I write are supposed to "contain" a meaning. The verbal expression can be so formalized, so rigid, so filled with already existing ideas that the idea I want to express can have all life squeezed out of it. On the other hand, the meaning I wish to express may have such a force and vitality… that it destroys the verbal container. The result is not a compact communication but an incoherence.
>
> (1967, p. 141)

Fragmentation, Flexibility and Rigidity

In his formal-abstract conceptualisation of the containing process, Bion placed emphasis on *flexibility* (non-rigid integration, or resilience of the *container*) as the way for the new sensorial data to be integrated with previous knowledge and allow mental adaptation, i.e. *learning by experience*. This is the foundation of the state of mind of the individual who can retain his knowledge and experience and yet be prepared to reconstruct past experiences in a manner that enables him to be receptive to a new idea (Bion, 1962, p. 93).

As discussed in the previous chapter, these are the characteristics of the *mind* and of emotionally meaningful information processing, or as Robert Langs (1996) called it the "emotion-processing mind". Hinshelwood (1987, 1999) tried to define the process of emotional containment in the interpersonal field using three dimensions: cohesiveness (of the container), disturbance (of the emotional contents) and flexibility (of the containment process). He defined three main possible outcomes (Hinshelwood, 1999): rigidity, fragmentation or flexibility.

a) "In the first variety, the container reacts to the intrusions by becoming rigid and refusing to respond to what has arrived in it, with the result that the contents, the contained, lose form or meaning".
b) The second would be a "flexible relationship, one in which the contained enters the container and has an impact on it, whilst the container and its shape and function also modify the contained".
c) "The third type is rather the opposite of the first, in which the contained is so powerful that it overwhelms the container which bursts or in some way loses all its own form and functions. A mother's mind can literally go to pieces, and she panics or even breaks down".

Intra-Personal or InterPersonal Emotional Containment?

A pertinent question refers to the problem of *where* the containment occurs. This problem can be addressed in two separate dimensions: the *individual-or-group* level, and the *contents-or-container* level. With regards the fragmented containment, where does the fragmentation occur; in the contained, in the contents, or in the system as a whole?

At the level of the individual, the containment process and consequently the containment deficits can be seen as taking place in the individual's own psychic apparatus. However, in the larger picture of the individual as a social being, it can be suggested that an interpersonal containment system must be implicated in the containment deficits. At the level of contents versus container, the problems in emotional containment can be associated with a) defects of the container (rigidity-fragility), b) excessive intensity and impact of the sensory contents (excessive arousal) or c) both factors at the same time.

Self and Interactive Regulation

We will suggest now that the main ideas and concepts described under the broad term of *emotional regulation* can be included in this general theoretical scheme of *emotional containment*, so that much of the literature about emotional regulation can be contextualised in the light of the above proposed emotional containment types (rigid, fragmented, flexible). This is in our view important because there is very little empirical research on the emotional containing paradigm in comparison with the amount done on the emotional regulation paradigm.

According to James Grotstein,

> Self-regulation, or modulation, is a term which has recently re-emerged from the infant development literature [...] to indicate that the newborn infant [...] requires its mother attuned intervention (interactional regulation to modulate until such time as these external interventions have been internalised as part of the self).
>
> (Grotstein, 1991, p. 12)

These processes are seen also as vitally important for the survival of the individual. The baby must, from birth to two months, be able to form basic homeostatic cycles and rhythms of sleep/wakefulness, feeding/elimination, activity/passivity, quiescence and crying[7] (Chatoor et al., 1984; Lichtenberg, 1989). Note the equivalence of these basic homeostatic functions with the initial "preconceptions", described above as proposed by Bion. The accomplishment of these biologic homeostasis cycles is followed by the ability to mobilise and engage in increasingly complex forms of interaction, which must also be regulated, but now at the level of psychologically experienced feelings (Lichtenberg, 1989).

The mutual regulation model stresses the interactivity of child and mother in the process of emotional regulation; when the mother accurately reads the message conveyed by the infant's behaviours and responds appropriately, she enables the infant to self-regulate (Tronick and Gianino, 1989). Also here, the caregiver is seen as relying on his own interpretation of the sense data relative to the emotions aroused by the child's needs.[8] For instance, Mary Ainsworth's definition of *sensitivity* involved (a) noting that a signal had occurred, (b) interpreting it accurately, (c) responding promptly and (d) appropriately (Hesse and Main, 1999). Then, the caretaker can impose a regulatory response with more or less flexibility. There is also the assumption of a process of "internalisation" of some sort, be that of a successful or of impaired regulation interactions. This internalised representation will be used as a non-conscious implicit guide to one's interactions with other partners (e.g. Tronick and Gianino, 1989, p. 65).[9]

Complementary of Containment and Regulation

We will suggest now that the concepts of containment and of emotional regulation can, in their basic principles, be seen as describing equivalent phenomena; they differ in their models for interpreting what is happening.

Regulation of Homeostasis by Feedback

The idea of emotional regulation as described above seems to be grounded in the cybernetic ideas of homeostasis regulation by feedback processes, of which one of the simplest examples is the regulation of temperature by feedback in a thermostat (Carver and Scheier, 1998; pp. 13–14, 26–27). This makes the model quite appropriate to describe the experience and regulation of emotional intensities and of biological cycles in relation to an optimal balanced state, directly linked with the realm of biological regulation of somatic states.

Spatial-Imagistic Experience

On the other hand, the concept of containment seems to be metaphorically grounded in the geometric mechanism of *projection*. In this sense it is directly linked with the experience of the human body in the spatial environment and of its own body parts in space and in relation one to another, and to other objects. This seems to be more appropriate to describe the emergence of phantasies and dream-like imagery, in other words, representations of emotional states as "things" and objects, the borders between inside and outside, and the different experienced-imagined regions of the body and the "self".

Complementarities

Although we are unable to treat this subject in depth here we would, however, like to suggest that both models could be seen as complementary in the sense that they represent different vertexes of observation on the same phenomena.[10] Finally, the introjection of faulty, deficient and disturbing interpersonal processes in the form of what Kleinian tradition metaphorically called the *bad breast* (Bion, 1962, pp. 34–35, 97) has also a clear parallel in the assimilation, into the child's *core affective representation*, of a dismissive relation with the caretakers (Tronick and Gianino, 1989).

Conclusion

The present chapter argued the importance of containment of raw emotional experience, stating that Bion viewed such process as comprising three different modes: flexible, fragmented and rigid. The fragmented and rigid modes can be seen as complementary forms of containment-regulation deficits. An oscillatory dynamic of mental rigidity and mental fragmentation was already suggested early on by Bion in one of his group papers (1952, pp. 174–175). Furthermore, Hinshelwood (1987, pp. 232–235) described how the intensification of the rigidity dimension of emotional containment, through bureaucracy, excessive regulations and impermeable borders in a community can be interpreted as a protection against the feeling of emotional fragmentation, by use of what he calls "*numbing*" and "*ossification*"; the rigid containment strategies can be viewed as ways of reducing the emotional arousal and excitation levels and the associated high intensity of distress characteristic of the experience of emotional fragmentation.

On the other hand, Bion (1962, 1970) elaborated at length the cases where the container-contained relation failed in such a way that the sense impressions correlated with emotional experiences did not cohere into a container, a mental structure (a preconception, a conception or words). This corresponds to experiences without psychic meaning (Grotstein, 1999; Hinshelwood, 2003). This model was used by Bion to understand the disorganisation of thinking and perception characteristic of psychotic states (Bion, 1962, 1967). However, it is important to distinguish the psychotic state of mind, and some pre-psychotic features of the fragmented state of mind. In psychosis we could say the subject loses the ability to distinguish between exteroceptive and interoceptive sensorial data, i.e., what stimuli come from the internal milieu and what come from the external world, and hence loses contact with a socially shared common sense (1962, pp. 50–51). However, in psychotic hallucinatory-delusional states, the internal emotional reality is perceived everywhere, everything in the external world is imbued with personal-emotional meanings (albeit very primitive and idiosyncratic). This should be distinguished from fragmentation proper. In fact, some people suffer severe psychological trauma without suffering a psychotic episode, or even without developing other full-blown psychological disorders such as major depression (e.g. Heim et al., 2001). Hence, we believe that it is useful to reserve the construct of mental fragmentation, or psychic disintegration, to denote states previous to any psychical organisation of defences, denoting only the overwhelming mounting of excitation in the psyche ("accretions of stimuli in the psyche"; Bion, 1962, p. 7) characteristic of the traumatic state in itself, which W. Cannon (1942) had called psychological shock and which can itself lead to death by somatic exhaustion. Bion's model remains to this day a source of inspiration and, it is argued, also a model that can provide bridges with other currents of psychology, thus withstanding the test of time.

Notes

1 Damasio states: "the imaged account is… generated from structures capable of receiving signals from maps which represent… the proto-self" (2000, p. 192).
2 As already mentioned in the meta-narrative above, the target-container of these "projected parts" is emotionally aroused by them and must then deal with an emotional state now "in its hands".
3 See also the concept of "fixed action patterns" (Gross; 1999).
4 "I shall abstract for use as a model the idea of a container into which an object is projected… the latter we shall designate by the term contained… container and contained are susceptible of conjunction and permeation by emotion. Thus conjoined or permeated or both they change in a manner usually described as growth. When disjoined or denuded of emotion they diminish in vitality, that is, approximate to inanimate objects" (1962, pp. 90–96)
5 According to Bion, initially incoherent sense impressions are experienced as in the schizoid paranoid position, but without the feeling of being persecuted (1962).
6 For Bion, conceptions and words represents hypothesis about the world; the process "abstracts successively more complex hypothesis and finally whole systems of hypothesis which are known as scientific deductive systems" (1962, p. 94).
7 "In facilitating the establishment of homeostasis in these infants, the caregiver plays a critical role. She must be able to provide both a physical and emotional environment in which the infant can balance and regulate both internal and external stimuli" (Chatoor et al., 1984).
8 "If she does not respond, his regulatory efforts may fall, and he becomes disorganized… The interaction has been characterised as a dyadic system in which the infant and the mother attempt to achieve the culturally valued goal of a shared positive emotional state" (Tronick and Gianino, 1989).
9 "The infant will develop a representation of his interaction with his mother as generally well regulated and reparable […] he will then apply this representation of other and self to guide his interactions with other partners, because it will in part structure his performance and emotional state with them" (Tronick and Gianino, 1989, p. 65).
10 Marans and Adelman (1997), for instance, explicitly used both notions when proposing that regulation of affective states and containment of anxiety and terrors are among the factors included in the sense of "psychological safety". An example that might clarify these complementarities could be the containing and regulatory functions of nursery rhymes or lullabies used to sooth and regulate sleep and anxiety states in infants.

References

Bion, W.R. (1952) Group dynamics: A review. *International Journal of Psychoanalysis* 32(2): 26–31.
Bion, W.R. (1959) Dream work alpha. In *Cogitations*. London: Karnac, 1992, pp. 62–68.
Bion, W.R. (1962) *Learning from Experience*. London: Karnac Books.
Bion, W.R. (1967) *Second Thoughts*. London: Karnac Books.
Bion, W.R. (1970) *Attention and Interpretation*. London: Tavistock; reprinted Karnac (1984), also in *Seven Servants* (1977).
Cannon, W.B. (1942). Voodoo death. *American Anthropologist* 44: 169–181.
Carver, C.S. and Scheier, M.F. (1998). *On the Self-Regulation of Behavior*. New York: Cambridge University Press.
Chatoor, I., Schaefer, S., Dickson, L. and Egan, J. (1984). Developmental approach to feeding disturbances. *Infant Behavior and Development* 7: 71. https://doi.org/10.1016/S0163-6383(84)80133-2

Damasio, A. (2000). *The Feeling of What Happens: Body, Emotion and the Making of Consciousness*. London: Vintage.

Edelman, G. (1992) *Bright Air, Brilliant Fire: On the Matter of the Mind*. New York: Basic Books.

Freud, S. (1895b) A reply to criticisms of my paper on anxiety neurosis. *SE* 3: 121–139. London: Hogarth Press, 1957.

Gediman, H.K. (1984). Actual neurosis and psychoneurosis. *International Journal of Psychoanalysis* 65: 191–202.

Gergely, G. and Watson, J. (1996). The social biofeedback theory of parental affect-mirroring. *International Journal of Psychoanalysis* 77: 1181–1212.

Gross, J. (1999) Emotion and emotion regulation. In Pervin, L. A. and John, O. P. (Editors) *Handbook of Personality: Theory and Research* (2nd ed.) (525–552). New York: Guilford.

Grotstein, J. (1991) Nothingness, meaninglessness, chaos, and the Black Hole III: Self and interactional regulation and the background presence of primary identification. *Contemporary Psychoanalysis* 27(3): 1–33.

Grotstein, J. (1999) *O Buraco Negro* [The Black Hole]. Lisboa: Climepsi.

Heim, C., Newport, D.J., Bonsall, R., Miller, A.H. and Nemeroff, C.B. (2001) Altered pituitary-adrenal axis responses to provocative challenge tests in adult survivors of childhood abuse. *American Journal of Psychiatry* 158(4): 575–581.

Hesse, E. and Main, M. (1999) Second generation effects of unresolved trauma in nonmaltreating parents: Dissociated, frightened and threatening parental behavior. *Psychoanalytic Inquiry* 19(4): 481–540.

Hinshelwood, R.D. (1987) *What Happens in Groups. Psychoanalysis, the Individual and the Community*. London: Free Associations.

Hinshelwood, R.D. (1989a) *A Dictionary of Kleinian Thought*. London: Free Associations.

Hinshelwood, R.D. (1989b) Social possession of identity. In Richards, B. (Editor) *Crises of the Self* (75–83). London: Free Association Books.

Hinshelwood, R.D. (1999) Countertransference. *International Journal of Psychoanalysis* 80: 797–818.

Hinshelwood, R.D. (2003) Group mentality and "having a mind". In Lipgar, R. and Pines, M. (Editors) *Building on Bion: Roots* (181–197). London: Jessica Kingsley.

Horowitz, M.J., Wilner, M. and Alvarez, W. (1979) Impact of event scale: A measure of subjective stress. *Psychosomatic Medicine* 41: 209–218.

Imbasciati, A. (1989). Towards a psychoanalytic model of cognitive processes: Representation, perception, memory. *International Review of Psychoanalysis* 16: 223–236.

Imbasciati, A. (2006) *Constructing a Mind: A New Base for Psychoanalytic Theory*. London: Brunner-Routledge.

Krystal, H. (1988) *Integration and Self-Healing: Affect, Trauma, Alexithymia*. Hillsdale: Analytic Press.

Lane, R.D. and Garfield, D.A. (2005) Becoming aware of feelings: Integration of cognitive-developmental, neuroscientific, and psychoanalytic perspectives. *Neuropsychoanalysis* 7(1): 5–30.

Langs, R. (1996) *The Evolution of the Emotion-Processing Mind*. London: Karnac Books.

Leff, J. (1973) Culture and the differentiation of emotional states. *British Journal of Psychiatry* 123: 299–306.

Lichtenberg, J. (1989) *Psychoanalysis and Motivation*. Hove and London: Analytic Press.

Marans, S. and Adelman, A. (1997). Experiencing violence in a developmental context. In Osofsky, J. D. (Editor) *Children in a Violent Society* (202–222). New York: The Guilford Press.

Panksepp, J. (1998) The periconscious substrates of consciousness: Affective states and the evolutionary origins of the self. *Journal of Consciousness Studies* 5: 566–582.

Panksepp, J. (2000) Fear and anxiety mechanisms of the brain: Clinical implications. In Bittar, E.E. and Bittar, N. (Editors), *Biological Psychiatry* (157–178). Stamford, CT: JAI Press Inc.

Panksepp, J. (2005) Commentary to "becoming aware of feelings". *Neuropsychoanalysis* 7(1): 40–55.

Pennebaker, J.W., Czajka, J.A., Cropanzano, R. and Richards, B.C. (1990) Levels of thinking. *Personality and Social Psychology Bulletin* 16: 743–757.

Sachar, E.J., Kanter, S.S., Buie, D. et al. (1970) Psychoendocrinology of ego disintegration. *American Journal of Psychiatry* 126: 1067–1078.

Schmidt, L.A. and Schulkin, J. (1999) *Extreme Fear, Shyness and Social Phobia: Origins, Biological Mechanisms and Clinical Outcomes*. New York: Oxford University Press.

Schumacher, J., Eisemarm, M. and Brahler, E. (1999) Looking back on parents: The Questionnaire of Recalled Parental Rearing Behaviour (QRPRB). *Diagnostica* 45(4): 194–204.

Spitz, R.A. and Wolf, K.M. (1946) Anaclitic depression – An inquiry into the genesis of psychiatric conditions in early childhood. *Psychoanalytic Study of the Child* 2: 313–342.

Sundin, E.C. and Horowitz, M.J. (2002) Impact of event scale: Psychometric properties. *British Journal of Psychiatry* 180: 205–209.

Taylor, G.J. (1987) *Psychosomatic Medicine and Contemporary Psychoanalysis*. Madison, WI: International Universities Press.

Tronick, E. and Gianino, A. (1989) The transmission of maternal disturbance to the infant. In Gomes-Pedro, J. and Patricio, M.F. (Editors) *Biopsychology of Early Parent-Infant Communication* (63–68). Lisbon: Fundacao Calouste Gulbenkian.

Vaillant, G.E. (1979) Health consequences of adaptation to life. *American Journal of Medicine* 67(5): 732–734.

Van der Kolk, B.A., McFarlane, A.C. and Weisaeth, L. (1996) *Traumatic Stress: The Effects of Overwhelming Experience on Mind, Body, and Society*. New York: Guilford Press.

Wisdom, J. (1959) On a differentiating mechanism of psychosomatic disorder. *International Journal of Psychoanalysis* 40: 134–146.

Chapter 3

On Containment and Holding
A Short Introductory Note

Tiago Mendes

Introduction

After World War II, the British psychoanalytical society was undergoing internal struggles, culminating in the development of different groups. This period characterised by internal differences was also, paradoxically, a time of intense creativity and discovery which gave rise to new and exciting concepts, as psychoanalysts travelled different routes. Two authors remain particularly influential to this day, namely Wilfred Bion and Donald Winnicott, who were exploring analytical ideas with psychotic patients (Bion 1959) and evacuee children (Abram 2007) respectively. Their work with these diverse groups gave rise to rich formulations, that became some of the more enduring and successful concepts in psychoanalysis: Bion's Containment (1962) and Winnicott's Holding (1960). Although tracing their roots to different psychoanalytic traditions and contexts (Hinshelwood and Abram 2018), as time passed by, both concepts have appeared to intertwine, to some extent, being increasingly used with the same meaning in the psychoanalytic literature, as Ogden (2004) duly noted. Despite their similar nature, both rooted in the baby-mother relationship, psychoanalysts do tend to distinguish them, as different concepts that highlight different phenomena, although closely related ones.

As such conceptual enmeshment seems to have transposed to the *systems psychodynamics* tradition, the present chapter is intended to provide some clarity on both traditions, as it might be useful for practitioners in the field. Although a thorough distinction between both concepts and their further developments is not the aim of this chapter, it must be stated that both have been the subject of recent efforts at providing a comparative inquiry (Aguayo and Lundgren 2018; Hinshelwood and Abram 2018; Ogden 2004). Furthermore, it is suggested in this chapter that careful distinction between the concepts is needed when applying them, either in clinical practice or in the context of organisations, as they may highlight different phenomena. Nonetheless, a word of caution is required in the sense that this book is focused mainly on Containment. Hence Winnicott's work is addressed for the single purpose of conceptual clarification/distinction, without the aim of chiselling a detailed depiction of its origins.[1] Furthermore, as a personal disclaimer, my

DOI: 10.4324/9781315146416-5

own research has dwelled more within the confines of the Kleinian tradition than within the rich and fertile tradition arising from Winnicott's work, which I am less familiar with.

On Containment

Within the Kleinian tradition, Bion's concept of Containment, as it is known today, is firmly connected to one of Melanie Klein's most influential ideas, that of projective identification (Bott Spillius et al. 2011; Hinshelwood 1991). The idea of projecting parts of the self into the object was a concept which gained a huge interest in the Kleinian group at the time, although Klein described projective identification as an aggressive phantasy. Nonetheless, Bion seemed to be the one who first brought it to light in a more articulate form (Bott Spillius et al. 2011; Hinshelwood 1991) when he argued that projective identification may not only be an omnipotent defensive mechanism, but also a fundamental mechanism of communication, thus having a normal role to play in human development. In fact, while addressing the problem of thinking, Bion (1962) describes the "normal" form of projective identification, separating it from the abnormal, pathological form.

Bion's realisation that projective identification might have a normal form led to further theoretical developments, namely the theory of Containment. It is thus deeply grounded in projective identification, of which it is an expansion where this mechanism is used not solely for evacuatory purposes but also with a communicative intent (Bell 2001; Bion 1959, 1962; Bott Spillius et al. 2011; Grotstein 2007, 2009a, 2009b; Hinshelwood 1991, 1994; Mawson 2011; Riesenberg-Malcolm 2001; Sandler 2009; Souder 1988; Steiner 2000). At the genesis of Containment is also Bion's theory of linking, of how things are linked, not just on the outside, but also linked from within (Bion 1959).

Regarding Containment, Bion argued that when faced with distressing feelings, such as a fear of dying, the baby would project them into their mother. The mother, facing her baby's discomfort and crying, would be able to understand these unbearable, shapeless feelings and transform them through her capacity for *rêverie* – her capacity to "day-dream" and imagine what could be distressing her baby, which Bion considered a factor of alpha-function (1962). Thus, the baby would reintroject a more shaped, transformed form of their feelings, which would no longer be harmful. But the transformed elements are not the only things which are introjected in the process. As has been argued, the mother's ability to transform and give meaning to the baby's experience is also introjected (Bott Spillius et al. 2011; Fonagy and Target 2003; Hinshelwood 1991; Lopéz-Corvo 2005, Sandler 2005). At the basis of this concept seems to be Bion's earlier description of a patient in "Attacks on linking" (Bion 1959; Hinshelwood 1991; Lopéz-Corvo 2005; Sandler 2005). And, it is argued, the description of this patient as well as Bion's abstraction of the role of the mother remained cornerstones throughout the constant development of the theory of Containment.

Bion gave an excellent description of a patient who attempted to use the analyst in order to place his *fears of death* inside him, with the phantasy that they would be modified and could then be re-introjected in a more tolerable form. Bion describes how "the patient had felt [...] that I evacuated them so quickly that the feelings were not modified, but had become more painful" (Bion 1959, p. 312). Thus the patient seemed to feel that his own feelings were so quickly disposed of, that in fact he was denied entrance inside Bion's mind and his fear of death became more painful. A violent cycle then ensues, where the patient forcefully tries to gain access to Bion's inside.

> Associations from a period in the analysis earlier than that from which these illustrations have been drawn showed an increasing intensity of emotions in the patient. This originated in what he felt was my refusal to accept parts of his personality. Consequently he strove to force them into me with increased desperation and violence. His behaviour, isolated from the context of the analysis, might have appeared to be an expression of primary aggression. The more violent his phantasies of projective identification, the more frightened he became of me. There were sessions in which such behaviour expressed unprovoked aggression, but I quote this series because it shows the patient in a different light, his violence a reaction to what he felt was my hostile defensiveness.
>
> (Bion 1959, p. 312)

Now the last part of the paragraph is quite interesting, since Bion describes how the patient's behaviour was in fact a reaction to the analyst's hostility. That is, it was not a hostile attack destined to control the object, but in fact the patient was desperately trying to gain access to Bion and becoming increasingly more desperate with the analyst's apparent refusal. In a stroke of genius, Bion linked this idea with the patient's early experience of his mother and abstracted from what was happening in the analytic session what sort of mother the patient might have experienced in his childhood. As Bion (1959, p. 313) described, "I felt that the patient had experienced in infancy a mother who dutifully responded to the infant's emotional displays".

This is quite an impressive account, and it certainly is from this experience and extrapolations that Bion abstracted his model of Containment, thus some of the main characteristics of this description must be highlighted. Bion presupposes the prototype for the adaptive form of Containment, where the mother is able to tolerate and give meaning and shape to the baby's projection of their fear of death. In such a case both mother and baby are enriched in the relation and there is mental development. On the other hand, Bion describes a dutiful mother, although presupposing two different models of behaviour for her, which are the prototype for his later development of two mal-adaptive forms of Containment. Bion states in this regard that the patient' mother "could not tolerate experiencing such feelings and reacted either by denying them ingress, or alternatively by becoming a prey to the anxiety which resulted from introjection of the infant's feelings" (Bion 1959, p. 313).

In one case the mother reacts to the child dutifully, that is, without emotionally linking with her baby, and with impatience. Although Bion does not mention it, the element of impatience seems also to presuppose an element of irritation, as if saying "stop bothering me". This mal-adaptive form will go on to be developed as his idea that the container crushes the contained. The other reaction of the mother was when she becomes a prey to anxiety, which Bion argues probably happened on rare occasions. This seems to be the prototype for Bion's description of a mal-adative form of Containment where the contained rips the container. Thus, it is clear that as far back as 1959, Bion was already struggling with a model of mother-baby interaction which presupposes one adaptive form, as well as two mal-adaptive forms.

Later on, in *Learning from Experience* (1962) where Bion first uses the term Containment to describe these ideas, Bion's model entails only two possible outcomes of the container/contained relation: an adaptive form where container and contained must adapt to each other in an active process between both parts which promotes emotional growth; or a mal-adaptive form that seems to be detrimental to both. Bion was probably still coming to grips with his model of Containment when he described it in this manner as a two-dimensional model. The concept was later expanded by Bion (1970), no longer just seen in terms of baby/mother, but also enlarged to individuals and society, as in the case of the mystic and the establishment. Either the establishment (container) is capable of Containing the mystic's (contained) creativity and innovation, or the establishment crushes such creativity – or the mystic shatters the establishment. That is, the relation between the two concepts includes three possible outcomes: it is either beneficial to both (adaptive), or it impairs the container (mal-adaptive) or it impairs the contained (mal-adaptive). Thus, again we are faced with a three-dimensional model, encompassing a second form of mal-adaptive Containment, which, it is argued by Hinshelwood (1991), traces its roots all the way back to Bion's 1959 paper and the mother that became a prey to emotion. In this text Bion expands the relation between container and contained as being applicable to different levels ranging from intra-individual to the relation between individuals and society, also describing how it might apply to the relation between words and meaning.

Containment has ever since been successfully applied to the analytical situation stating how the analyst might act as a container for the patient's projections, which they then transform into a more tolerable form. Nonetheless, it must be noted that this concept has evolved, or at least been used with different meanings. In *The New Dictionary of Kleinian Thought* it is argued that although the notion of Containing has become a decisive concept for most British forms of psychoanalytic psychotherapy inside and outside the Kleinian group of psychoanalysts, although this now often means that it is used imprecisely (Bott Spillius et al. 2011, pp. 279, 280). In fact, Containment seems to be used in the literature, usually while referring to the analytical setting, with the meaning of Containing (Bott Spillius et al. 2011; Hinshelwood 1991). But as seen previously three modes of Containment may exist, comprising a rigid, fragmented and flexible form.[2] I am referring here to the process by which the analyst receives the intolerable emotional projections of the patient and transforms them into something more tolerable, which can be re-introjected by the patient. Its two-dimensional quality (contained/uncontained) seems to be based on Bion's description of Containment in *Learning from Experience* (1962). Bion used the mathematical notation of alpha function to refer to the process of transforming beta-elements into alpha-elements, although Containing seems to be more commonly used. Containment is also used to refer to a three-dimensional model encompassing one adaptive and two mal-adaptive forms (Hinshelwood 1994; Lopéz-Corvo 2005; Sandler 2005), as mentioned previously. In this case there is an attempt to separate between two mal-adaptive forms and attribute a more precise meaning to each form. On other occasions Containment is used in connection with the violent omnipotent forms of projective identification, by referring to the object as Containing a part that the individual projected. Hence, in this case, it is used in order to describe the function executed by the object in projective identification, although not necessarily the normal, benign form of projective identification. Such complex formulations and usages possibly create the need for conceptual clarification.

On Holding

As with the case of Wilfred Bion, Donald Winnicott was also a prolific psychoanalytic author whose work can be divided into several distinct phases, whereby he constantly revisited some of his ideas, bringing different concepts and perspectives to a more mature form. In the present instance, the development of the *Holding Environment* has been attributed to the second phase of his work, where he focused on "*Transitional phenomena*", which lasted from 1945 to 1959 (Abram 2007). This can be traced to his specific work with children evacuated during the course of World War II, as Jan Abram argued (2018). The impact of such displacement on the children was enormous, and it was the genesis of therapeutic residential responses, such as that pioneered by Barbara Dockar-Drysdale, with whom Winnicott was closely associated (Crociani-Windland 2013; Kasinski 2003). The impact of displacement and the disruption inflicted on the children certainly made an impression on Winnicott who, being a paediatrician, already was experienced with and attuned to the importance of the relationship between mothers and infants.

At the time, Winnicott seemed to have been interested in the relationship between the mother and the baby from early on, and the capacity of the mother to provide an environment where the baby felt *held* since, from the beginning of its life, the baby is fully dependent on a caregiving figure; this gave rise to the famous statement "There is no such thing as an infant" (Winnicott 1960), referring to the maternal care required to sustain and maintain a baby, both in the physical as well as in the psychological sense. In this context, Winnicott posited that a specific environment was required to care for the baby, a Holding environment with a *good enough mother* (Winnicott 1953), that would not only dutifully perform her role, but also care and love her baby. The role of the good enough mother is depicted by Winnicott as one that delineates a path for the baby from "complete adaptation to the infant's needs" (Winnicott 1953, p. 94), towards a slow and incrementally increasing exposure to failure and frustration, mitigated by the child's own increasing ability to tolerate frustration. In this regard, the baby is completely dependent on the mother (or the person providing a maternal role), who not only takes care of the baby's physical needs, but also, as Winnicott's states, the "main reason why in infant development the infant usually becomes able to master, and the ego to include, the id, is the fact of the maternal care, the maternal ego implementing the infant ego and so making it powerful and stable" (1960, p. 587).

Winnicott described in detail what he perceived was the developmental path through which the infant progresses from the mother's *"ego support"* to a more mature form whereby they achieve differentiation. This pathway would lead the child from a stage of absolute dependence, passing through a stage of relative dependence leading to a stage moving towards independence[3] (Winnicott 1960), whereby transitional phenomena would play a key role in the transition. In this regard, in a more meta-psychological note, it must be stated that contrary to Klein, Winnicott adhered to Freud's (1914) view of primary narcissism, that the baby has diverted its instincts into its own body and is, therefore, absent from developing object relations from birth. This preconized developmental pathway, from "absolute dependence" to "towards independence" also constitutes the path from pleasure principle and autoerotism, to form object relationships and abide to the reality principle (Winnicott 1960, p. 588). Nonetheless, Winnicott informs us that such a developmental path does not constitute the whole of his theory, but only half, since the other half is comprised by the mother's ability to provide care, and her ability to attune herself to the baby's needs. Winnicott described in this aspect the role of what he termed *Primary Maternal Preoccupation* (Winnicott 1956a), a preconized temporary state, whereby the mother adapts "delicately and sensitively to the infant's needs at the very beginning" (Winnicott 1956a, p. 302). In this sense, Winnicott's description of the good enough mother that provides for a Holding environment is in itself a psychoanalytic theory of emotional maturation. While debate abounds on Winnicott's meta-psychological views (see Fulgencio 2015; Girard 2017), their separation from the ideas of the Kleinian group is noted[4] and seems well established.

A further note in this matter is required, since it has been understood that Winnicott focused mainly in the overwhelming importance of the external context surrounding the child, the environment in which children were raised, as opposed to the intrapsychic world. Such interest in the outside world, as it were, is patent in some of his publications, such as a paper discussing anti-social tendency in children, where Winnicott (1956b) vividly depicts how emotional deprivation and anti-social tendencies in children appear intertwined. Nonetheless, as Jan Abram has argued, Winnicott's "primary focus, and indeed his most significant clinical innovation, is on the environment-individual set-up" (2018, p. 142). That is, that Winnicott was not solely focused on the external environment, but in the specific interrelation between context and child, and its outcomes. As in the case of Bion, Winnicott's vibrant ideas and contributions became hallmarks of the psychoanalytic tradition, gaining increasingly more attention in current psychoanalytical thought, which constantly turns to his formulations (Caldwell and Joyce 2014; Lanyado 1996; Rappoport 2012).

On Containment and Holding

Having addressed some key aspects of both concepts, it is now time to address their points of contact and key differences. As mentioned earlier, different authors have pointed to the fact that both concepts are increasingly seen as intertwined, or at least that their differences are subsumed (Caldwell 2018; Girard 2017; Ogden 2004, 2016). And in fact, when one reads different accounts of psychoanalytically informed interventions, either in the clinical context, or in the application of psychoanalytic thought to different contexts, both concepts seem to be used in a rather disparaging manner, ranging from being interchangeable, to complementary, and utilised as if to highlight different phenomena (e.g. Caldwell 2018; Conti 2017; Diamond 2014; Goldberg 1989; Hyman 2012). In some cases, it seems they are even depleted of their original meaning or used in a very different light from how they were originally coined. Although one might argue that such broad use may in fact stem from both concepts' success, and that key psychoanalytic ideas may, and in fact should, evolve as our theoretical understanding progresses, still there is a strong case to be made for added clarification and distinction regarding similar concepts stemming from different traditions. Not an easy task given that, among other reasons, both concepts are vernacular words commonly used in English.

Still, interest in comparative perspectives within psychoanalysis has grown in the past few years, including fruitful advances in comparative understanding of both Bion's and Winnicott's ideas and influences (Aguayo and Lundgren 2018; Hinshelwood and Abram 2018; Riesenberg-Malcolm 2001). Such efforts have ranged from attempts at clarification of the different origins, contexts and influences that gave rise to such ideas (Hinshelwood and Abram 2018; Riesenberg-Malcolm 2001), to attempts at joining the concepts into a more unified version. The latter has been suggested in *The New Dictionary of Kleinian Thought* (Bott Spillius et al. 2011) as one where Holding can be described as a broad umbrella term, within which a specific process such as Containment might be seen as being subsumed (Bott Spillius et al. 2011, p. 283). Thus in this perspective, Containment could be seen as a specific component of the Holding environment. Also, there are points of similarity, not least of which is the fact that both Holding and Containment derive from the baby-mother interaction. Furthermore, both concepts describe theories of emotional maturation, highlighting developmental pathways from early infancy towards emotional maturity.

Even if such concepts do share many commonalities, it must be noted that they arose from analytical work with very different clients. And, perhaps more interestingly, at different epistemological stages in these authors' careers. Nonetheless, the distinction between both concepts usually tends to follow along other lines and the concepts tend to be separated on the basis of allegiance to Freud's idea of primary narcissism (Freud 1914). While Winnicott based Holding on this concept, Bion adhered to Klein and to her idea that object relations exist from the beginning of life, thus departing from Freud's notion of primary narcissism while considering that from the beginning the baby has an Ego, albeit a rudimentary one, and strives to evacuate its fear of dying into the mother. This distinction was emphasised by Riesenberg-Malcolm (2001, p. 170) who states that Winnicott conceptualises this early stage as a "merger, as expressed in holding" while in the case of Bion "it is a relationship between the two in which the infant's ego participation is active", while also recognising that the mother's participation in the relationship extends beyond a simple "physical contact". More recently, Caldwell (2018), a known Winnicottian, reiterated this idea by stating that contrary to Bion's description of the baby's ability to project its own feelings into the mother, in Winnicott's model there is no room for a rudimentary ego capable of such complex mental activities. Nonetheless regarding both authors' views of Freudian drives, it must be noted that, as has been highlighted in recent years, both Klein and Winnicott were not drive-theorists *per se* (Hinshelwood and Abram 2018), and that their formulations should be understood in the particular context of the British Psychoanalytic Society of the time.

Symington and Symington (1996) also distinguish between the concepts, arguing that there are three main differences between them. First of all, while Holding describes what can be seen as a passive process, whereby the Holding environment sets the stage for the child's development, Containment in contrast refers to an active process. Symington and Symington draw on the idea that the container should not simply be seen as a passive entity in the process, but in fact actively struggling to give shape and meaning to the contained, an important distinction. A second point concerns a closely related idea, which is that while Holding happens in the external environment, the container may also lay in the internal world. Andre Green (1975) also seemed to adhere to this notion since, as he addressed the problems arising from the development of psychoanalytic theory in the 70s, he stated that "Winnicott's 'holding' refers to the care of the external object, Bion's 'container' to internal psychic reality" (Green 1975, p. 10). Finally, the sensorial quality of the Holding environment plays a key role in this distinction. In fact, while Containment is mostly non-sensorial, if one draws on Bion's own descriptions, Holding has a more sensorial quality to it as Caldwell and Joyce (2014) argue. In this sense, Winnicott stressed the integration of psyche and soma into a single unit (Caldwell and Joyce 2014), while positing that the body plays a key role in the development of psychical structure (Caldwell 2018). This view of Holding as a more passive process than Containment, although shared by several authors, is not the only one. Goldberg (1989), for instance, argued that the Holding environment should be "actively sought and created – or discovered – within the therapist" (p. 448), a process which, for him, is different from Containing. However, Goldberg makes interchangeable use of Holding and Containing to describe his own work with clients, while considering the *Containing function* as analogous to the *environmental hold*.

Furthermore, one might make a case regarding the Holding environment as concerning solely, or at least mainly, the external environment, instead of the internal, phantasised one. Such a stance might be particularly seductive to those using the psychoanalytic framework in working with organisations. Nonetheless, Jan Abram's work makes a careful suggestion regarding Winnicott's own interest in intrapsychic life, and not solely in the external environment.

Although a complex and quite contemporary topic, this brief digression into some of the distinctions between the concepts in the literature seems to highlight that there is still a long journey ahead in carefully crafting a solid differentiation, if that is at all possible in the clinical arena. And in fact, carefully crafting the influences and links between the work of Klein, Bion[5] and Winnicott is still underway, as recent efforts have tried to uncover (Aguayo 2002; Caldwell 2018; Hinshelwood and Abram 2018). Such work will certainly be important to ensure that when providing clinical and organisational descriptions, practitioners do not solely rely on the concepts based on their theoretical affiliations.

Conclusion – An Ongoing Debate

The richness of psychoanalytic metapsychology certainly is in debt to the variety of its many schools and approaches. A long history, going back more than 100 years, also provides the fertile ground for a complex genealogical tree of concepts, of which Kleinian and Winnicottian traditions are main branches. Nonetheless, tracing the history of these concepts, highlighting their differences and points of contact, is not an easy task, not least due to the fact that Bion kept reformulating or, better still, readdressing his concepts in different ways, without leaving us clear indications for a definitive formulation. Winnicott's ideas seemed much more concerned with the external environment, a point that is made by several authors and that is again addressed in Chapter 10 of this book, when Susan Long suggests how containers can hold their contents. This also indicates a path for future discussion, trying to bridge the gap between the different traditions and see points of complementarity between both.

Though the debate across multiple traditions will certainly shed increasing light on the interrelations of psychoanalytic concepts, I argue that such debate might also be beneficial if transposed to the other contexts where the psychoanalytic tradition is being applied.

Notes

1 For the readers interested in exploring Winnicott's ideas, Jan Abram's work (2007, 2008) is an important starting point.
2 See Chapter 2 of this book for a more detailed account.
3 See Abram (2007, 2008) for a more detailed view of Winnicott's ideas on the matter, particularly the notion that Winnicott considered that "There is no such thing as 'independence' but only 'towards independence'" (p. 1207).

4 Winnicott initially started his work closely affiliated with Melanie Klein, who was the clinical supervisor of one of his cases. Their eventual theoretical separation, the context leading to such separation, and his role during the controversial discussions have been addressed in detail by several authors (Abram 2008; Aguayo 2002; Hinshelwood and Abram 2018). Regarding Winnicott's perceived influence of his own work on Bion's subsequent ideas, see Caldwell (2018).
5 See Caldwell (2018) for an assessment of some of Winnicott's influences on Bion's work.

References

Abram, J. (2007) *The Language of Winnicott*. 2nd Edition. Abingdon, Routledge.

Abram, J. (2008) *Donald Woods Winnicott (1896–1971): A brief introduction. International Journal of Psychoanalysis*, Vol. 89, pp. 1189–1217.

Abram, J. (2018) Holding and the mutative interpretation. In Hinshelwood, R.D. and Abram, J. (eds) *The Clinical Paradigms of Melanie Klein and Donald Winnicott: Comparisons and Dialogues*. Abingdon, Routledge, pp. 140–147.

Aguayo, J. (2002) *Reassessing the clinical affinity between Melanie Klein and D.W. Winnicott (1935–1951): Klein's unpublished "Notes on baby" in historical context. International Journal of Psychoanalysis*, Vol. 83, pp. 1133–1152.

Aguayo, J. and Lundgren, J. (2018) *Introduction to a comparative assessment of W.R. Bion and D.W. Winnicott's clinical theories. British Journal of Psychotherapy*, Vol. 34, pp. 194–197.

Bell, D. (2001) Projective identification. In Bronstein, C. (ed.) *Kleinian Theory: A Contemporary Perspective*. London, Whurr, pp. 148–165.

Bion, W.R. (1959) *Attacks on linking. International Journal of Psychoanalysis*, Vol. 40, pp. 308–315.

Bion, W.R. (1962) *Learning from Experience*. London, Tavistock Publications.

Bion, W.R. (1970) *Attention and Interpretation*. London, Karnac Books.

Bott Spillius, E., Milton, J., Garvey, P., Couve, C. and Steiner, D. (2011) *The New Dictionary of Kleinian Thought*. Abingdon, Routledge.

Caldwell, L. (2018) *A psychoanalysis of being: An approach to Donald Winnicott. British Journal of Psychotherapy*, Vol. 34, No. 2, pp. 221–239.

Caldwell, L. and Joyce, A. (2014) *Essentially Winnicott: Creating psychic health. British Journal of Psychotherapy*, Vol. 30, No. 1, pp. 18–32.

Conti, M. (2017) The case study of Jacob: Childhood sexual abuse and the limitations of the holding environment. *Psychoanalytic Social Work*, Vol. 24(1), pp. 18–36.

Crociani-Windland, L. (2013) Towards a psycho-social pedagogy as a relational practice and perspective. *Organizational and Social Dynamics*, Vol. 13, No. 2, pp. 127–146.

Diamond, M. (2014) *Metaphoric processes and organisational change: A contemporary psychoanalytic perspective. Organizational and Social Dynamics*, Vol. 14, pp. 104–129.

Fonagy, P. and Target, M. (2003) *Psychoanalytic Theories: Perspectives from Developmental Psychopathology*. London, Whurr.

Freud, S. (1914b) On narcissism. In *The Standard Edition of the Complete Psychological Works of Sigmund Freud*, Vol. XIV, pp. 67–102. London, Hogarth Press.

Fulgencio, L. (2015) *Discussion of the place of metapsychology in Winnicott's work. International Journal of Psychoanalysis*, Vol. 96, pp. 1235–1259.

Girard, M. (2017) *Early and deep: Two independent paradigms? International Journal of Psychoanalysis*, Vol. 98, pp. 963–984.

Goldberg, P. (1989) *Actively seeking the holding environment – Conscious and unconscious elements in the building of a therapeutic framework. Contemporary Psychoanalysis*, Vol. 25, pp. 448–476.

Green, A. (1975) *The analyst, symbolization and absence in the analytic setting (on changes in analytic practice and analytic experience). International Journal of Psychoanalysis*, Vol. 56, pp. 1–22.

Grotstein, J. (2007) *A beam of intense darkness*. London, Karnac Books.

Grotstein, J. (2009a) *But at the same time and on another level*, Vol. I. London, Karnac Books.

Grotstein, J. (2009b) *But at the same time and on another level*, Vol. II. London, Karnac Books.

Hinshelwood, R.D. (1991) *A Dictionary of Kleinian Thought*. Second edition. London, Free Association Books.

Hinshelwood, R.D. (1994) Attacks on the reflective space: Containing primitive emotional states. In Schermer, V. and Pines, M. (1994) *Ring of fire: Primitive affects and object relations in group psychotherapy*. Hove, Routledge, pp. 86–206.

Hinshelwood, R.D. and Abram, J. (2018) *The Clinical Paradigms of Melanie Klein and Donald Winnicott: Comparisons and Dialogues*. Abingdon, Routledge.

Hyman, S. (2012) *The school as a holding environment. Journal of Infant, Child & Adolescent Psychotherapy*, Vol. 11, No. 3, pp. 205–216.

Kasinski, K. (2003) The roots of the work: Definitions, origins and influences. In Ward, A., Kasinski, K., Pooley, J. and Worthington, A. (eds) *Therapeutic Communities for Children and Young People*. London, Jessica Kingsley, pp. 43–64.

Lanyado, M. (1996) *Winnicott's children: The holding environment and therapeutic communication in brief and non-intensive work. Journal of Child Psychotherapy*, Vol. 22, No. 3, pp. 423–443.

Lopéz-Corvo, R. (2005) *The Work of W.R. Bion*. London, Karnac Books.

Mawson, C. (ed.) (2011) *Bion Today*. Abingdon, Routledge.

Ogden, T. (2004) *On holding and containing, being and dreaming. International Journal of Psychoanalysis*, Vol. 85, pp. 1349–1364.

Ogden, T. (2016) *Destruction reconceived: On Winnicott's "The Use of an Object and Relating Through Identifications". International Journal of Psychoanalysis*, Vol. 97, pp. 1243–1262.

Rappoport, E. (2012) *Creating the umbilical cord: Relational knowing and the somatic third. Psychoanalytic Dialogues*, Vol. 22, pp. 375–388.

Riesenberg-Malcolm, R. (2001) Bion's theory of Containment. In Bronstein, C. (ed.) *Kleinian Theory: A Contemporary Perspective*. London, Whurr, pp. 165–180.

Sandler, P.C. (2005) *The Language of Bion*. London, Karnac Books.

Sandler, P.C. (2009) *Dreaming, Transformation, Containment and Change: A Clinical Application of Bion's Concepts*, Vol. I. London, Karnac Books.

Souder, J. (1988) *Projective Identification: Comparison and Discussion of Four Views*. Rosemead School of Psychology, Biola University.

Symington, N. and Symington, J. (1996) *The Clinical Thinking of Wilfred Bion*. London, Routledge.

Steiner, J. (2000) *Containment, enactment and communication. International Journal of Psychoanalysis*, Vol. 81, pp. 245–255.

Winnicott, D.W. (1953) *Transitional objects and transitional phenomena a study of the first not-me possession. The International Journal of Psycho-Analysis*, Vol. 34, No. 2, pp. 89–97.

Winnicott, D.W. (1956a) Primary maternal preoccupation. In Winnicott, D.W. (1975) *Through Paediatrics to Psycho-Analysis: Collected Papers*. New York, Basic Books, pp. 300–305.

Winnicott, D.W. (1956b) The antisocial tendency. In Winnicott, D.W. (1975) *Through Paediatrics to Psycho-Analysis: Collected Papers*. Routledge, London, pp. 303–315.

Winnicott, D.W. (1960) *The theory of the parent-infant relationship. International Journal of Psychoanalysis*, Vol. 41, pp. 585–595.

Part II

Psychoanalysis Beyond the Couch

From the beginning, psychoanalysis attempted to expand its insights from the clinical context into diverse domains of human experience. Freud was particularly adamant in expanding such horizons, having written on such vast topics as society, war, culture and literature. His contributions range from his hypothesis on the functioning of primitive societies in *Totem and Taboo* (1913–1914), and the relation between the father and his children, to the narcissism of minor differences observable in countries that share a border and are culturally similar (Freud 1930).[1] Although his most influential work regarding groups and leadership seems to be *Group Psychology and the Analysis of the Ego* (Freud 1921). It must be noted that in this process, Freud was not oblivious to contemporary developments in social sciences, quite the opposite. However, some anthropologists, including Bronislav Malinovski, were unimpressed.

Such expansion of psychoanalytic thought beyond the borders of psychology and clinical work continued, even before Freud's death, and informed organizational thought, as well as other sciences. The present book section deals with the efforts carried through by different authors to expand psychoanalysis to different contexts, beyond the clinical setting. In doing so, psychoanalysis became a helpful tool to explore the psychosocial context in general, and the organizational setting in particular. Although Part II is not particularly focused on containment, it does set the scene for the constant cross-fertilization between psychoanalysis and the vast psychosocial scene, where organizational studies play a key role.

As such, the fourth chapter "The Early Days of the Tavistock Institute" (by Alice White), addresses a time that was ripe for the application of psychoanalytic thought to the war effort in World War II and the subsequent post-War period. From the seminal work of the Institute derives much of the work that set the basis for the systems psychodynamics approach. From Alice White's chapter, it is clear that psychoanalysis played a key role in the work carried out in the post-War period, that is, it not only informed what was being done, but psychoanalytic thought was also shaped by the experiments being carried out. A second point, derived from White's chapter, is the constant effort not to take psychoanalytic insights at face value, but in fact apply them to specific contexts and needs (not to mention political sensitivities). That is, a requirement in the cross-fertilization effort was the need for

DOI: 10.4324/9781315146416-6

adaptation of the conceptual framework. Sometimes this meant that such knowledge was adapted to meet the needs of different projects. Finally, psychoanalytic knowledge was not stagnant at the time they were carrying out such work – in fact the Tavistock group did more than simply applying Freud's ideas as they stood some years back. Close contact with contemporary developments of the British Psychoanalytic Society was maintained on an ongoing basis, as key members continued with personal analysis or were involved in the conceptual developments that were coming out of the fertile debates of the Society at the time.

If the application of psychoanalytic ideas beyond the couch has been a hallmark of psychoanalytic thought, methodological questions abound and may puzzle practitioners. The field comprises a vast array of applications, described in the literature from the simpler use of psychoanalytic insight to understand clients' motivations and needs, but without any psychodynamically informed intervention, as described by Eric Miller in his consultation work, to the more complex Group Relations based interventions in organizations. Notwithstanding the richness and innovation that arises from such applications, careful consideration must be employed regarding its methodology since linear adaptations of ideas originating from the clinical setting to different contexts may, if used incautiously, hinder the very goal of applying the psychoanalytic framework. The fifth chapter "Researching the Unconscious in Organisations" (by Kalina Stamenova and Tiago Mendes) reviews some of the more common methodologies in the field, exploring its virtues. The authors also argue that the key tenet that separates psychodynamic-informed methodologies from the ones used by other sciences, such as anthropology or sociology, is the nature of data. The use of counter-transferential material as key data is crucial in this school of thought, which is unique when compared with other schools.

The sixth chapter, "Operationalisation of Concepts in Psychoanalytic Research" (by Gillian Walker), bridges the conceptual building blocks with the practical needs of research. Clearly one of the problems in bridging the fertile grounds of psychoanalytic theory with everyday practice has been the ways in which such concepts should be operationalized. The rich vocabulary of Kleinian practice, designed to capture one's innermost phantasies and bring them to light, paradoxically also hinders the effort of operationalization of its concepts due to its complex language. Walker addresses the need for operationalization of concepts in psychoanalysis and delves into the origins of the need for operationalization. Her own research in sadomasochism is the basis for her operationalization of Bion's concept of containment as well as Klein's excessive projective identification, allowing for a clearer view of what one can observe through these lenses. To do so, Walker draws on authoritative sources, which bring uncontroversial material on how said concepts were devised, and proposes her own set of criteria devised to be applied to discrete elements, cases or observations. The endeavour of providing clarification builds the basis for future explorations of the concept.

Finally, the last chapter in Part II, "Cultural Differences Between Groups" (by R.D. Hinshelwood) addresses a key aspect in group and organizational cultures. If the culture of an organization provides a containing function for the stresses of those working in it, then there is a question about the merging of two organizations. Will the containing functions be compatible with each other? As Menzies (1959) showed in her research with the nursing service of a general medical hospital, the practice was very specifically designed to enable the nurses to cope with the emotional stress of patients frightened by their symptoms, illnesses, operations or death. If the unconscious collective containing methods of the cultures are different it is likely to undermine the containing function of culture. Several examples are discussed including the coming together of Freud's Wednesday meeting group in Vienna with Jung and the Burgholzli group in Zurich.

As a final reference, although these chapters, for the most part, are not concerned with containment *per se*, the effort to clarify the methodological concerns is a necessary step for the following part.

Note

1 *Totem and Taboo* came to light at a crucial time in the Viennese Psychoanalytic Society, which was struggling with Jung's dissension. One might also interpret it as a message for the psychoanalytic community as a whole.

References

Freud, S. (1913–1914) *Totem and Taboo*. In *The Standard Edition of the Complete Psychological Works of Sigmund Freud*, Vol. XIII, pp. vii–162. London: Hogarth Press.

Freud, S. (1921) *Group Psychology and the Analysis of the Ego*. In *The Standard Edition of the Complete Psychological Works of Sigmund Freud*, Vol. XVIII, pp. 65–144. London: Hogarth Press.

Freud, S. (1930) *Civilization and Its Discontents*. In *The Standard Edition of the Complete Psychological Works of Sigmund Freud*, Vol. XXI, pp. 57–146. London: Hogarth Press.

Menzies, I. (1959) The functioning of social systems as a defence against anxiety: A report on a study of the nursing service of a general hospital. *Human Relations*, 13: 95–121. Republished in Menzies (1988) *Containing Anxiety in Institutions*. Free Association Books; and in Trist and Murray (eds) (1990) *The Social Engagement of Social Science*. Free Association Books.

Chapter 4

The Early Days of the Tavistock Institute

Alice White

Introduction

Applying psychoanalysis to groups and organisations was and is a hallmark of the Tavistock Institute. It is equally well-known by psychoanalysts and those working in business schools, yet the way that psychoanalytic ideas were first transposed from the clinical context to groups and organisations, and the way that management and bureaucratic necessities likewise shaped psychoanalytic ideas and practices, are often overlooked.

Before Wilfred Bion developed the concept of 'containment' in his clinical practice, before Elliot Jaques' notion of the 'social defence system' became widely known, and even before there was a Tavistock Institute, the people who would establish the Institute were beginning to look at organisational pathology – and health – through a psychoanalytic lens.

This chapter explores the origins of 'containment' by showing some of the factors that influenced later developments. The work discussed here predates the use of the term 'containment', 'containing' or 'contained', but marks a time when Bion and colleagues were thinking deeply about how people's personalities develop, how people manage emotions, and how mental states might be projected and interpreted.

First, it provides a pre-history of the Tavistock Institute, describing how its members came to work together in applying clinical concepts to the British Army during World War II. As the scale of the conflict became apparent, traditional clinical practice became impossible for some psychoanalysts. At the same time, psychologists were looking for new ways to apply their skills. Work investigating 'problem' officers brought together the people who would later form the Tavistock Institute, and their efforts to establish War Office Selection Boards and Civil Resettlement Units had a significant impact on the development of their ideas and methods. During the course of this work, the psychologists had opportunities to think, study and test their ideas about what constituted positive ways of developing and engaging with the world, rather than primarily addressing the difficulties of patients seeking help, as they had in clinical practice previously.

DOI: 10.4324/9781315146416-7

Next, this chapter covers how this 'invisible college' group that formed to solve wartime problems made plans to continue and develop their early work. From the very outset, this involved conflict between individuals within the group who had differing visions and priorities. Whilst Bion wanted the space to explore promising new concepts, Rees wanted to ensure that programmes were not shut down by disapproving military management. There were also difficulties at an organisational level as the group found themselves between the worlds of psychoanalysis and management. Whilst this was an intellectually fertile area, there were many challenges to their hopes of continuing to apply clinical ideas to organisations, not least of which involved finding funding.

Following this is a brief discussion of the ideas that stemmed from the cross-fertilisation between psychoanalysis and business. Work for the National Coal Board, Glacier Metal Company and the Ahmedabad Manufacturing and Calico Printing Company are perhaps the best-known examples.

The chapter concludes with a summary of the context for how the Tavistock group brought psychoanalytic ideas into their work with organisations, and how much of this history is yet to be explored.

A Pre-History of the Tavistock Institute

The Tavistock Institute rose from the ashes of World War II. In fact, the very plans to create the Institute were referred to by Bion and colleagues as 'Operation Phoenix'. Because of this, it is impossible to fully understand the work of the Institute in applying psychoanalytic ideas to organisations without first knowing a little about the wartime work.

Psychologists Go to War

One of the fundamentally interesting things about the military projects where psychoanalytical ideas were applied to organisations is how they ever came about. Psychoanalysts did not simply decide to take their expertise and apply it to a passive Army. The motivations to seek new outlets to apply their knowledge were both intellectual and financial.

Between the World Wars, psychology, psychiatry and psychoanalysis in Britain were not as clearly demarcated as in Germany or America, and there were relatively few academic departments devoted to psychological research[1] (Thomson 2001; Richards 2000; Ellesley 1995; Hayward 1995).

Whilst the lines between different types of psychology were not clearly drawn to the layperson at this time, there were differences between different groups. For instance, Frederick Bartlett's department at Cambridge shunned social psychology and favoured laboratory experiments and cognitive approaches, and the Tavistock

Clinic, established in 1920 to see patients for one-to-one psychoanalytic therapy, was disapproved of both by psychiatrists at the Maudsley and by Ernest Jones and his group at the British Psycho-Analytic Society (E. Trist 2008; H.V. Dicks 1970; Fraher 2004).

Regardless of their theoretical position, during the interwar period, many psychologists were still in the early stages of establishing their remits and trying to win funding, establish teaching programmes and contracts for work (Jones and Rahman 2009). For example, Tavistock Clinic staff had already expressed an interest in going beyond solely working with individuals in difficulty; they wanted to expand their scope to include organisations, 'the employer and managerial classes' (Bunn, Richards and Lovie 2001; 'The Tavistock Clinic: Effective Results of Treatment' 1938). Working for the military offered practitioners a chance to prove the value of psychology and to work in new ways with a different type of client.

Moreover, funding was a concern even before the war for many psychological organisations and with many clients departing London due to the war, the need to find new avenues for work became more urgent. At the Tavistock Clinic, for instance, staff had recently volunteered to go unsalaried due to financial challenges (H.V. Dicks 1970). Working for the military presented a temptation in that the services had enormous funding capabilities during the war.

However, it initially appeared quite unlikely that the Army (considered the most 'hidebound' and 'patrician' of the military services) would be willing to use the services of psychologists[2] (Turner 1956, 14, 295; Cannadine 1990, 607). And many psychiatrists and psychoanalysts found their skills were not particularly in demand. Some analysts relocated their practices to the suburbs and countryside because their patients had moved in order to avoid bombing. Some opted to work for the emergency medical services at places such as Mill Hill or Westfield, where there were very few patients at times but where different psychological approaches mingled and many informal professional connections were made (H.V. Dicks 1970; E. Trist 2008; Trahair 2015). Others who offered their services to the military were ignored (Ahrenfeldt 1958; H.V. Dicks 1970; White 2016c).

This began to change when, due to his networks, J.R. Rees of the Tavistock Clinic was commissioned as the Consultant to the Army at Home, which was one of only two positions created for psychiatrists in the British Army at the outbreak of the war (Thalassis 2004, 83–84). Rees allocated colleagues to Area Commands where they worked closely with military colleagues on problems that were pressing in their particular area.

An important factor in initiating and maintaining psychologists' Army work was the way that they integrated with the organisation: Rees' colleagues noted that he had a 'genius for "roping in" lay support' for psychoanalytical work; Ronald Hargreaves reportedly devoured all of the Army field manuals; and Bion was seen by Army colleagues as 'a large, outspoken man, a physician of repute and a fighting soldier, who had won the DSO [Distinguished Service Order] commanding a tank at Cambrai' (H. Dicks 2009; Belhaven 1955). Psychiatrists were known as 'trick cyclists' and viewed with suspicion by many both in the rank-and-file and in senior ranks, so such efforts to demonstrate that they were relatable figures were vital in gaining trust and acceptance of their work.

Officer Selection

Once psychologists had established relationships with their local commanders, the first task that seemed ideally suited for the application of psychoanalytic skills was to assist the Army with 'problem' officers (White 2016a). Erik Wittkower, Thomas Ferguson Roger and John Bowlby framed the problem psychoanalytically, explaining that men were failing in their roles as trainee or newly trained officers because the way that they were relating to others made them poorly suited for the role. In addition to dealing with the immediate problem presented by these men, the psychologists offered to apply their skills prophylactically and assist with selection by weeding out those vulnerable to breakdown or unsuited to leadership (E.L. Trist and Murray 1990).

Career soldiers who actively sought new ways to solve Army problems with officer quality and selection facilitated the application of psychological ideas. In some cases they initiated the investigations (Colonel Vinden had seen German psychological selection methods in use before the war and was keen to try something similar in Britain), whilst in others they were open to proposals and made opportunities for experimentation to take place by providing time, soldiers and physical space (White 2016a; French 2001; Crang 2000). Early work applying psychoanalysis to organisations grew from the middle ranks of the Army organisation rather than being commissioned from the top. It was only once the initial experiments showed impressive results that they reached the attention of the War Office, and the War Office Selection Boards (WOSBs) were officially established.

WOSBs drew upon a variety of tools that blended psychological and military methods. Originally, the Army pressed to go ahead with a system that simply added an intelligence test and a psychiatric interview to the original Army Command Interview Board, but Eric Trist, Isabel Menzies and others at the Edinburgh Board continued to develop and refine a battery of tasks intended to provide information for interviews and make them more focused. Each task was intended to help show who might be vulnerable to breakdown in a commanding position due to issues such as anxiety that the men they commanded were more intelligent than them, or difficulty dealing with people in authority over them.

The approved WOSBs selection methods included 'intelligence' tests of mental ability, psychological 'pointers' (self-description, word association, thematic apperception), interviews, questionnaires and group tasks or discussions. Some methods were considered potentially useful and tried, but could not be made to work at an organisational level. Rorschach inkblots were deemed impossible to administer under Board conditions and could not be interpreted by Sergeant Testers who had limited psychological training (White 2016a).

Tasks were more intended to establish whether a person had sufficient resources to manage stress, without trying to artificially recreate a stress situation, unlike

German officer selection tests that looked at performance under stress by introducing stressful stimuli, including electric shock (White 2016a).

The 'leaderless group' task is perhaps the best-known innovation of the WOSBs. It has been described as 'a two-person idea', but in the literal sense far more people than Bion and his analyst John Rickman helped to develop the method (Foresti 2011). An unnamed Military Testing Officer initiated the use of a practical problem that a group were left to solve without being assigned roles by the assessor. The psychological staff initially accepted this addition to the testing battery to make the tests appear 'hands-on' and military enough, but soon Bion saw an opportunity to analyse candidates' social relations in practice. At this point, the original task given to the group was demoted to the 'set' problem as the 'real' problem that made the test valuable concerned the candidates' object relations ('Chapter 7: The Work of the MTO, Quasi-Real-Life Situations', n.d.; White 2016a). In addition to providing an analytical framework for interpreting the physical leaderless group tests, Bion also experimented with having leaderless groups select a discussion topic and then direct their discussion of it.

Bion and Rickman also extensively discussed how the psychiatric interview should function, though it was Rickman who wrote the notes on the psychiatric interview technique (Rickman, 1944). Emphasis was placed upon the importance of the psychiatrist as uniquely able to consider the way that previous experiences shaped the way that people interact with others and how 'most deeply ingrained attitudes appear to be created out of the earliest experiences with others... those who satisfy his earliest needs, above all his mother and father' ('Chapter 4: What Should be Tested and Job Analysis', n.d.). Unconscious processes in relation to WOSBs were explicitly discussed in terms of object relations. There are no references in discussion papers about containing or reverie (either in relation to psychiatrist or mother), or to raw experiences.

There was, however, an emphasis on candidates' abilities to think and articulate under pressure. The psychiatric staff sought to develop and refine methods that could help to identify things that a person could not articulate about themselves. Psychological staff of WOSBs argued that 'in the selection setting, oblique techniques were imperative'. Oblique methods were projection techniques and included the psychological pointers, leaderless group tasks and the psychiatric interview, all of which used 'apparently neutral material to obtain clues to "what he cannot or will not say about himself"' ('Chapter 5: Chapter on Interviews', n.d.) Notable examples include thematic apperception and word association tests, for which blank or truncated answers indicated 'blocking' or an inability to think in relation to certain stimuli. This is never framed in terms of beta-elements, however.

Civil Resettlement Units

Once the first WOSBs were established, it did not take long before they spread across the United Kingdom and beyond. WOSBs were established for other British and allied forces; Elliot Jaques' first connection with the growing Tavistock group began when he helped to bring the new WOSB procedures into use in the Canadian Army (Kirsner 2004).

One of the new applications for the techniques was at No. 21 WOSB, where Bion began to investigate possibilities of selecting repatriated prisoners of war (POWs). A.T.M. Wilson was also working with POWs and was keen to put into practice analytic principles suggested by work Bion had begun with 'therapeutic communities' at Northfield Military Hospital, whereby groups participated in therapeutic discussions with an analyst present to support participants in helping each other. Bion felt that this was 'rash'. However, when a scheme of Civil Resettlement Units (CRUs) was approved by the War Office in February 1944, it was Wilson who was chosen to lead by Rees, rather than Bion. Bion's preference to explore an idea in more detail lost out under pressure to speedily establish a programme (White 2016a).

Despite their rapid deployment, there was a great deal of psychological thought underpinning CRUs. Even the term 'resettlement' indicates a core principle; that participants were sensitive to the idea that they might be 'damaged' in some way and would not be willing to participate in a visibly analytic scheme that might sully their reputations in the military or with potential employers following demobilisation. Bion explained that they would 'be employing psychiatric machinery; but the machinery need not cause irritation by creaking' (W.R. Bion 1945). CRUs were innovative and influential because their psychoanalytic foundations were obscured.

Just as the 'real' psychological problem set to leaderless groups was concealed by a 'set' task, the therapeutic aspect of CRUs was to be complemented and concealed by a work experience element. Wilson, Trist and Menzies immediately began engaging industrial federations, trade associations, the Ministry of Pensions and the Ministry of Labour to secure support for the new resettlement programme. He spoke the language of his audience, advising them that 'good personnel management is not a humanitarian affair but is satisfactorily reflected in the annual reports of companies' and arguing that far from being 'an impractical and starry-eyed idealist', he was actually being very cautious to avoid the unrest that followed the previous World War (Wilson 1945). Wilson's approach worked and it was less than two months from the first meetings to the date when the first CRU opened its doors on 31 May 1944.

The CRUs are another example of a way that clinical expertise was applied at an organisational level in order to prevent harm, rather than treat problems once they arose. Wilson and his colleagues hoped that CRUs might operate on the Northfield principles, and CRUs are today often mentioned as a post-script to the Northfield Experiments; they are just one way that the therapeutic community ideas were applied. But CRUs are an example of how the Tavistock group took analytic principles beyond the clinical setting and into business and industrial organisations. Applying psychoanalysis to the resettlement organisation was dependent upon it not appearing to be overtly psychological, just as the WOSBs tests were most successful when they carried a military veneer to cover their psychological underpinnings (White 2016a).

Disagreeing on Principles

The expansion of the psychological work from officer selection into the new realm of POW resettlement, however, did not mean that there was total acceptance of these methods nor agreement on how to proceed. Important people were concerned about the use of psychoanalysts and their expertise within the British Army. The Prime Minister, Winston Churchill, was particularly alarmed about their work, stating that it was 'very wrong to disturb large numbers of healthy normal men and women by asking the kind of odd questions in which the psychiatrists specialise' (Churchill 1942). In the popular discourse, psychoanalysis was linked with taboo topics such as sex, and some senior military figures were uncomfortable with the possibility of questions that strayed beyond whether a man wanted 'to push a bayonet into some German's guts' (Belhaven 1955).

As their influence and work spread, Churchill convened an Expert Committee to investigate the work of psychologists and psychiatrists in the British military. The psychologist members of the committee persuaded their peers very quickly of the utility of their work. They then usurped the Committee's original purpose and instead used it to agree amongst themselves on territories for their work to be applied, and to invite prospective clients to view their work in action, ostensibly as independent judges of the work but actually to advertise their services to captains of industry and other influential figures (White 2016a).

Churchill and other senior figures' worries were not solely about psychoanalysis, though, and were not assuaged by the Committee's reassurance that psychoanalysis was not probing inappropriately into soldiers' sex lives. The most influential supporter of the WOSBs, Sir Ronald Adam, was known for his left-leaning politics, which was also a concern for those opposed to WOSBs (Addison 2013). The battle over who should choose officers was a microcosm of larger social debates between those advocating for the preservation of conservative systems and those favouring a liberal meritocracy (White 2016b). The traditionalists' concerns appeared to be borne out at the WOSB where Wilfred Bion was working: he began a 'regimental nomination scheme' by which soldiers were able to elect via a secret ballot their own candidates to be sent for officer training (Eric Trist 1985). Once word got out about this scheme, it was rapidly shut down amidst 'accusations of encouraging and development of Soviets' in the Army (Trahair 2015, 103).

Psychoanalysis being applied to an organisation represented modernisation. Sometimes, that made it appealing: one of the reasons that WOSBs were rolled out was because the Army needed to be seen to be addressing concerns that its promotion structure was outdated and unmeritocratic. On the other hand, it also made it threatening to those satisfied with the status quo.

Practical Psychology

The application of analytic methods at an organisational level also presented frustrations for the psychologists. The Tavistock group who had formed from Clinic staff and others working on WOSBs and CRUs referred to themselves as the Invisible College, after the scholars who went on to form the Royal Society (H.V. Dicks 1970).

This gives an indication of the scale of their hopes and ambitions, and Bion had hoped that the Army might be their Schiehallion – a place where they could rigorously test their principles as the Royal Society had tested the mean density of the Earth on the Scottish mountain. However, by December 1944, Bion felt that 'psychiatric work [in the Army] is at a standstill except for the activity of the Tavistock group in its attempts to snatch some glittering prize of publicity with which to deck itself in civil life' (Vonofakos and Hinshelwood 2012).

It is understandable that Bion would feel bitter about the sincerity of his colleagues' commitment to their practice. His regimental nomination scheme was halted by Rees, he was removed from Northfield military hospital because his colleagues feared that either Bion would 'blow up... the whole of Army psychiatry... or one of the Big Guns would fire at us', and he had lost out to Wilson on the POW work too (Bion 2012, 58).

The Tavistock group were described as having 'no profound grasp of psychopathology', and Bion may have agreed with this judgement when projects that he was just beginning to conceptualise were either halted or thrust into practice before they were fully developed. However, the group's skills lay 'in the way of practical psychology... in the tactful handling of negotiations' (Adrian Stephen 1943, as quoted in King 1989, 17) Applying analytic techniques at an organisational level required compromises that not everyone was comfortable making: practicality and willingness to experiment were put ahead of insistence on theoretical rigour.

The analysts' work for the Army was not only dependent upon finding the right balance of methods that would be acceptable to the organisation, it was also about knowing when to forge ahead and when to desist from following ideas that were intellectually promising but threatened the relationship with their clients. The continuation of the collaboration (and the funding it provided) was only possible because of careful diplomacy. All that Bion could hope for was 'a new attempt in peace time with a properly trained and determined team who are prepared first of all to apply the Schichallion scheme themselves, and then apply themselves to the Schichallion scheme' (Vonofakos and Hinshelwood 2012).

Establishing the Tavistock Institute

The WOSBs helped to select men to take on new responsibilities from hundreds of thousands of candidates, and tens of thousands of repatriated POWs were supported by CRUs on their return to civilian life and employment. Both projects also played a vital part in facilitating new opportunities for the post-war work of the psychologists themselves. The connections they had forged with influential figures from business and industry, and the ideas and methods they had begun to apply in their work with organisations, opened new prospects. Henry Dicks noted that:

> There is no doubt... that the kind of experience gathered in the Army, perhaps especially by the psychologists who joined us after the war, had an impact on the development of personality assessment techniques based on psychodynamic principles which has characterised the Tavistock's services.

> (H.V. Dicks 1970, 310)

To keep the Invisible College group together and to facilitate their continued experimentation in applying analytical ideas at an organisational level, a new organisation was established: the Tavistock Institute.

In spirit, the Institute represented the new start that 'Operation Phoenix' implied. Though WOSBs generated a significant insight amongst the psychological staff into new ways that they could apply their knowledge, the psychiatrists were surplus to requirements and removed from Army WOSBs at the end of the war. Future projects would be inspired by, but separate from, this former work.

Perhaps indicating that the group felt that in leaving the Army, they were moving past the need to compromise their principles for practical reasons, Rees was ousted from leadership of the new organisation. Despite this shift, Bion was not elected to the management committee (H.V. Dicks 1970).

In practice, though the Tavistock Clinic and Tavistock Institute were officially different organisations, this was in name and funding only during the years immediately following the war. Ideas crossed back and forth from the clinical setting to the organisational setting, and vice versa. Whilst Tavistock Institute staff were working on projects for organisations, they were often simultaneously seeing patients or in analysis (Fraher 2004; Trahair 2015).

Immediately after the war, all of the staff of the new Institute, many of whom had backgrounds in other social sciences, entered psychoanalytic training (Pines 2000). This ensured that the subsequent work with organisations conducted by this staff had a common intellectual grounding.

Accounts indicate that the atmosphere was intense in these early years, as the Institute staff did indeed attempt to apply their methods to themselves as well as to others. Bion's role 'was stressful much of the time' and 'despite the denial mechanisms in the group the impact was profound; two members developed duodenal ulcer symptoms before the group finished, and three decided to have personal analysis subsequently' (Sutherland 1985).

Another challenge in pursuing this new direction was that they no longer had the Army paying their salaries, and, in departing from the clinical setting, clinical funding streams were no longer available to the Institute. They were informed by well-placed friends just before the creation of the National Health Service that it categorically would not encompass the sort of prophylactic organisational-level work they intended to conduct (H.V. Dicks 1970).

Post-War Projects

Fortunately, the WOSBs and CRUs had enabled the Tavistock group to build relationships with influential figures in industry, and word had spread about their work. Concerned about the economy, the Ministry of Labour formed a Productivity Committee headed by Stafford Cripps, who had sat on the Expert Committee and was therefore familiar with the Tavistock group's war work. The Human Factors Panel of Cripps' Committee sanctioned three Tavistock Institute projects. There were thus immediate opportunities to continue developing the Group Relations concepts that had begun to form during the war.

One of the Human Factors projects involved work for the Glacier Metal Company. This arose directly from the war work in the sense that the Medical Officer from Glacier had attended a wartime meeting with Wilson and the head of the company became interested in the Institute's methods before there was an Institute. The project at Glacier enabled staff including Trist, Jaques and A.K. Rice to begin to reconcile 'the way that individuals operate psychologically with the way social systems operate'. It was in the book about this work, *The Changing Culture of a Factory*, that Jaques introduced anxiety as binding together individuals' unconscious phantasies when they were members of an organisation (Hinshelwood 2008).

Work with the National Coal Board (NCB), another of the Human Factors projects, was initially hampered by the Institute staff's lack of influential connections. The NCB work is known in management schools today because it is considered the origin of the socio-technical systems approach, which reconsidered how groups work with new technologies. The projects nearly did not happen though: it was only because one of the Institute's new trainees, Ken Bamforth, was a former miner that they were able to begin (E.L. Trist and Bamforth 1951). Even with this connection, the work started and stopped several times; the Institute staff evidently felt it very important to their burgeoning ideas to persist despite these challenges.[3]

Trist described the Glacier and NCB projects as where the Institute found its identity. Rice built upon the Group Relations ideas developed at Glacier and the NCB in his work at the Ahmedabad Manufacturing and Calico Printing Company. This work enabled the Institute staff to develop their ideas and the global networks involved also facilitated the popularisation of their approach (Banerjee 2015). The importance of the early work of the Institute is now being reassessed by historians of management, who argue that some innovations traditionally accredited to American groups actually originated with the Tavistock in the UK (Banerjee and Cooke 2012; Burnes and Cooke 2013).

Conclusion

This chapter has not revealed a dramatic or unexpected earlier origin for the first mentions of containment, raw experience, receptive reverie or alpha-function, or for evidence of these elements beginning to form in the writings of Bion or his colleagues.

However, there is a notable gap in the literature between Bion's experiences of World War I, thought to have influenced his development of ideas of containment when he later reflected upon them, and his experiences from the 1950s of marriage and working with psychotic patients, when he began to write about ideas of containment. This chapter offers suggestions of where Bion might have had opportunities to develop his ideas relating to his own role and to how people think, or are unable to think, under pressure, and how others can facilitate or block this. It suggests projects that may have prompted his thinking in directions that led towards containment, though most of these were abruptly halted before he had much opportunity to develop his thinking in the way that he wanted.

The people that came together during World War II brought together ideas from psychoanalysis, organisational studies and beyond, and this cross-fertilisation resulted in the birth of the Tavistock Institute, whose work continued in this tradition.

The application of psychoanalytic methods to the organisation of the British Army had initially worked much like clinical analysis, looking at individuals with less than optimal functioning. The expansion to group-level application occurred informally initially, via local experiments that were supported by military commanders seeking a new approach to managing. Psychoanalytic, psychological and military methods mingled together to produce tools such as the leaderless group test, projective tests, and new approaches to interviewing.

The Tavistock group's experimentation gave rise to a range of new practices and ideas but was curtailed by practical considerations such as what military staff would accept and time limits before POWs returned and required services. This frustrated Bion but gave rise to the practical psychology that so appealed to postwar clients because it had produced demonstrable results.

Large projects for Glacier, for the NCB and in Ahmedabad grew out of the war work on selection and resettlement. At these projects, Institute staff continued to develop their application of psychoanalysis to organisations and develop the idea of Group Relations, and the projects were influential both within the Institute and around the world. However, these projects were often difficult to conduct and were insufficient to cover the Institute's financial needs.

The Tavistock group noted with surprise that 'visitors [to the boards] wanted to take over the new methods with little, if any, preliminary critical inquiry regarding their appropriateness for selection tasks other than finding potential officers' ('Chapter 1: Introduction', n.d.). The unquestioning acceptance that psychological methods could be applied in different situations is reflected in management literature, which often discusses methods but lacks interrogation of the principles that guided the psychological staff who applied them.

Throughout World War II, Bion railed against constraints that limited careful consideration of the underlying principles behind the methods that he and his colleagues were involved in developing. He continued to challenge his colleagues at the post-war Tavistock, and it is possible that there is more to be said on containment and institutions. The most potentially valuable sources in which to examine the way that early thinking about containment and the concepts around it might have intersected with post-war projects are likely to be the notes of the Institute staff. My examination of these notes has yielded little evidence of Bion's influence, and no mention of containment. But there are extensive notes on these projects and therefore opportunity for closer examination of how thinking on these projects shifted over time, which might be a fruitful source for those hoping to interpret the development of concepts and their subtle influence in the Institute's work.

I thus conclude this chapter with a call to action. Understanding the historical context of later developments is valuable, yet there is a great deal still to be explored. The newly catalogued archives of the Tavistock Institute offer ample opportunities to study this early period before 'containment' and 'social defence systems' had been formally written-up; I hope that we will soon see a flourishing of scholarship on this era.

Notes

1 Because there was not a formalised difference or training path to these careers at this time in history, this chapter will refer to psychologists as a term to cover those of various types of training and practice, though many of those at the centre of this history had psychoanalytical interests, had undergone analysis or were trained analysts.
2 For their part, the other two armed forces saw the potential value of psychological expertise, but not analysis, to their work much earlier. The Royal Navy sought the services of the National Institute of Industrial Psychology, who had experience in time and motion studies and in selecting young people to train for technically skilled jobs; and the Royal Air Force used Frederick Bartlett's team of applied psychologists based at the University of Cambridge to investigate factors such as fatigue, vision and stimulants upon flying ability (Edwards 1939; Vernon 1947; 'The psychology of skill' 1947; White 2016a).
3 The role of unions in supporting and shaping the NCB studies has not yet been fully explored by researchers but archive materials indicate a close collaboration between the Institute and the National Union of Mineworkers and potentially a new dimension to consider in how psychoanalysis was applied to organisations.

References

Addison, Paul. 2013. *Churchill on the Home Front, 1900–1955*. Faber & Faber.
Ahrenfeldt, Robert H. 1958. *Psychiatry in the British Army in the Second World War*. Routledge & K. Paul.
Banerjee, Anindita. 2015. *Global Networks and Their Influence on Shaping and Popularisation of Post-World War II Management Theory: The Particular Case of the Generalisation of Tavistock Institute's Sociotechnical Systems Theory*. Lancaster University.
Banerjee, Anindita, and Bill Cooke. 2012. *How Human Relations Got Its Name: The Journal As Boundary Object*. Tavistock Institute of Human Relations. https://web.archive.org/web/20240523192613/https://www.tavinstitute.org/whats-on/how-human-relations-got-its-name
Belhaven, Lord Robert Alexander Benjamin Hamilton. 1955. *The Uneven Road*. John Murray.
Bion, W.R. 1945. 'Return from Stalag'. *The British Medical Journal* 1 (4406): 844–845.
Bion, W.R. 2012. *All My Sins Remembered: Another Part of a Life & The Other Side of Genius: Family Letters*. Karnac Books.
Bunn, Geoffrey C., G.D. Richards, and A.D. Lovie. 2001. *Psychology in Britain: Historical Essays and Personal Reflections*. BPS Books.
Burnes, Bernard, and Bill Cooke. 2013. 'The Tavistock's 1945 invention of organization development: Early British business and management applications of social psychiatry'. *Business History* 55 (5): 768–789.
Cannadine, David. 1990. 'The Second World War'. In *The Decline and Fall of the British Aristocracy*. Yale University Press.
'Chapter 1: Introduction'. n.d. In *Unpublished WOSBs Write-Up MSS*.
'Chapter 4: What should be tested and job analysis'. n.d. In *Unpublished WOSBs Write-Up MSS*.

'Chapter 5: Chapter on interviews', n.d. In *Unpublished WOSBs Write-Up MSS.*
'Chapter 7: The work of the MTO, quasi-real-life situations'. n.d. In *Unpublished WOSBs Write-Up MSS.*
Churchill, Winston. 1942. 'Prime Minister's personal minute'. WO 259/75. The National Archives.
Crang, Jeremy A. 2000. *The British Army and the People's War, 1939–1945.* Manchester University Press.
Dicks, H.V. 1970. *Fifty Years of the Tavistock Clinic.* Routledge & K. Paul.
Dicks, Henry. 2009. 'John Rawlings Rees'. In *Munk's Roll: Lives of the Fellows,* Online Edition, VI: 387. Royal College of Physicians. https://history.rcplondon.ac.uk/inspiring-physicians/john-rawlings-rees
Edwards, Lieut.-Commander Kenneth, *Sunday Times* Naval Correspondent. 1939. 'The Navy goes in for psychology'. *The Sunday Times,* 6 August. Gale NewsVault.
Ellesley, Sandra. 1995. *Psychoanalysis in Early Twentieth-Century England: A Study in the Popularization of Ideas.* PhD, University of Essex.
Foresti, Giovanni. 2011. 'Rediscovering Bion and Rickman's leaderless group projects'. In *International Forum of Psychoanalysis,* 20: 103–107. Taylor & Francis. www.tandfonline.com.chain.kent.ac.uk/doi/abs/10.1080/0803706X.2011.570788.
Fraher, Amy Louise. 2004. *A History of Group Study and Psychodynamic Organizations.* Free Association Books.
French, David. 2001. *Raising Churchill's Army.* Oxford University Press.
Hayward, Rhodri. 1995. *Popular Mysticism and the Origins of the New Psychology, 1880–1910.* University of Lancaster. EThOS, The British Library.
Hinshelwood, R. 2008. 'Systems, culture and experience: understanding the divide between the individual and the organization'. *Organisational and Social Dynamics* 8 (1): 63–77.
Jones, Edgar, and Shahina Rahman. 2009. 'The Maudsley Hospital and the Rockefeller Foundation: The Impact of Philanthropy on Research and Training'. *Journal of the History of Medicine and Allied Sciences* 64 (3): 273–299.
King, Pearl. 1989. 'Activities of British psychoanalysts during the Second World War and the influence of their inter-disciplinary collaboration on the development of psychoanalysis in Great Britain'. *International Review of Psycho-Analysis* 16 (15): 14–33.
Kirsner, Douglas. 2004. 'The intellectual odyssey of Elliott Jaques: From alchemy to science'. *Free Associations* 11 (2): 179–204.
Pines, Malcolm. 2000. *Bion and Group Psychotherapy.* Jessica Kingsley.
Richards, Graham. 2000. 'Britain on the couch: The popularization of psychoanalysis in Britain 1918–1940'. *Science in Context* 13 (2): 183–230.
Rickman, J. 1944. 'A symposium on the psychiatric interview in officer selection'. A.M.D. 11 45/03/8, Tavistock Institute Archives.
Star, Susan Leigh. 2010. 'This is not a boundary object: Reflections on the origin of a concept'. *Science, Technology & Human Values* 35 (5): 601–617.
Sutherland, J.D. 1985. 'Bion revisited: Group dynamics and group psychotherapy'. In *Bion and Group Psychotherapy,* edited by Malcolm Pines. Routledge & Kegan Paul.
Thalassis, Nafsika. 2004. *Treating and Preventing Trauma: British Military Psychiatry during the Second World War.* University of Salford. University of Salford Institutional Repository.
'The psychology of skill'. 1947. *The British Medical Journal* 1 (4511): 890–891.
'The Tavistock Clinic: Effective results of treatment'. 1938. *The British Medical Journal* 1 (4037): 1118–1119.
Thomson, Mathew. 2001. 'The popular, the practical and the professional: Psychological identities in Britain, 1901–1950'. In *Psychology in Britain: Historical Essays and Personal Reflections,* edited by G.C. Bunn, A.D. Lovie and G.D. Richards. BPS Books.
Trahair, Richard. 2015. *Behavior, Technology, and Organizational Development: Eric Trist and the Tavistock Institute.* Transaction Publishers.

Trist, E.L., and K.W. Bamforth. 1951. 'Some social and psychological consequences of the longwall method of coal-getting: An examination of the psychological situation and defences of a work group in relation to the social structure and technological content of the work system'. *Human Relations* 4 (1): 3–38. https://doi.org/10.1177/001872675100400101.

Trist, E.L., and Dr Hugh Murray. 1990. *The Social Engagement of Social Science: The Socio-Psychological Perspective*. Free Association Books.

Trist, Eric. 1985. 'Working with Bion in the 1940s: The group decade'. In *Bion and Group Psychotherapy*, edited by Malcolm Pines. Routledge & Kegan Paul.

Trist, Eric. 2008. '"Guilty of enthusiasm", from *Management Laureates*, Vol. 3, Ed. Arthur G. Bedeian (Jai Press, 1993)'. *The Modern Times Workplace*. www.moderntimesworkplace.com/archives/ericbio/ericbio.html.

Turner, Ernest Sackville. 1956. *Gallant Gentlemen: A Portrait of the British Officer, 1600–1956*. M. Joseph.

Vernon, P.E. 1947. 'Research on personnel selection in the Royal Navy and the British Army'. *American Psychologist* 2 (2): 35–51. https://doi.org/10.1037/h0056920.

Vonofakos, Dimitris, and Bob Hinshelwood, eds. 2012. 'Wilfred Bion's letters to John Rickman (1939–1951): The letters'. *Psychoanalysis and History* 14 (1): 64–94.

White, Alice. 2016a. *From the Science of Selection to Psychologising Civvy Street: The Tavistock Group, 1939–1948*. PhD, University of Kent. https://kar.kent.ac.uk/55057/

White, Alice. 2016b. 'Governing the science of selection: The psychological sciences, 1921–1945'. In *Scientific Governance in Britain, 1914–1979*, edited by Charlotte Sleigh and Don Leggett. Manchester: Manchester University Press. www.manchesteruniversitypress.co.uk/9780719090981/

White, Alice. 2016c. 'Silence and selection: The "trick cyclist" at the War Office Selection Boards'. In *The Silences of Science: Gaps and Pauses in the Communication of Science*, edited by Felicity Mellor and Stephen Webster. Routledge.

Wilson, A.T.M. 1945. 'Some psychological aspects of resettlement: An address by Lt. Col. A.T. Macbeth Wilson to the Ministry of Production: Harrow District Mutual Aid Organisation, report of 15th inter-group meeting'. CRUs (PsOW): Papers/Talks/Contributions, Box 377625502. Tavistock Institute Archives.

Chapter 5

Researching the Unconscious in Organisations

Kalina Stamenova and Tiago Mendes

Introduction

Psychoanalysis is essential in understanding the unconscious in individuals and groups, organisations and society at large, as it may offer concepts quite useful for social science such as unconscious phantasy, the anxiety-defence model or projective identification and containment. Organisations experience various dynamics and while some can be understood by using rational thinking and decision-making, other dynamics are hidden and unavailable for thinking and understanding. People join various organisations and bring with them their emotions, creating unique organisational cultures, shaped by several forces, while also being confronted with experiences that trigger deeply held anxieties in their work contexts.

Below organisational practices, policies and structures, or what we could define as the surface of the organisational and social life, lie hidden dynamics which can be more clearly illuminated through the lenses of psychoanalytic ideas and thinking. We trace back these ideas to Freud's anthropological thesis *Totem and Taboo* which attempted to create the 'first bridge from psychoanalysis to social science' (Hinshelwood 2008, p. 117). There has been fruitful cross-fertilisation between psychoanalysis and social science leading to the application of psychoanalytic thought to anthropology (Devereux 1978; Ewing 1992; Molino 2004), sociology (Craib 1989; Hunt 1989; Rustin 2001), literature and predominantly in organisational studies leading to the conceptualisation of culture as a psycho-social process (Trist 1950). Despite such rich endeavours, there are inherent difficulties when one tries to apply psychoanalytic concepts to social sciences. The path has not been trailed without bumps in the road. Several criticisms of the approach abound, some even in Freud's days, as in the case of Malinowski, who opposed Freud's attempts to expand his ideas to social science. Even within the psychodynamic community, criticisms abound regarding attempts to use other methods alongside clinical psychoanalysis. Such criticisms, although understandable given that the psychoanalytic methodology and theory were constructed, first and foremost, from clinical experience, nonetheless prevent the use of psychoanalytic rich insights in other sciences, thus insulating psychoanalytic knowledge from contributing to other fields. In the end, such efforts may lead to

DOI: 10.4324/9781315146416-8

keeping psychoanalytic insights siloed and sterilised. To us, such would be the demise of psychoanalytic knowledge.

This chapter addresses those challenges, but also explicates the virtues and pit-falls of taking psychoanalysis outside of the couch, as it were, of expanding its conceptual building beyond the clinical setting and, by doing so, casts a psycho-analytically informed glance upon social experiences. This is not a novel path, as Freud himself continued to push the boundaries of the science he coined beyond its original perimeter. Nevertheless, it is a path that is argued must be trodden with careful consideration, to prevent simplistic analogies between social phenomena and clinical phenomena. In the chapter, we review the methodologies in the field which have successfully integrated psychoanalytic concepts and understanding, arguing that they bring to the fore different but complementary lenses and epis-temological paradigms to explore beneath-the-surface phenomena. But it should be noted that this chapter is not focused only on containment, but on reviewing the methodologies that research the unconscious in organisations while addressing their key issues. We hope that such a review will bring added clarity to methodo-logical considerations that are inherent to using containment as a tool to explore the dynamics of social settings.

The Beginning – Doing Psychoanalytically Informed Research

The development of psychoanalytic conceptualisations is deeply rooted in clinical practice (Dreher 2000; Rustin 2001; Wolff 1996), however, attempts to reproduce the clinical approach while researching organisations fall short of understanding the multiple layers involved in its dynamics, to say the least. Doing research within the psychoanalytic framework poses several problems to the researcher regard-ing what kind of methodological approach to use. The Unconscious, as Freud described it, is only pictured through clues left behind, by inferring from the avail-able data. Freud's method was an indirect one, by resorting to free associations of dreams he attempted to probe the unconscious meaning of human behaviour, with well-known results (Freud 1900). Whilst Freud never attempted to directly analyse children, Melanie Klein started to work with very young children and her technique was also based on free associations, though in this case, she argued that the child's play could be seen as the infant equivalent of free associations in adults (Klein 1926, 1955). Both Freud and Klein grounded their discoveries in clinical evidence extracted from analytic work.

Two major currents in the development of psychoanalytic theory seem to exist: the supporters of the use of data stemming from the clinical setting as the main source of data; the supporters of psychoanalytic research using 'scientific' meas-ures in the development of psychoanalysis. The first tendency, closer to the origins of psychoanalysis, argues that clinical data should continue to be the main source of data for psychoanalysis since it was this kind of data which gave psychoanalysis its rich conceptual building. This position has staunch adherents in Andre Green (cited in Sandler et al. 2000) who argued that all major psychoanalytic concepts appeared out of clinical practice, and Peter Wolff (1996), to name only a few. The other position argues that psychoanalysis should prove and verify its claims and that the only way to do so is through the use of reliable and widely accepted measures. This current approach also has staunch supporters such as Peter Fonagy (1996). Controversy over the reliability of both sets of data for psychoanalysis has long been debated, with supporters of each position defending their approaches to research. But it should be noted that data of the second kind is very rare in the psychoanalytic approach to organisations.

In the specific case of organisational studies, psychoanalytic research has had a long and less troublesome history – starting with Bion's experiments with groups (Bion 1961) and later the work of the Tavistock Institute where Jaques's (1955) and Menzies Lyth's (1960) research led to the development of some very innovative concepts by applying psychoanalytic thinking to organisations. Menzies Lyth studied the dysfunctions of a particular social system in a hospital and found out that the specific practices the nurses in the hospital employed served a particular purpose of defending against the painful experiences of the hospital staff caring for ailing and dying patients. When applying psychoanalytic concepts to social science, it is perhaps important to bear in mind the influence of social systems and structures on individuals and how these systems and structures resonate with the internal world of people in organisations; this is where the explorations of Jacques and Menzies Lyth differ. While Jacques thought that people import their anxieties into the organisation and thus co-create the social defences, Menzies Lyth found out that it was the anxiety stirred by the organisation's primary task, i.e. taking care of people in pain stirred particular unconscious phantasies, which led to the use of social defences in the organisation. The psychoanalytic concept of containment can be very helpful in understanding this conundrum as it elucidates the complex interrelations between container-contained, or between an organisation and its members. Indeed, numerous organisational studies have used the concept of containment to study specific organisational cultures (Broeng 2022; Cooper & Dartington 2019; Smith 2019; Sanfuentes et al. 2018; Ruck 2007; James & Huffington 2004).

In addition, social science researchers have been trying to understand a wide range of organisational problems. For instance, Stein has investigated the critical period of disasters and the link with the ability to tolerate anxiety (Stein 2004); the organisational propensity to create a manic culture and its relation to the 2008 credit crisis (Stein 2011); the influence of past unsuccessful paternal figures on present leadership and the Oedipal struggles in the family history of Enron to understand problems with authority (Stein 2007); the 'fantasy of fusion' about introducing the single currency in the EU (Stein 2016); and the gang aspects of work organisations and intra-organisational ganging dynamics (Stein & Pinto 2011). Visholm explores the influence of sibling rivalry in self-managing teams and the psychodynamic processes in hierarchies and self-managing teams. This author emphasises the need for leadership via containing in postmodern organisations (Visholm 2021). Kenny

(2012) uses psychoanalytically informed interpretations and data analysis to study power in organisations. Fotaki and Hyde (2015) examine organisational blind spots as an organisational defence mechanism. Clancy et al. (2012) develop a psychoanalytic theoretical framework to study disappointment in organisations while Nossal (2013) elaborates on the use of drawings as an important tool to access the unconscious in organisations. The issues these studies have been trying to articulate are far-ranging, but they all try to illuminate the unconscious in organisations and contribute to understanding the culture of an organisation.

Psychoanalytic concepts have also been used in educational research – to study educational relations in their natural context (Adamo 2008), and containment for disruptive adolescents (Adamo & Serpieri 2010); Shim (2012) studies teachers' interactions with texts from a psychoanalytic perspective. Different educational research questions and areas have also been studied. Carson (2009) explores the potential of psychoanalysis to broaden the understanding of self in action research on teaching and cultural differences in Canada. Glynos and Lapping (2018) study the dynamics affecting graduate teaching assistants, and McKamey (2011) researches immigrant students' conceptions of caring.

Moreover, the concept of counter-transference has been used increasingly in organisational and social science research where the mind of the researcher and their feeling states in the observational field can be used to better understand unconscious processes. Using counter-transference can become an invaluable tool in additional data collection. Several studies elaborate on how counter-transference can help better understand what is happening. Devereux (1967) discussed how using counter-transference can illuminate what might be happening in the research field. The research of Froggett and Holloway (2010) and Hollway (2010) discusses the researchers' emotional responses during the research. Several studies discuss how counter-transference can be used to illuminate previously unrecognised material (Hansson & Dybbroe 2012; Roper 2003, 2014; Theodosius 2006; Arnaud 2012). There have also been critiques on the use of transference and counter-transference in extra-clinical research emphasising the danger of attributing researchers' feelings to research subjects and observational fields (Frosh & Baraitser 2008; Frosh 2010).

The question of the use of counter-transference in fieldwork brings us back to psychoanalytic theory and the place occupied in it by counter-transference. Indeed, for Freud, only transference was seen as data, as counter-transferencial responses were seen as resistances by the psychoanalyst which needed to be dealt with through personal analysis (Freud 1910; Laplanche and Pontalis 1973; Bott Spillius et al. 2011). Melanie Klein also seemed to be quite reluctant concerning the uses of counter-transference, suspecting it could be used by analysts as a defence against their inadequate interpretations (Hinshelwood 1991; Bott Spillius et al. 2011), and Paula Heimman's publication of a paper on counter-transference (Heimann 1950) may, in fact, be a key aspect in her leaving the Kleinian group in the 50s (Hinshelwood 1991; Bott Spillius et al. 2011). Nonetheless, currently, counter-transference is one of the most important aspects of the clinical setting (Bateman and Holmes 1997) and is widely accepted as a useful source of data in psychoanalysis.[1]

Psychoanalytic concepts can, therefore, be useful instruments in the minds of researchers and organisational consultants and their understanding is crucial to how they can be used in organisational work and research to make sense of paradoxical occurrences.

The Presence of the Unconscious in the Life of Groups and Organisations – Some Methodological Questions

It should be noted that, if one considers that unconscious processes are present and impact our daily lives, through the decisions we make, how we perceive reality or how we interact with others, then such processes certainly abound when one addresses the lives of groups and organisations. As outlined by the growing body of research above, the unconscious does influence organisational cultures. The question that arises regards the methodologies used to bring to light such phenomena that delve beneath the surface. Gabriel (1999) already emphasised that most research makes use of observations, interviews and questionnaires, and this seems to be the case in classic studies such as Menzies Lyth's (1960) work with the nursing service and Miller and Gwynne's (1972) work with young people who were physically disabled, or more recent studies (Willshire 1999; Freeman 2005), to name but a few. Nonetheless, in such studies, although several made use of interviews, observation also played a key role. And, observing what was happening at the organisations, how people were doing their job seemed to be one of the most important research tools, if not the most important. Although the data collected in the vast majority of the cases are not accessible and evaluating the evidence gathered is difficult, it nevertheless seems that many of the examples used in the description of social defences against anxiety were collected from participant observation.

Psychoanalytic Understanding and Concepts in Qualitative Research

A wide range of qualitative methodologies have used psychoanalytic concepts to understand the unconscious in groups and organisations as part of both data collection and analysis – in interviewing, observational studies and visual methodologies.

Innovative interviewing methods such as the Free Association Narrative Interview (Hollway & Jefferson 2008) offer a psychoanalytically informed model of qualitative research by paying attention to the intersubjective dynamics of the interview setting itself. In addition, the Reverie Research Method developed by Holmes (2018) is informed by psychoanalytic principles and has also been used in interviews – both in data collection, i.e. within the interview itself, and in data analysis. It utilises the researcher's receptivity to 'emotional experience in which he or she may experience imagistic responses ("reveries"), which may then be linked to research data in order to better understanding the participant' (p. 1). Interviewers can form and use interpretation-like responses in the moment of the interview based on their subjective emotional experience triggered by a dreamlike state and indicating data related to unconscious content.

The method has the following components:

a) focused attention on the participant, his/her body posture and gestures as well as words;
b) establishing within the researcher an inner containing space; into which
c) enteroceptive responses – 'pit of the stomach feelings'; – and
d) visual imagery may arise;
e) transforming these sensations into thoughts; which, finally, may be
f) verbally communicable;
g) which then can be assimilated into a research hypothesis. (Holmes 2018, p. 64)

To be able to use reverie in their studies researchers need to be able to hold a hypothesis in mind, contain their research uncertainty and related anxieties which might create barriers to emerging reverie states and they also need to stay focused on the present moment in the research interview.

Socioanalytic interviewing is another prominent development in interviewing research and practice used in organisational research which uses the concepts of the system as a whole and, in particular, social defence systems against anxiety. Long (2018) elaborates that it is possible to study unconscious dynamics in organisations by integrating psychoanalysis and systems theory into a new field – socioanalysis – 'the dynamic field of human systems' (p. 43) where 'the object of research is the system-as-a-whole – whether a group, an organisation or a society' (p. 45). A peculiar distinguishing feature of the socioanalytic interview is that an interviewee represents something on behalf of the whole system – group, organisation etc. Through the conceptualisations of a person-in-a-role as the smallest discriminated part of an organisation and the fact that an organisation is made up of multiple interacting roles, which are interrelated to each other and the whole system, the socioanalytic interview enables researchers to study the whole system, its interdependent subsystems with their unconscious dynamics and its impact on the organisational culture. Within the socioanalytic conceptual framework, an interviewee might be representative of various subsystems. By interviewing people in the organisation, the researchers can study the unconscious dynamics of various subsystems within the whole system. 'The identification of unconscious processes relies on noting repetitions and patterns in behaviour' (Long 2018, p. 49). The methods demonstrate that it is possible to study systemic defensive processes in organisations, including splitting and denial.

Role Analysis

Another interesting development closely related to the socioanalytic interview is organisational role analysis (ORA), first described by members of the Grubb Institute of Behavioural Studies, London and was very much influenced by the thinking and the applications of the Group Relations Tradition of the Tavistock Institute of Human Relations (Long 2013; Newton 2013). The method was conceptualised as 'a window in organisational life' (Krantz & Maltz 1997, p. 139) and it is designed to develop insight and understanding of both the conscious and unconscious influences of people in organisations by using the concept of a person-in-a-role as the intersection of a person and an organisational system, that is to say where the individual and the system meet. It is theorised that a person-in-a-role holds conscious and unconscious internalised objects (in Kleinian terms, 'objects' and 'part-objects') of the broader system or 'system domain' (Bain 1998) that they belong to. So, in a way, people in an organisation become representative 'members' of this system domain thus enabling understanding of the whole system.

In organisational consultancy, ORA is a method of working with people to enable them to fulfil their roles effectively. Newton (2013) emphasises the evolution and the variation of the method. ORA does not focus on solving problems because leaders tend to focus on solving problems for which they already have solutions. Instead, it focuses on the iterative processes of hypothesising and testing hypotheses in the work environment (Motsoaledi & Cilliers 2012). Current research using the method includes experiences of first-year master students (Cilliers & Harry 2012) and the unconscious role behaviour of academic research supervisors (Cilliers 2017).

Observational Studies

Various observational methods using psychoanalytic understanding have also been used in research into groups and organisations (Hinshelwood & Skogstad 2000; Elfer 2018; Stamenova 2018). Psychoanalytically informed observational methods evolved from infant observation pioneered by Esther Bick in 1964 and use the psychoanalytic concepts of anxiety and defences against it, projective identification, containment, transference, and counter-transference.

Psychoanalytic observations have been used in a wide range of studies:

- in psychoanalytically informed social anthropological studies to observe a mosque (Shuttleworth 2012)
- in psychoanalytically informed ethnographic research in educational settings (Price, 2006)
- within an interdisciplinary research design to study children's transitions to nursery (Datler et al. 2010)
- in organisational settings in health care – Hinshelwood & Skogstad (2000) use the conceptual model of social defence systems against anxiety to study the culture of healthcare organisations and generate some hypotheses; a study in this area by Datler et al. (2009) focuses on studying unconscious defences against primitive emotions in nursing homes; Vonofakos (2008) explores the different types of anxieties in psychiatric organisations.

Visual Methodologies

Mersky and Sievers (2018) have developed two visual methods for studying unconscious dynamics in organisations – **social photo-matrix (SPM)** and **social dream drawing (SDD)** – to pinpoint unconscious processes in organisations using a socioanalytic theoretical framework. They define socioanalysis as psychoanalysis applied to organisations and society and elaborate on Long's ideas of 'associative unconscious – a matrix of thought that links members of a community at an unconscious level' (Long in Mersky and Sievers 2018, p. 145). Perhaps the psychoanalytic concepts of unconscious phantasy and projective identification can be quite helpful here to elaborate the formation of such matrices of thought. Another theoretical perspective that the authors draw on is social dreaming developed by Gordon Lawrence. The unconscious of an organisation can be "accessed to and amplifications of dreams that organisational role-holders share with one another. The *'container'* [my italics] in which these dreams are shared and associated is termed the 'matrix'" (Mersky and Sievers 2018).

The SPM developed by Sievers (2003, 2008) is an experiential learning method to study the unconscious in organisations and its aim is to experience the unconscious of the organisation through collective viewing of photos taken by participants and examining the collective associations to the participants' photos thus aiming to reveal the hidden processes in an organisation. The idea that there is an unconscious phantasy behind each conscious activity (Isaacs 1948) is helpful to understand the methodology. When someone takes a photograph there is an unconscious relationship between the photographer and the object they are taking. When the photograph is shared with participants in the social photo matrix, they add their associations thus creating a matrix and opening a transitional space between real and unreal. The associations and thoughts are then available for thinking and making sense of (Mersky and Sievers 2018). What is important for this psychoanalytic research method is that the collected data is not approached with a firm set of operational criteria but rather a loose set of preconceptions that need saturation.

SDD also uses visual materials, but the methodology differs from SPM. Participants are also asked to bring visual materials to the matrices, in this case drawings of personal dreams, but there are some important differences: 'What particularly distinguishes SDD from social dreaming and the social photo-matrix is the intensive associative work done with the dream drawings of individual participants. It is through the associative work of the group that the individual dreamer becomes more and more aware of the deeper issues reflected in the original dream material' (Mersky & Sievers 2018, p. 151). It seems the focus of research in SDD is the individual in the organisation as a means of accessing the unconscious both in individuals and the organisation.

Both methods can generate rich data by using photographs, pictures and the associations of the participants in the process. Mersky and Sievers emphasise the importance of the role of containment of the group of participants taking part in these methodologies and the task at hand. Researchers need to be able to contain their own experiences as well as the experiences of the participants.

Another rather innovative method is using systems psychodynamic **Listening Posts** to collect data about the unconscious (Cilliers & Harry 2012; Greyvenstein & Cilliers 2012) through unstructured design using free-floating conversations led by experienced convenors managing task and time boundaries.

Methodological Issues

As seen above, the psychodynamic field not only offers a conceptual building to explain the behaviour of groups, organisations and social contexts but also provides different methodologies devised to capture the unconscious in the life of groups and organisations. These are important contributions that bring to the fore a vast array of methods, but also a different lens applied to different contexts outside the consulting room. And in fact, that can be seen in different disciplines such as the case of anthropology, sociology or managerial studies. Although these disciplines also share some methodologies, the following question requires further exploration: how is the psychoanalytic method different from the methods used by other disciplines? We can say that the difference is connected with what is considered to be the nature of the data in such approaches and, connected with this point, the role of the observer/researcher in these traditions.

In fact, to use the example of participant observation, in ethnographic research the aim of the researcher is to blend in as much as they can, in order to disrupt as little as possible what is being observed. Its main goal is to observe without interfering, and as such several strategies are used in order to gain acceptance and prevent any disturbance. In such cases, this may mean that the researcher should live and dress as a member of a tribe, as in the case of anthropology. In this case, what is considered as data are the observations in themselves, the observed facts, and it is in order to preserve them that the observer merges with the environment while fully recording his/her observations as field notes. This is very different from psychoanalytically based research, where the emotional reaction of the observer is also of paramount importance in the research process and is considered as data. Katherine Ewing (1992), a psychoanalytically trained anthropologist, argued that the difference between the two traditions concerns the fact that the anthropological method is based on the rule of the least interference in the object of observation, while the psychoanalytic technique is essentially the process of observing one's own participation in dialogue with another (Ewing 1992), a fundamental difference. In psychoanalytic observation (Hinshelwood and Skogstad 2000; Hunt 1989; Rustin 2001), the observer takes for granted that they will interfere in the environment. It is an unavoidable consequence of research, since observing without interfering is impossible, as has also been increasingly stated by anthropologists (Crapanzano 2004). The researcher will then observe that interference and how the environment was disturbed by their presence (transference) and will use a psychoanalytic tool, their own internal response to what is being observed (countertransference). Hunt (1989), in a comparison between a psychoanalytic perspective on field work and a sociological perspective, also criticises the denial of the impact on the subject of the presence of the observer or, when it is acknowledged, the rigidification of the role of the observer as somewhat in-humane or, in some cases, as excessively strategic in order to gain the trust of the subjects and have access to observations. The researcher also emphasises the role of the interrelation between subject and object as valid data and not so much as interference, as sociological approaches tend to consider.[2] As Ewing asserts (1992), the difference between the two research traditions lies in the fact that in the psychoanalytic tradition, disturbances are no longer perceived as 'noise' that needs to be reduced, as in the above described traditions, but rather as data to be acknowledged and explored. This is a fundamental difference between psychoanalytically informed observation from other traditions, where the observer's feelings should be taken into account as data in themselves. The psychoanalytic method does not maintain the illusion that a fact can be observed in its pure form since the observer always interferes with the object observed (Crapanzano 2004), perhaps even in the case of covert participant observation. This characteristic of the method is clearly an advantage, as it allows for the researcher to make use of a range of data that is not used in other traditions, namely their own emotional reactions towards what is being observed (counter-transference).

On the side of organisational studies, Fotaki, Long and Schwartz (2012), while emphasising the numerous contributions stemming from the psychoanalytic field to organisational behaviour, nonetheless state that psychoanalytic knowledge remains on the outskirts of managerial science. Several reasons may be pointed out, from psychoanalysis's own stance as a discipline to the focus on the 'dark side of behaviour' (Fotaki et al. 2012, p. 1106). Nonetheless, here the question of the nature of data remains important since transferential and counter-transferential data from client interventions is key in psychodynamically informed action research projects. And in fact, as Arnaud argues psychoanalysis sheds light on and allows managers to better manage relations, especially on the unconscious dynamics at play, by bringing a different methodology through the lens of transference phenomena.

Still, the links between both fields remain complex. Arnaud (2012) in an insightful paper described three aspects that prevent psychoanalytic insights from being integrated within organisational studies. First of all, the theoretical underpinnings of psychoanalysis are not easy to grasp and make complex assertions that are particularly hard to operationalise. Secondly, Arnaud warns of the dangers of transposing psychoanalytic concepts, which originate in the clinical contexts for the most part, literally into the organisational sphere without adaptation. Finally, the neutral and non-judgmental stance characteristic of psychoanalysis clashes with the decision-making process present in managerial enterprises. Furthermore, phenomena appearing at the individual level may not translate necessarily to the context of groups, organisations or cultural groups.

All these criticisms are particularly valid. Although much is to be gained by elucidating the dynamics of organisations, careful consideration is to be made when using analogies between the consulting room and vast, more complex systems. As Bion carefully advised in *Transformations*, for an analogy to be valid the relation between both parties must remain equal. If psychoanalysis is to bring its distinct viewpoint and value proposition through its understanding of human intersubjectivity, it must also be clear about its limitations and interconnection with other adjacent disciplines.

Conclusion

The chapter has aimed to provide an overview of research into the unconscious of groups and organisations. The abundance of research in organisations, groups and individuals in extra-clinical settings using psychoanalytic methods, conceptualisations and understanding is truly heartening. It shows that a) psychoanalysis can be used outside the clinical setting, b) the overview illuminates paradoxical occurrences in organisational life and c) it provides evidence for the existence of unconscious processes and dynamics unavailable for rational thought.

Notes

1 As a side note, other psychological disciplines such as systemic theory were also very concerned with the role of the observer. In first-order cybernetics it was considered that the observer lay outside the system and, as such, could observe the system impartially, a similar stance to anthropological or sociological fieldwork. Nonetheless, in second-order cybernetics the observer (or therapist) is considered to be a part of the system and, as such, his/her own reactions are also a part of the system. As such, the idea that the observer neutrally observes the object has also been rejected in systemic theory (Richardson 2003). And the stance of second-order cybernetics bears several similarities with psychoanalytic theory, both considering that the observer is not neutral and that he/she impacts on what is being observed. By asserting that counter-transference can be seen as essential data, the psychoanalytic stance seems to have preceded second-order cybernetics. This seems to be an important link that the two theories share.
2 Although certain currents of sociology seem increasingly interested in psychoanalysis as a way of exploring unconscious meaning and emotions with greater in-depthness than the traditional approaches in the field (see Theodosius 2006)

References

Adamo, S., 2008. Observing Educational Relations in Their Natural Context. *Infant Observation*, 11(2), pp. 131–146.
Adamo, S. & Serpieri, S.A., 2010. A Containing Environment for Disruptive Adolescents in Search of an Identity. *International Journal on School Disaffection*, 7(2), pp. 29–39.
Arnaud, G., 2012. The Contribution of Psychoanalysis to Organisation Studies and Management. *Organisation Studies*, 33(9), pp. 1121–1135.
Bain, A., 1998. Social Defenses Against Organizational Learning. *Human Relations*, 51(3), pp. 413–429.
Bateman, A. & Holmes, J., 1997. *Introduction to Psychoanalysis – Contemporary Theory and Practice*. London: Routledge.
Bion, W., 1961. *Experiences in Groups*. New York: Brunner-Routledge.
Bott Spillius, E., Milton, J., Garvey, P., Couve, C. & Steiner, D., 2011. *The New Dictionary of Kleinian Thought*. Abingdon: Routledge.

Broeng, S., 2022. Lost in the Present Moment – An Action Research Study on Employee Experience of Involvement in Change Processes in the Public Sector in Denmark. *Organizational and Social Dynamics*, 22, pp. 66–82.

Carson, T., 2009. Teaching and Cultural Difference: Exploring the Potential for a Psychoanalytically Informed Action Research. In: S. Noffke & B. Somekh, eds. *The Sage Handbook of Educational Action Research*. London: Sage, pp. 347–357.

Cilliers, F., 2017. The Systems Psychodynamic Role Identity of Academic Research Supervisors. *South African Journal of Higher Education*, 31(1), pp. 29–49.

Cilliers, F. & Harry, N., 2012. The Systems Psychodynamic Experiences of First-Year Master's Students in Industrial and Organisational Psychology. *SA Journal of Industrial Psychology*, 38(2), pp. 117–126.

Clancy, A., Vince, R. & Gabriel, Y., 2012. That Unwanted Feeling: A Psychodynamic Study of Disappointment in Organizations. *British Journal of Management*, 23(4), pp. 518–531.

Cooper, A. & Dartington, T., 2019. The Vanishing Organization: Organizational Containment in a Networked World. In: C. Huffington, W. Halton, D. Armstrong & J. Pooley, eds. *Working Below the Surface*. London: Routledge.

Craib, I., 1989. *Psychoanalysis and Social Theory: The Limits of Sociology*. Hertforshire: Harvester Wheatsheaf.

Crapanzano, V. 2004. Anthony Molino in Conversation with Vincent Crapanzano. In A. Molino (ed.), *Culture Subject Psyche: Dialogues in Psychoanalysis and Anthropology*. Connecticut: Wesleyan University Press, pp. 63–79.

Datler, W., Datler, M. & Funder, A., 2010. Struggling Against a Feeling of Becoming Lost: A Young Boy's Painful Transition to Day Care. *Infant Observation: International Journal of Infant Observation and Its Applications*, 13(1), pp. 65–87.

Datler, W., Trunkenpolz, K. & Lazar, R., 2009. An Exploration of the Quality of Life in Nursing Homes: The Use of Single Case and Organisational Observation in a Research Project. *Infant Observation*, 12(1), pp. 63–75.

Devereux, G., 1967. *From Anxiety to Method in the Behavioural Sciences*. The Hague: Mouton & Co.

Devereux, G. (1978) *Ethnopsychoanalysis: Psychoanalysis and Anthropology as Complementary Frames of Reference*. London: University of California Press.

Dreher, A. 2000. *Foundations for Conceptual Research in Psychoanalysis*. London: Karnac Books.

Elfer, P., 2018. Psychoanalytic Observation in Nurseries. In: K. Stamenova & R.D. Hinshelwood, eds. *Methods of Research into the Unconscious*. New York: Routledge, pp. 126–142.

Ewing, K. (1992) Is Psychoanalysis Relevant for Anthropology? In: T. Schwartz, G. White & C. Lutz, eds. *New Directions in Psychological Anthropology*. Cambridge: Cambridge University Press, pp. 251–268.

Fonagy, P., 1996. Commentaries. *Journal of the American Psychoanalytic Association*, 44, pp. 404–422.

Fotaki, M., Long, S., Schwartz, H. (2012) What Can Psychoanalysis Offer Organization Studies Today? Taking Stock of Current Developments and Thinking About Future Directions. *Organization Studies*, 33(9), pp. 1105–1120.

Fotaki, M. & Hyde, P., 2015. Organizational Blind Spots: Splitting, Blame and Idealization in the National Health Service. *Human Relations*, 68(3), pp. 441–462.

Freeman, E., 2005. *Caring Beyond Boundaries: A Case Study Using Social Defence Theory and Inter-Group Relations Theory*. PhD dissertation, unpublished.

Freud, S., 1900. *The Interpretation of Dreams*. In: *The Standard Edition of the Complete Psychological Works of Sigmund Freud*, Vol. IV, pp. IX–627. London: The Hogarth Press.

Freud, S., 1910. *The Future Prospects of Psycho-Analytic Therapy*. In: *The Standard Edition of the Complete Psychological Works of Sigmund Freud*, Vol. XI, pp. 139–152. London: The Hogarth Press.

Froggett, L. & Hollway, W., 2010. Psychosocial Research Analysis and Scenic Understanding. *Psychoanalysis, Culture and Society*, 15(3), pp. 281–301.

Frosh, S., 2010. *Psychoanalysis Outside the Clinic*. London: Palgrave Macmillan.

Frosh, S. & Baraitser, L., 2008. Psychoanalysis and Psychosocial Studies. *Psychoanalysis, Culture and Society*, 13(4), pp. 346–365.

Gabriel, Y., 1999. *Organizations in Depth*. London: Karnac Books.

Glynos, J. & Lapping, C., 2018. Psychical Contexts of Subjectivity and Performative Practices of Remuneration: The Movement of Desire in Teaching Assistants' Narratives of Work. *Journal of Education Policy*, 33(1), pp. 23–42.

Greyvenstein, H. & Cilliers, F., 2012. Followership's Experiences of Organisational Leadership: A Systems Psychodynamic Perspective. *SA Journal of Industrial Psychology*, 38(2), pp. 1–10.

Hansson, B. & Dybbroe, B., 2012. Autoethnography and Psychodynamics in Interrelational Spaces of the Research Process. *Journal of Research Practice*, 8(2).

Heimann, P. (1950) On counter-transference. *International Journal of Psycho-Analysis*, 31, pp. 81–84.

Hinshelwood, R., 1991. *A Dictionary of Kleinian Thought*. 2nd ed. London: Free Association Books.

Hinshelwood, R.D., 2008. Social Science and Psychoanalysis: Marriage or Infection? *Organisational & Social Dynamics*, 8(2), pp. 115–137.

Hinshelwood, R.D. & Skogstad, W., 2000. *Observing Organisations*. Abingdon: Routledge.

Hollway, W., 2010. Conflict in the Transition to Becoming a Mother: Psycho-Social Approach. *Psychoanalysis, Culture and Society*, 15(2), pp. 136–155.

Hollway, W. & Jefferson, T., 2008. The free association narrative interview method. In: L. Given, ed. *The Sage Encyclopedia of Qualitative Research Methods*. Sevenoaks, CA: Sage, pp. 296–315.

Holmes, J., 2018. *A Practical Psychoanalytic Guide to Reflexive Research*. 1st ed. London: Taylor and Francis.

Hunt, J., 1989. *Psychoanalytic Aspects of Fieldwork*. London: Sage.

Isaacs, S., 1948. The Nature and Function of Phantasy. *International Journal of Psycho-Analysis*, 29, pp. 73–97.

James, K. & Huffington, C., 2004. Containment of Anxiety in Organizational Change: A Case Example of Changing Organizational Boundaries. *Organizational and Social Dynamics*, 4, pp. 212–233.

Jaques, E., 1955. Social Systems as a Defence against Persecutory and Depressive Anxiety. In: M. E. A. Klein, ed. *New Directions in Psychoanalysis*. London: Tavistock.

Kenny, K., 2012. Someone Big and Important: Identification and Affect in an International Development Organization. *Organization Studies*, 33(9), pp. 1175–1193.

Klein, M., 1926. The Psychological Principles of Infant Analysis. In J. Mitchell (ed., 1987) *The Selected Melanie Klein*. New York: Free Press, pp. 57–68.

Klein, M., 1955. *The Psycho-Analytic Play Technique: Its History and Significance*. In: J. Mitchell (ed., 1987) *The Selected Melanie Klein*. New York: Free Press, pp. 35–54.

Krantz, J. & Maltz, M., 1997. A Framework for Consulting to Organizational Role. *Consulting Psychology Journal: Practice and Research*, 49(2), pp. 137–151.

Laplanche, J. & Pontalis, J.B. (1973) *The Language of Psychoanalysis*. London: Karnac Books.

Long, S., 2013. *Socioanalytic Methods*. 1st ed. London: Karnac.

Long, S., 2018. The Socioanalytic Interview. In: K. Stamenova & R. Hinshelwood, eds. *Methods of Research into the Unconscious*. New York: Routledge.

McKamey, C., 2011. Uncovering and Managing Unconscious Ways of 'Looking': A Case Study of Researching Educational Care. *Psychodynamic Practice*, 17(4), pp. 403–417.

Menzies Lyth, I., 1960. A Case-Study in the Functioning of Social Systems as a Defence Against Anxiety: A Report on a Study of the Nursing Service of a General Hospital. *Human Relations*, 3(2), pp. 95–183.

Mersky, R.R. & Sievers, B., 2018. Social Photo-Matrix and Social Dream Drawing. In: *Methods of Research into the Unconscious; Applying Psychoanalytic Ideas to Social Science*. Abingdon: Routledge, pp. 145–168.

Miller, E. & Gwynne, G. (1972) *A Life Apart*. London: Tavistock Publications.

Molino, A. (ed.) (2004) *Culture Subject Psyche: Dialogues in Psychoanalysis and Anthropology*. Connecticut: Wesleyan University Press.

Motsoaledi, L. & Cilliers, F., 2012. Executive Coaching in Diversity from the Systems Psychodynamic Perspective. *SA Journal of Industrial Psychology*, 38(2), pp. 32–43.

Newton, J., 2013. Organisational Role Analysis. In: S. Long, ed. *Socioanalytic Methods*. London: Karnac, pp. 205–224.

Nossal, B., 2013. The Use of Drawing as a Tool in Socioanalytic Exploration. In: S. Long, ed. *Socioanalytic Methods*. London: Karnac, pp. 67–91.

Price, H. (2006) Jumping the Shadows: Catching the Unconscious in the Classroom. *Journal of Social Work Practice*, 20(2), pp. 145–161.

Richardson, C. (2003) The Contribution of Systemic Thinking and Practice. In: A. Ward, K. Kasinski, J. Pooley and A. Worthington, eds. *Therapeutic Communities for Children and Young People*. London, Jessica Kingsley.

Roper, M., 2003. Analysing the Analysed. *Oral History*, 31(2), pp. 20–32.

Roper, M., 2014. The Unconscious Work of History. *Cultural and Social History*, 11(2), pp. 169–193.

Ruck, G., 2007. Reflective Practice in Child Care Social Work: The Role of Containment. *British Journal of Social Work*, 37(4), pp. 659–680.

Rustin, M. 2001. *Reason and Unreason: Psychoanalysis, Science and Politics*. London: Continuum.

Sandler, J., Sandler, A. & Davies, R. (2000). *Clinical and Observational Psychoanalytic Research: Roots of a Controversy*. Madison, WI: International Universities Press.

Sanfuentes, M., Espinoza, T. & Navarro, B., 2018. Dilemmas and Conflicts of Various Professional Roles within a Human Service Agency. *International Journal of Applied Psychoanalytic Studies*, 15, pp. 264–278.

Shim, J.M., 2012. Exploring How Teachers' Emotions Interact with Intercultural Texts: A Psychoanalytic Perspective. *Curriculum Inquiry*, 42(4), pp. 472–496.

Shuttleworth, J., 2012. Infant Observation, Ethnography and Social Anthropology. In: C. Urwin & J. Sternberg, eds. *Infant Observation and Research: Emotional Processes in Everyday Lives*. Hove, New York: Routledge.

Smith, H., 2019. Omniscience at the Edge of Chaos: Complexity, Defences and Change in a Children and Families Social Work Department. *Journal of Social Work Practice*, 33(4), pp. 471–480.

Sievers, B., 2003. Against All Reason: Trusting in Trust. *Organizational and Social Dynamics*, 3(1), pp. 19–39.

Sievers, B., 2008. Pictures from Below the Surface of the University: The Social Photo Matrix as a Method for Understanding Organisations in Depth. In M. Reynolds and R. Vince eds. *Handbook of Experiential Learning and Management Education*. Oxford: Oxford University Press.

Stamenova, K., 2018. Comparative Analysis of Overlapping Psychoanalytic Concepts Using Operationalisation. In: K. Stamenova & R.D. Hinshelwood, eds. *Methods of Research into the Unconscious*. New York: Routledge.

Stein, M., 2004. The Critical Period of Disasters: Insights from Sense-Making and Psychoanalytic Theory. *Human Relations*, 57(10), pp. 1243–1261.

Stein, M., 2007. Oedipus Rex at Enron: Leadership, Oedipal Struggles, and Organizational Collapse. *Human Relations*, 60(9), pp. 1387–1410.

Stein, M., 2011. A Culture of Mania: A Psychoanalytic View of the Incubation of the 2008 Credit Crisis. *Organization*, 18(2), pp. 173–186.

Stein, M., 2016. 'Fantasy of Fusion' as a Response to Trauma: European Leaders and the Origins of the Eurozone Crisis. *Organization Studies*, 37(7), pp. 919–937.

Stein, M. & Pinto, J., 2011. The Dark Side of Groups: A 'Gang at Work' in Enron. *Group & Organization Management*, 36(6), pp. 692–721.

Theodosius, C., 2006. Recovering Emotions from Emotional Management. *Sociology*, 40(5), pp. 893–910.

Trist, E. (1950) Culture as a Psycho-Social Process. In: E. Trist & H. Murray (eds, 1990) *The Social Engagement of Social Science*, Vol. 1. London: Free Association Books, pp. 539–545.

Visholm, S., 2021. *Family Psychodynamics in Organizational Contexts: The Hidden Forces That Shape the Workplace*. 1st ed. London: Routledge.

Vonofakos, D., 2008. *Differentiating Anxiety, Defence and Reality-Oriented Functioning in the Psychodynamics of Social Systems: Observing the Unconscious Cultures of Psychiatric Institutions*. University of Essex, unpublished PhD dissertation.

Willshire, L. (1999) Psychiatric Services: Organizing Impossibility. *Human Relations*, 52(6): pp. 775–804.

Wolff, P. (1996) The irrelevance of infant observations for psychoanalysis. *Journal of the American Psychoanalytic Association*, 44, pp. 369–392.

Chapter 6

Operationalisation of Concepts in Psychoanalytic Research

Gillian Walker

A crucial problem for psychoanalysis is not only the 'plethora of competing theories but the relatively weak methods' available (Hinshelwood 2008, 503). Outside clinical practice there seems to be a lack of generally accepted research methods. There is a clear need for recognised and acceptable methodological frameworks that are both valid and reliable in psychoanalytic research. Flawed methodology corrupts hypothesis formation and negates claims to the veracity, validity and reliability of research endeavours. Sustained misconceptions of a theory lead to invalid applications causing failure in the scientific process (Boag 2006, 74–86). Psychoanalysis should be able to evidence and verify its claims, and accepted, reliable methods of research should be applied to psychoanalytic theory (Fonagy et al. 1996). In my contribution to this book, I discuss something of the attempts to address these concerns in psychoanalytic research.

Formal research involves testing of theoretical models which by their nature are composed of generalisations and concepts. To gather data for research purposes means that such generalisations have to be 'distilled' to extract *observable phenomena*. In psychological and mental health research many of such observables are subjective and not necessarily quantifiable. Great care needs to be taken in identifying those observables which give a valid indication of the general concept. I am going to show that identification of observable criteria is achieved by 'operationalisation of concepts'.

The principle of operationalisation was first established in physics but quickly spread to other disciplines. Applied to complex, often abstract phenomena (e.g. Einstein's theory of relativity), the principle is that, 'all theoretical terms must be defined via those operations by which they are measured' (Campbell 1920, 132). The process of defining such operations and measurements was termed operationalism (Bridgman 1927). In the 1930s psychologists (at Harvard University), finding themselves struggling with epistemology and problems of measuring psychological phenomena, successfully adapted the principle (Skinner 1931; Stevens 1935; Boring 1945).[1] From then on the principle of operationalisation has spread to other disciplines as diverse as: education (Stamenova, 2013), sexuality (Walker 2021), organisational changes (Boey and Hede 2001), the study of emotion (Brown 2000), infants at risk (Briggs, 1997), social defence systems (Mendes 2012) and so

DOI: 10.4324/9781315146416-9

on. Stamenova and Hinshelwood (2018) provide examples of how operationalised assessment devices have been created for diverse psychoanalytic research projects (Sanfuentes 2008; Vonofakos 2009; Walker and Hinshelwood 2018).

Operationalisation, establishing a comprehensive set of observable phenomena,[2] is a form of 'abductive reasoning', a form of logical inference that seeks the simplest and most likely conclusion from a set of observations. As I have previously explained (Walker and Hinshelwood, 2018), operationalisation is often described as the duck test:[3]

> If it looks like a duck, swims like a duck, and quacks like a duck. Then it probably is a duck.

One concludes from the characteristic features of a thing, that it is, or is not, a duck. It is a duck because it looks and behaves like a duck. The determination of *observable features* can then be applied to other phenomena. Observations have to be made with a *reliable instrument*, an assessment device that, applied to other data determines whether something is, or is not, a duck. The key is 'observable features'; the process of determining those features is *operationalisation*.

Simply put the task of operationalisation is to refine terminologies and identify observable characteristic features. This includes classification, categorisation, establishing inclusive/exclusive criteria, attribution to, or restriction to, a specific object or group and so forth. Taking the taxonomist as an example the task is to identify shared features or structural characteristics in order to determine the allocation of a given life form to one genus or another. A process of refinement will identify separate species within that genus. A child struggles to differentiate between a horse and a cow until he learns by a process of refinement, by operationalisation, what is and what is not a cow. Both animals will always have the 'set-in-stone' characteristics of mammals, but each species has its own distinctive, observable characteristics that the child learns to recognise. The outcome of psychic developmental processes is to create a stereotype – of horse and of cow. Piaget termed such stereotypes 'schemata', patterns of thought or behaviour that organise and categorise information and the relationship between them. Research may seek to generalise and create general terms but those terms need to be precise and have exact meaning and thus everyone will have the same understanding of a given concept.

Illustrative examples include the *Diagnostic and Statistical Manual* (DSM) and the *International Classification of Disease* (ICD). In medicine, a stereotype or schema equates to a complex or a syndrome, that is, something that consists of a cluster of features or characteristics. Comprehensive works like these aim to aid the clinician in diagnosis by identifying a set of features to assist in identifying a given disorder. Some unrelated disorders share common observable features, some concepts remain unclear, somewhat fuzzy, and so difficult to categorise. A differential diagnosis may rest upon one significant feature, its presence or absence.

In his introduction to DSM (V)[4] Insel[5] stated that the strength of DSM was in its *reliability* – all clinicians using the same terms in the same way – however, its shortcomings lie in the issue of *validity*. Simply put, does the DSM define, qualify, measure (in the loosest sense) what it sets out to measure. The quality of validity confers authority, efficaciousness and applicability based on well founded, sound and to-the-point logic 'against which no argument or objection can be fairly brought' (Insel 2013).

However, what if we want to study unconscious processes? How do we pin down something as incorporeal as the unconscious? How can we say 'look there', we can see excessive projective identification (PI^e)? Does psychoanalysis have an equivalent to DSM? Does something like *The Language of Psychoanalysis* (Laplanche and Pontalis 1980), or Hinshelwood's *Dictionary of Kleinian Thought* (1989), go some way to fulfil this need? It is the purpose of any dictionary to give a precise and accurate definition of a word, a thing, a concept; by default it will also indicate what something is not. A robust effort to accurately define psychoanalytic concepts was made in the *Psychodynamic Diagnostic Manual* (PDM-2, Lingiardi et al., 2017). Other endeavours include Davis et al. (2000), Akhtar (2018) and Skelton (2006).

The therapeutic encounter may not be reducible to a manual, although as Lemma argued 'much can be learnt from those approaches that attempt, however imperfectly, to pin down what it is that psychoanalysts do'. And that to make explicit what it is that psychotherapy does, and to make the clinical process accountable, requires operationalisation of the terms and concepts of the work (Lemma 2015, xiii). Crucially, subjective experience and its complexity require that specific qualities should be reduced to precise operationalised indicators to reduce the impact of subjective variables in research (Holway and Jefferson 2012; Holmes 2018). Essentially, an in-depth definition that does justice to the complexity and ambiguity of unconscious processes allows construction of empirically implementable research tools (Parth and Loeffler-Stastka 2015).

I posited the question above as to whether it is possible to say something like 'look, there is projective identification'. I am going to show how the essence of two theoretical psychoanalytic concepts, Klein's projective identification (PI^e), and Bion's model of normal projective identification (PI^n) can be 'captured' by the operationalisation process. I will then describe, utilising my own research (Walker 2021), how I operationalised Bion's container-contained model, how I created a data assessment device, and how I applied that device to novel data derived from a study of sadomasochism. I will argue that both 'reliability', but in particular 'validity', can be conferred upon psychoanalytic research by operationalisation of concepts.

Operationalisation: The Process

I am going to describe the operationalisation process beginning with the following example from Hinshelwood (2008). Hinshelwood demonstrated that clarification of terminologies or establishing 'semantic boundaries' could show whether there is a difference between Freud's notion of *repression* and Klein's notion of *splitting*.

Semantic analysis of the literature aimed to establish the core elements under investigation by defining the 'semantic territory' of each concept. Differences in terms established whether the two were semantic alternatives for similar clinical phenomenon, or whether the two were in fact different concepts. Hinshelwood described a two-step process of 'semantic rigour' to establish the *core elements* of a concept (510).

1. A fair assessment from *authoritative sources*, from the two separate theoretical schools.

   Authoritative sources are scholarly works against which, as Insel said, 'no argument can be fairly brought'. By scrutinising the psychoanalytic literature for comparison, Hinshelwood determined instances where both concepts appeared to overlap in semantic terms and where they distinctly diverged.

   Followed by:

2. Identification of *observable* critical moments from *clinical material*.

   Clinical material can be taken in the broadest sense to include not only individual psychotherapy patients, but also observation of groups, organisational structures and so on.

   There are two points I want to take forward. The first is 'authoritative sources' and the second reiterates what I have already explained – identification or extrapolation of 'observable criteria'.[6]

Authoritative Sources

The utilisation of those sources that can rightfully be determined authoritative cannot be underestimated. DSM and ICD are authoritative sources. A dictionary aims to define fully and succinctly what a word means, and therefore what it doesn't mean; it is an authoritative source. We refer to a renowned expert in a given field as 'an authority'. Freud's original texts are authoritative, Klein's original texts are authoritative, Bion's original texts are authoritative. As I describe the operationalisation process, I will show why the use of 'authoritative sources' avoids methodological flaws in regard to the project's validity. Robust accurate operationalisation of the concepts under investigation means a project is more than likely to be measuring what it says it is measuring, or observing what it claims to be observing.

Identification of Observable Criteria

I operationalised normal projective identification, and the container-contained model from Bion's own works (1959, 1962a, 1962b). However, given my own difficulty in understanding Klein's excessive projective identification from her own work (1946, p. 9), I turned to another authoritative source, Hinshelwood's *A Dictionary of Kleinian Thought* (1989). Under the entry of projective identification,

Hinshelwood provides a short, succinct definition of Klein's excessive projective identification thus:

> Projective identification was defined by Klein in 1946 as the prototype of the aggressive object-relationship, representing an anal attack on an object by means of forcing parts of the ego into it in order to take over its contents or to control it… It is a 'phantasy remote from consciousness'… a belief in certain aspects of the self being located elsewhere, with a consequent depletion and weakened sense of self identity, to the extent of depersonalisation.
>
> (Hinshelwood 1989, p. 179)

Operationalising Klein's Excessive Projective Identification (PI^E)

I said Hinshelwood provides a 'short' definition but look what it gives us:

a) an anal attack
b) an attack upon the object
c) the use of force with respect to another
d) a bid for control over another
e) a deeply unconscious phantasy
f) a belief that one can relocate parts of oneself
g) a depleted ego
h) a weakened sense of self.

These can be distilled to reflect a number of superordinate themes clarifying and operationalising Klein's model of PI^e. There is, in unconscious phantasy:

- Aggression and attack against another **(violence)**.
- A depletion of self-identity and weakening of the sense of self **(self-destruction/ ego-depletion)**.
- The belief that one can relocate parts of one's ego **(splitting)** into another psyche **(excessive projective identification)**, or at least elsewhere.
- Force against, and the striving for control over another **(omnipotence)** with forced occupation of another psychic space **(intrusion)**.

If these characteristic features can be observed in a given data set, then I argue it can be said the data shows the presence of discrete elements of excessive projection. Discrete elements may be seen to interact so that excessive projective identification is observed as a process.

I have laboured Klein's PI^e because its introduction was vital to Bion's own theoretical developments with recognition of a 'normal' projective identification (PI^n). Normal projective identification is a feature of the container-contained process,

Klein's version of PI^e is not. The 'evacuative' characteristics of PI^e *should not be observable* in the project's data sets. Not appreciating the differences between the two creates a 'pit-fall' in the methodology, specifically in the project's validity. My own 'almost pit-fall' occurred when I was operationalising 'masochism'. Taking Krafft-Ebing (1886), Hartwich (1959), DSM and ICD and other 'authoritative sources' I was initially mistakenly led to operationalise pathological masochism. In fact I needed the subject cohort within which masochism was specifically associated with BDSM.[7] This form of masochism, as Freud stated (1924), is not deemed pathological. Such an error would have led to identification of the wrong subject group thereby misdirecting and completely undermining and invalidating the whole research project.

Operationalising Normal Projective Identification (PI^n)

Whereas Klein's PI^e is thought of as an evacuative device Bion came to see that projective identification could occur as a more normal means of communication. I have described the operationalisation of Klein's PI^e above by utilising an accepted 'authoritative source'. I am now going to show operationalisation of the containing process, using Bion's own works. Bion described his realisation that there was a normal communicative form of projective identification thus:

> Throughout the analysis the patient resorted to projective identification with a persistence suggesting it was a mechanism to which he had never been able sufficiently to avail himself… a mechanism of which he had been cheated… which led me to suppose that the patient felt there was some object that denied him the use of projective identification.
>
> (1959, 312)

And:

> When the patient *strove to rid himself* of *fears of death* which were felt to be *too powerful for his personality* to continue he *split off his fears* and *put them into me*, the idea apparently being that if they were *allowed* to *repose there long enough* they would *undergo modification by my psyche* and could be *safely reintrojected*… the patient had felt that I evacuated them so quickly that the feelings were not modified, but had become more painful.
>
> (1959, 312, my emphasis)

These two important observations introduce what would become the mature model of containment theory in the 1962 *Learning from Experience* (1962b). That the patient's communications need to be sufficiently intrusive for the analyst to 'get hold of' confers upon the recipient of PI^n an active role. That the patient continues to try, despite repeated failures, infers the need for a very particular response. The patient's emotional intensity increased, he became frustrated because the analyst was not receiving his projections, or more specifically the projected parts of the patient's own ego.

I am assuming of the reader some knowledge of Bion's development of the container-contained model[8] and offer a summary. In response to an uncomfortable experience, say hunger, the infant experiences what Bion called an '**intolerable thought**', the fear that he is dying. The infant's primitive mind, unable to think thoughts, **projects**/ejects these awful 'feelings' towards another mind, that of the maternal object. The intention is to communicate the need for understanding and for subsequent action. The infant achieves this by **splitting** off that part of the ego that has created the awful feelings. Bion named these unprocessed experiences **beta-elements** (ß-e). It is the role of the maternal mind to act as an auxiliary mind. The mother in a state of **maternal reverie**, in tune with and focused on her baby, psychically accepts-introjects the infant's projected ß-e. The maternal mind has the capacity to 'think' the infants proto-thoughts with her **maternal alpha-function** (α-f). The early infant does not yet have the capacity to processes ß-e into **alpha-elements** (α-e). ß-e are denuded of their horror by maternal α-f, α-e are then returned to the infant in such an ameliorated or modified state that the infant can safely **re-introject** them. He is reassured and mollified, he feels comforted and safe, he is not going to die. Failure on the part of the maternal mind to accept the infant's projections leaves the infant with what Bion referred to as an experience of 'nameless dread'. Maternal reverie occupies the space between projected ß-e and maternal α-f. A suitable analogy is of a porous membrane through which projections, raw data, can enter, be broken down, and processed, into nutritional sustaining elements. Bion used the metaphor of physical digestion. Maternal reverie is therefore a feature of, and a requirement for, maternal alpha-function. This functional process remains with us and continues to operate. We soothe a frightened distressed friend by taking in (introjecting), sharing and 'holding' their fears and anxiety. When able to share with an able 'other' the friend feels understood and supported. The uncontained horror is contained by the maternal container in the guise of the friend. The maternal figure unable to do this leaves the infant/friend alone with their horror. The sufferer is unable to do anything other than eject/project or try and cope as best they can alone. When uncontained projections move around a group, the function of the group is to contain, process and ameliorate anxiety. However, like the inadequate mother, like the infant who is in such a state they cannot be comforted, the group/organisation can fail.

Operationalised Model of the Container-Container Process

When analysing data we are looking for evidence of:

- **INTOLERABLE EXPERIENCE-THOUGHTS**. In 1962, this idea included splitting off an accompanying ego-function.[9] The experience that one is having, as well as the ego-function that has created the experience, are both part and parcel of 'I', of the 'self'. The intolerable thought is a perception. For the infant 'I am hungry' is akin to a fear of dying. They are *aware* of their feelings but this is pre-symbolic. Lacking the thinking capacity to understand their fears, those fears and primitive ego functions are split off – **SPLITTING**.

- In order to rid the self of the intolerable thoughts/experiences, they are projected *into* another mind along with the split-off ego-function[10] – **EGO-DEPLETION**. Both ego-function and the experience (I, the self) are split off, attributed to another mind, and felt and perceived to be within the other. This is accomplished by projective identification – **PI[n]**.
- The projected thoughts repose (sit) within another (auxiliary) mind – **MATERNAL REVERIE**. The auxiliary mind, focused on the subject, attentive and receptive, provides temporal and psychic space for the projections.
- Within the auxiliary mind, there is modification of the intolerable thought, modification provides meaning and proposes action – **ALPHA-FUNCTION**. Within the maternal psyche there is change, conversant with amelioration of that deemed intolerable – **MODIFICATION**.
- The modified thought becomes safe enough to be 'thought' or, to the primitive ego, 'felt'. **ALPHA-ELEMENTS** are reintrojected along with an accompanying ego-function and so it is an ego-developing process. The introjection of a modifying object then becomes an internal object or part of the self – **REINTROJECTION**.
- There is a return of ego-function along with the now modified intolerable experience. The mother's modifying ego-function is added to the infant's ego-function, serving to develop the infant's ego – **CONTAINMENT and GROWTH**.

In essence:

- 'Something intolerable' in one mind is **UNCONTAINABLE**.
- Something intolerable is 'relocated', put inside, projected into, communicated to, another mind that will hold it, **A CONTAINER**.
- Something intolerable is 'held within' the container whilst it undergoes change, it is subject to 'modification', that deemed intolerable undergoes amelioration, **CONTAINMENT**.
- Something has changed to such an extent that it can be **CONTAINED**.

Following extrapolation of the core characteristics of the container-contained model by thorough scholarly research, using authoritative sources, a data assessment device, an interpretative tool, can be designed. The design of an assessment device for my research was by establishing 'a set of questions' that interrogated the data. The device consists of a set of four questions, each question represents an element in Bion's model. Questions are put to the data. Responses evidence whether discrete elements of the container-contained process can be shown to emerge at critical moments in the data.

I set out the assessment device below. It was the goal of my own research project, on the basis of empirical findings, to offer an original and alternative concept of masochism. As examples I will add a short note from my own research (Walker, 2021) analysing a BDSM 'scene'.[11] To aid understanding I will give a précis of some novel data to which I applied the assessment device (four questions).

Example Data

Data was obtained by observing a filmed documentary[12] BDSM scenario taking place at a professional establishment providing the services of professional dominatrices. A male client (M) has asked for punishment and humiliation at the hands of a 'Mistress'. 'M' is prone to starting fights and bar brawling, he reports 'phantasies of genocide and mayhem'. In the scene 'M' is seen crawling on all fours with a Mistress atop him as if riding side-saddle. 'M' is 'ridden' to a lavatory where he is ordered to lick the toilet seat. After doing so he vomits profusely. Throughout the scene the Mistress speaks to him in a softly encouraging manner. Once he has vomited, with his head still in the toilet, the Mistress smacks the toilet seat down on the back of his head and flushes the toilet. The Mistress walks off softly tittering. 'M' explains to the film maker that he comes for 'ritual humiliation' in order to 'expunge' himself of 'all the shit' in his head.[13] Once he has a session with a dominatrix his violent phantasies and need to brawl are relieved. He reports his feelings towards the dominatrix as those of relief and gratitude. To me, the film observer, the client looks and sounds somewhat 'soporific'.

Assessing the Container-Containing Process: An Assessment Device

Q1. Is there evidence of Something Intolerable: has something intolerable been projected?

It may never be known what the something intolerable is. It may be unconscious and remains unconscious, a primitive infantile, pre-symbolic experience. In my study of BDSM my main subject (M), reported feeling terrible anger and despair, he reported phantasies of genocide and mayhem (beta-elements). The origins of his intolerable experiences may not be known even to him. Nevertheless, it is clear that something is difficult or impossible to contain and help from elsewhere is being sought. My argument was that through BDSM, physical pain was equal to emotional pain.

Q2. Is there evidence of Splitting and Projection (PI^n) – what has gone, what has been put elsewhere?

Is there evidence of ego-depletion on the part of the subject? What ego-functions appear to be missing? In this case 'M' has surrendered his autonomous powers such as decision making and self-mastery. In the BDSM scene this is called power exchange (PE$_x$). The submissive (masochistic) partner willingly gives him/herself up to the whims and directions of the dominant partner.

Q3. Is there evidence of Relocation: where has it been put?

Have those ego-functions appeared elsewhere, in a relationship with someone or something, (in the analyst, in the family, in the group, in the BDSM scene)? Is someone or something, accepting, taking in, worries and concerns, offering promise of a containing experience (maternal reverie)? I argued that in the BDSM scene, the subject's pain was projected into the dominatrix, her job was to accept (introject) and 'hold' that pain thereby acting as a pain container.

Q4. Is there evidence of change?

- **What has changed – albeit in the short term?**
- **How has the intolerable been managed/modified?**
- **What effect/change can be observed/reported?**
- **Has anxiety reduced, has distress and worry been alleviated and thus contained?**

Can positive change be observed, what are those observations? Has worry and concern reduced, has fear been ameliorated in such a way that it is now manageable (maternal alpha-function and alpha-element reintrojection)? In my study the main subject (M) reported feeling he had been 'expunged' of his horrible, uncontainable anger, he felt he had been released from 'all that shit' in his head.

My hypothesis was that emotional pain, translated into physical pain, could be dealt with, traversed. Traversal of pain was a journey that led to victory over pain. My subject 'M' expressed feeling great fortune and gratitude to his dominatrix. Her actions, taking in his pain and returning it to him in a form he could cope with (given that this was often very very painful), ameliorated his pain. This left him feeling what by observation appeared to be a deep sense of relaxation. That is, a BDSM experience enabled the subject to temporarily cope with his terrible intolerable thoughts.

Discussion

Struggling from the beginning to justify its discoveries, psychoanalysis has come to see that verifiable claims are dependent on methodology. As mainstream interest has slowly moved away from quantitative behavioural research, efforts by psychoanalytic researchers to develop legitimate qualitative methodologies have increased. The principle of operationalising complex abstract concepts, like unconscious processes, is playing a greater part in psychoanalytic research. I have described the process of operationalising concepts as a two-step process of scholarly work. In the first instance, identification of 'authoritative sources' is mandatory. Freud, Klein, Bion, their contemporary and later colleagues, provide a plethora of original and erudite texts. The history of psychoanalytic thinking, its idea and developments, are unquestionably well recorded and accessible. For the researcher looking specifically into groups and organisations and the containing experience

I refer them once again to the Essex University (UK) PhD studies of Sanfuentes (2008), Vonofakos (2009), Mendes (2012) and Stamenova (2013).[14] These researchers, and Hinshelwood (2008) and myself, all used original, primary sources to operationalise psychoanalytic concepts. Secondary sources do have their place when ideas have been developed and expanded upon, but particularly when ideas are unclear and need elucidation and clarification. I showed this when I utilised Hinshelwood's dictionary to give a full but succinct exposition of Klein's excessive projective identification. Clarity of definition, allowing for specific characterisation of the mechanisms under investigation, avoids 'erosion of meaning and usefulness' (Hinshelwood 2008, 510). As I have described in terms of validity, if the definition of a concept is lacking, or understanding is erroneous, this will more than likely undermine the whole research project.

Having established a clear definition of a concept or phenomenon it is then possible to reduce or translate the characteristic features of a concept into a set of observable phenomenon. Increased success depends on the researcher's knowledge of their field and subject, and on their own creativity.

Conclusion

This book shows how containment theory can be applied to containment in organisations. Projects vary, each researcher has designed a methodology to suit their own research needs. My own research project was not specifically about organisations. However, one can see that the professional organisation that 'M' frequented was one that took in and accepted something he felt was 'intolerable'. His unwanted feelings were worked through and with his immense gratitude, a process which relieved his troubled mind. I have shown that operationalisation of the container-contained model, or aspects of it, should remain true to the theory, tenets and mores of Bion's own theory. I have shown how this was achieved in my own project. I have explained that the integrity of research outcomes is dependent on methodology. To conclude, I have shown that psychoanalytic concepts can be robustly empirically researched, that reliable methodology can be applied to psychoanalytic research and that psychoanalysis can evidence and verify its claims.

Notes

1 Leading to a symposium on operationalisation (1945) to which Bridgman was invited to contribute.
2 Or perhaps one distinguishing or differential feature.
3 Claims to the origin of the phrase 'Duck Test' vary. It is usually attributed to Emil Mazey, Secretary-Treasurer at the United Workers labour meeting (1946) when accusing members of communism.
4 A massive attempt to characterise every known medical disorder.
5 Then director of the National Institute of Mental Health (USA).
6 Hinshelwood used an inductive method. He states that a deductive approach would result in a set of predictive identifiers.

7　Bondage-domination-sado-masochism.
8　I refer to Bion's three works through which the container-container model can be seen to emerge, 'Attacks on linking' (1959), 'A theory of thinking' (1962c), coming to fruition in *Learning from Experience* (1962).
9　I find it helpful to think of an ego-function like an envelope of ego wrapped around or containing the experience that the ego-function has itself created. Freud provided examples of ego-functions in *Formulations on Two Principles of Mental Functioning* (1911).
10　In 1946 Klein explained this as 'nothing matters really' in someone who loses all their feelings. They lose the ego-function of being aware of their feelings as that ego-function has been split off and consequently annihilated.
11　BDSM provides a sado-masochistic, made-up scenario, referred to as a 'scene'. Much like an act in a play, there is often an agreed script of sorts, each participant plays an agreed role. Limitations and boundaries are agreed beforehand.
12　'Fetishes' (2005). Nick Broomfield director.
13　I provide an ad verbatim account in Chapter 9 of *Methods of Research into the Unconscious* (Staminova and Hinshelwood, 2018).
14　All available in Essex University Library.

References

Akhtar, S. (2018 [2009]) *Comprehensive Dictionary of Psychoanalysis*. London: Routledge.
Bion, W.R. (1959) Attacks on linking. *International Journal of Psychoanalysis* **40**: 308–315.
Bion, W.R. (1962a) A psychoanalytic study of thinking. *International Journal of Psychoanalysis* **43**: 306–310.
Bion, W.R. (1962b) *Learning from Experience*. London: Heinemann.
Bion, W.R. (1962c). A theory of thinking. In *Second Thoughts: Selected Papers on Psychoanalysis*. New York: Jason Aronson.
Boag, S. (2006) Freudian repression: The common view and pathological science. *Review of General Psychology* **10** (1): 74–86.
Boey, W.H., and Hede, A. (2001) Resistance to organisational change: The role of defence mechanisms. *Journal of Managerial Psychology* **16** (7): 534–548.
Boring, E.G. (1945) A review of general psychology: The use of operational definitions in science. *Psychological Review* **52** (5): 243–245.
Bridgman, P.W. (1927) *The Logic of Modern Physics*. London: MacMillan.
Briggs, S. (1997) *Growth and Risk in Infancy*. London: Jessica Kingsley.
Brown, J. (2000) What is a psychoanalytic sociology of emotion? *Psychoanalytic Studies* **2** (1): 35–49.
Campbell, N.R. (1920) *Physics: The Elements*. Cambridge: Cambridge University Press.
Davis, R., Sandler, A. and Sandler, J. (2000) *Clinical Observational Psychoanalytic Research: Roots of a Controversy – Andre Green and Daniel Stern*. London: Routledge.
'Fetishes' (special edition) (2005) DVD. Directed by Nick Broomfield. Metrodome Distribution.
Fonagy, P., Leigh, T., Steele, M., Steel, H. Kennedy, R. Mattoon, G. and M. Gerber, A. (1996) The relation of attachment status, psychiatric classification, and response to psychotherapy. *Journal of Consulting and Clinical Psychology* **64** (1): 22–31.
Freud, S. (1911) *Formulations on the Two Principles of Mental Functioning*. In *The Standard Edition of the Complete Psychological Works of Sigmund Freud, Volume XII*. London: Hogarth.
Freud, S. (1924) The economic problem of masochism. *Standard Edition of the Complete Psychological Works of Sigmund Freud* XIX: 155–170. London: Hogarth.
Hartwich, A. (1959 [1937]) *Krafft-Ebing's Aberrations of Sexual Life*. London: Staples Press.

Hinshelwood, R.D. (1989). *A Dictionary of Kleinian Thought*. London: Free Association Books.

Hinshelwood, R.D. (2008). Repression and splitting: Towards a method of conceptual comparison. *International Journal of Psychoanalysis* **89**: 503–521.

Holmes, J. (2018) *A Practical Psychoanalytic Guide to Reflexive Research: The Reverie Research Method*. London: Routledge.

Holway, W. and Jefferson, T. (2012) *Doing Qualitative Research Differently: A Psychosocial Approach* (2nd ed.). London: Sage Publication.

Insel, T. (2013). Transforming diagnosis. https://psychrights.org/2013/130429NIMHTransf ormingDiagnosis.htm

Klein, M. (1946). Notes on some schizoid mechanism. *International Journal of Psychoanalysis* **27**: 99–100.

Krafft-Ebing, R.V. (1886) *Psychopathia Sexualis*. Stuttgart: Ferdinand Enke.

Laplanche, J. and Pontalis, J.B. (1980 [1973]) *The Language of Psychoanalysis*. London: Hogarth.

Lemma, A. (2015) *An Introduction to the Practice of Psychoanalytic Psychotherapy* (2nd ed.). Chichester: Wiley.

Lingiardi, V., McWilliams, N., Bornstein, R.F., Gazzillo, F., and Gordon, R.M. (2017) *Psychodynamic Diagnostic Manual*. New York: Guilford Press.

Mendes, T. (2012) *Tasks, Emotions and Emotional Tasks: A Study of the Interconnection Between Social Defence Systems and Containment in Organisations* (PhD Thesis, Essex University Library).

Parth, K. and Loeffler-Statska, H. (2015) Psychoanalytic core competence. *Frontiers in Psychology* **6**: 356. doi:10.3389/fpsyg.2015.00356.

Sanfuentes, M. (2008) *Regression and Group Psychotherapy: Observing the Effect of the Group as a Whole on the Group Members 'Thinking'* (PhD Thesis, Essex University Library).

Skelton, R. (2006) *The International Encyclopaedia of Psychoanalysis*. Edinburgh: Edinburgh University Press.

Skinner, B.F. (1931) The Concept of the Reflex in the Description of Behaviour. *Journal of General Psychology* **5**: 427–458.

Stamenova, K. (2013) *Envy and Learning: A Psychoanalytical Observational Study of a Group in Education* (PhD Thesis, Essex University Library).

Stamenova, K. and Hinshelwood, R.D. (eds) (2018) *Methods of Research into the Unconscious: Applying Psychoanalytic Ideas to Social Science*. London: Routledge.

Stevens, S.S. (1935) The operational definition of psychological concepts. *Psychology Review* **42**: 517–527.

Vonofakos, D. (2009) *Differentiating Anxiety, Defence and Work-Related Functioning in the Social Dynamics of Social Systems: Observing the Unconscious Cultures of Psychiatric Organisations* (PhD Thesis, Essex University Library).

Walker, G.P. (2021) *BDSM – A Search for the Container-Contained Experience: An Object Relations Approach to the Problem of Masochism* (PhD Thesis, Essex University Library).

Walker, G.P. and Hinshelwood, R.D. (2018) 'Is it a bird, is it a plane?' In Stamenova, K. and Hinshelwood, R.D. (eds) *Methods of Research into the Unconscious: Applying Psychoanalytic Ideas to Social Science*. London: Routledge.

Chapter 7

Cultural Differences Between Groups

R.D. Hinshelwood

This chapter will give some initial thoughts to the working relationship between two groups where the different cultures of the groups interfere with each other. To a greater or lesser extent any working organisation will find some trouble in its working task, even if that is only an anxiety about getting it done and surviving as an organisation. But for many the task itself provokes anxiety. One could say that any care organisation or any hospitality organisation is going to be beset by the inevitable complexities of working with people. Manufacturing industries may have specific anxieties too – for instance factories making military hardware are faced, in overt or more likely hidden ways, with the ethics of fighting and killing.

As this book has argued these anxieties can frequently and almost inevitably be handled by developing attitudes and practices in the organisation which can avoid those anxieties and will support the individuals' own means for managing their anxieties. Those attitudes and practices form a part of its culture which in some way or other brings the members together around their common need to cope with the stress of the work.

However, if that system is disturbed it will threaten to expose and make conscious the latent anxiety the group members avoid. Such disturbance will be the encroaching or undermining of the containing attitudes and practices that the group culture has developed. When two groups which have evolved different methods of containing come together, they may undermine each other's containing cultures.

Group Dynamics

At this stage, I want to make an important distinction. More common is the description of a group dividing into two as the basis for expressing and dealing with a conflict in the culture of the originating group. However, this chapter is considering the coming together of two groups each of which has separately developed a culture for dealing with its own anxieties. The us-and-them dynamic between different groups is a commonplace. The fans of two different football teams identify themselves very differently. But more than that they give different evaluations of

DOI: 10.4324/9781315146416-10

each other – us good, them bad. Freud was impressed by the antagonism that can emerge between groups:

> It is always possible to bind together a considerable number of people in love, so long as there are other people left over to receive the manifestations of their aggressiveness.
>
> (Freud 1930, p. 114)

He called this the 'narcissism of minor difference'. Difference between groups, in fact difference of any sort, seems to automatically attract such evaluative judgements for the human being. As Freud had said: 'Expressed in the language of the oldest… "I should like to eat this", or "I should like to spit it out"' (Freud 1925, p. 237). The other group then represents, usually unrealistically, what has been spat out. This us-and-them dynamic is commonplace, and distorts the reality of each other to a small or large extent.

This may become stabilised as a persisting group dynamic. Its strength is enhanced by each group forming a solidarity supported by the otherness of the different other. However, this is a system of intergroup dynamics in which each culture *uses* the other. The us-and-them dynamic grows up in order to develop a cultural attitude to another group which allows the group to feel superior. This is frequently on a mutual basis – each group uses the other in the same superior way to project inferiority into. Ultimately, they come to need each other in order to sustain the self-enhancing projection of 'bad' into the other. It is the basis of problematic ethnic and gender relations. But this narcissism, I contend, can be exacerbated in a group by the need to resist the encroachment upon its defensive needs against an anxiety that threatens all the members, and which the group culture is evolved to contain.

Groups Coming Together

The dynamic I now want to discuss is where two groups have each evolved their containing attitudes and practices *without* reference to the other. Then the two groups find themselves coming closer and having to work together. Typically, this might be two commercial organisations that for extraneous reasons (usually financial) merge. Then the specific culture of one meets the specific culture of the other. The idiosyncratic character of each as it has grown up in relation to its task meets the character of the other. Attitudes clash, practices clash. The outcome is that each will find their attitudes and practices weakened or undermined, and the potential for containing anxiety is reduced. Stress and anxiety will surface for the individuals. They may be dealing with the same anxiety but dealing with it on the basis of two different cultures, or they may be dealing with different anxieties which have given rise to their own separate containing cultures.

There is only a modest literature on groups interacting in this way. A number of authors (Schalk, Heinen and Freese 2001, Broeng 2017, de Grouijer 2009, Cardona 2010, Fraher 2004) describe mergers of companies and organisations, and not surprisingly show the arousal of a persecutory anxiety about survival. The merger is experienced as threatening the survival of the organisation or more personally of individuals' jobs. Despite the quite reasonable side to these anxieties they may also provoke deeper phantasies. Jinette de Grouijer's book is titled *The Murder in Merger*, implying an intended destructiveness. The extensive description of her research showed:

> Many images of the merger... seemed infused with images of invasion and death. Furthermore a merger is the result of a pairing and conception between different organisations, evoking the 'Oedipal situation' and phantasies about the 'merging parents'.
>
> (de Grouijer 2009)

It is as if such a merger brings out quite basic destructive phantasies that previously were contained by defensive cultures. A rigidity may inevitably occur as an attempt to prevent too much anxiety being released.

In this chapter, I want to consider an example of each of two situations – one with two groups working together, the other merging. Both are in the healthcare services but very different aspects and historical epochs. The crucial elements we have to consider, I suggest, are:

- The nature of the anxiety
- The specific aspects of each culture that acts as a container of stress
- The success or otherwise of that containing culture

Experiences in the British National Health Service

This example derives from working in several hospital-based services within the NHS and derives from the period after 1990. At that time there was a movement to improve efficiency of the public services in general in Britain by re-modelling them on working organisations that operate within a market. The approach (in the 1990s) was to organise the NHS by developing the professionalisation of the management side. This involved increasing the size of such departments, and, particularly, the financial services. The culture of management groups as well as their training was increased to a university level and modelled on the management of the commercial sector.

In contrast was the long tradition of the culture of the healthcare professionals that the new management was destined to manage. These were cultured medical and nursing professions which had established positions for much longer and involving much greater training and apprenticeship requirements than the 20th century profession of management. There were therefore separate traditions.

Management Culture of a Commercial Organisation

Management services were derived from the management style of factory production with an untrained workforce. Such a working organisation is adapted to survival in a competitive market place with a focus on competition with rivals and ensuring the survival of the organisation by maximising profits for the owners and investors. The place of investors in such commercial organisations had been under discussion at the time and increasingly prioritised by business since the seminal article by Milton Friedman in the *New York Post* in 1970. Increasingly management focused on their anxieties to maximise profits, to ensure survival of the organisation amongst its competitors and to provide dividends for investors to avoid aggressive take-over bids. Then, second, the practices that followed focused on productivity and efficiency by making changes that constantly improved the products and services in advance of competitors, and also kept the most valuable staff through stimulating loyalty to the organisation and, as Weber said, to eliminate favouritism. In other words, practices evolved to work efficiently with physical raw materials – efficiency, impersonality and statistical accountability – are characterised by responses to the anxiety of a ruthless competition which spares no one. Much of this was at a conscious level addressing the reality of circumstances, though survival anxiety demanded considerable sacrifices at management and worker levels.

Healthcare Culture

Healthcare cultures differ in their anxiety and defences. First of all, anxiety is about death – not death of the organisation or of the healthcare workers but of the human 'raw material' they work with. Patients are people. Their survival is the purpose of the organisation, not the survival of the organisation as such. Practices have developed to cope with the particular stress of people frightened, in pain, mutilated, dying. For the work force, this involves a much greater sense of personal responsibility with the ever present threat of guilt and blame. Much of this is at a deep level, felt only unconsciously; as Menzies Lyth remarked in her study of a nursing practice: '[The] objective situation confronting the nurse bears a striking resemblance to the phantasy situations [of damage and death] that exist in every individual in the deepest and most primitive levels of the mind' (Menzies Lyth 1959, p. 46). The capacity for the organisation to provide a containment of the deadly responsibility and guilt has led to distinctive practices that support staff to cope. Similar coping practices exist in mental healthcare (see Hinshelwood and Skogstad 2000), as well as physical medicine and nursing.

I have offered these descriptions in order to emphasise the distinct contrasts between the two cultures, in terms of anxiety and the cultural practices which involve rigid defences.

Relations Between the Two Professions

This discussion has described two different cultures that have come together when commercial management was introduced into healthcare organisations. There is first of all a difference of anxiety. On one hand, management are focused on the survival of the organisation they are identified with, and on the other, the healthcare professionals are concerned for the illness and death of the people they treat. The contrast is striking and represents the two basic anxieties: the fear for one's own survival (the persecutory anxiety of the paranoid-schizoid position), and the concern for the injury or survival of others (known as depressive anxiety) (see Hinshelwood 1989).

So, each of the two professional groups develop practices focused on different anxieties. The management focus on financial and competitive market issues (prioritising the organisational business), and the care professions on the health of the persons in the beds (beset by the responsibility for the suffering). These are not completely contrasting as both the running of the organisation and the treatment of patients are important tasks within a hospital. There could be (and is) a potential creative division of labour. But the collaboration is made difficult by the rigidity of the unconscious focus in each culture deriving from the need to cope with different stresses. That rigidity comes from the need to contain the primary anxieties and it leads to an exclusiveness of the focus on each side. The alternative foci lead to a degree of resentment towards each other's approach. Often this is not personal as individuals from each profession may have good relations (though not always). It is a group dynamic in which good-bad evaluations are adopted and sustained as the narcissistic us-and-them dynamic described previously. An unfortunately toxic culture has developed on the basis of this dynamic in the worst instances.

It can be seen that however good personal relations are, there remains a fundamental cleavage between the two sets of anxiety – on one hand competition, and on the other, a rescuing care to protect from death. This is a fundamental cleavage in the service, arising from different anxieties. And they lead to different means of coping with those anxieties. On the one hand, there is a cultural attitude expressed as 'we can't possibly let the organisation collapse'; and on the other hand, an attitude expressed as 'we need whatever resources are necessary to avoid death'.

At a superficial level, the financing of services is seen from two different angles. Each potentially threatens the other. Management needs to protect the financial viability of the organisation, and the healthcare workers need to draw on whatever finances are needed. Whereas this is an understandable and conscious conflict the organisation has to cope with, the question is how the emotional anxieties can be contained without disturbing the culturally supported defences and thus exposing those intolerable anxieties defended against.

There is no doubt that at times, constructive meeting between the two separate interests can and does usefully happen. Listening to each other's concerns is an important element, plus the agreement with each other on some sort of give-and-take basis. Such a *contained* process is possible. At other times there is acrimony when the different interests simply clash, and consequences result from this. There can then be enduring resentment towards those who hold the purse-strings and hold the necessary opportunity to assert that power; and in the opposite direction, a resentment towards those who aggravate guilt about the suffering and deaths of patients.

This kind of contrast can be put in terms of the way the primary task is perceived – either survival of 'our' organisation, or survival of the patients. Such variance in the primary task was noted in different form in parts of a different organisation and commented on as follows:

> Managers' views of the primary task changed depending on their position in the hierarchy and structure of the organisation. At a Service-level, managers were emphatically user-focused, whereas senior Regional and Head Office managers developed more conceptual and intellectual perceptions of the primary task, since their work focused more on turning knowledge about practice into strategy and plans. As the emotions and stresses associated with creating and implementing strategy were different to those generated through direct client work, this was experienced by some regional managers as a source of tension and one which expressed itself in ambivalence to the strategic task, accompanied by a sense of guilt at shifting their focus away from clients.
>
> (Laughlin and Sher 2010, p. 11)

This was not a healthcare organisation but is mentioned here as a rare comparable example of the differing interpretations of the primary task that each appears rigid, when a more flexible form of containing would allow the different perceptions to work more closely together without either a loss of integrity or the exposure to the anxieties of the conflicting groups. In other words, the perception of the task by others needs to be contained in parallel with that of one's own perceptions. For instance, in a hospital the organisation may be in a dire position financially, and this has to be kept in balance with the needs of patients threatened with death. It is so easy for such a difficult balance to divide up into contrasting focuses of interest which compete with each other in rigid, unreconcilable and ultimately fractious ways.

It is the containment of such opposite tensions that this chapter is trying to draw attention to. Different cultural attitudes to the two stresses can undermine each other with the emerging of enduring anxiety and resentment between separate groups. Most usually such resentment is interpreted as merely jealousy and rivalry. But it is necessary to know how cultural methods of containment on both sides are subject to a hidden threat from each other because of the potential release of painful anxieties and stress.

Another very different version of this pulling apart of an organisational container will now be described.

Working in Vienna and in Zurich

In a previous publication (Hinshelwood 2018) I constructed the hypothesis that the professional groups of psychoanalysts which joined together in 1910 as the International Psychoanalytic Association had different cultures due to unconscious structures. This led to friction within the new organisation which could not be contained by conscious debate. And indeed, it would have needed some understanding of the unconscious dynamics between two groups with different cultural attitudes to the work done by the members of each group. Here I will emphasise that problem of psychological containing.

Sigmund Freud had developed his ideas in the 1890s in Vienna and began to form a small group of adherents from 1902 onwards. Slightly later a geographically separate group, in Zurich, drew on Freud's ideas which they learned from the published literature. The latter group formed around Eugen Bleuler at the Burgholzli Hospital, and was led by Carl Jung.

From the available material it could be shown that specific work anxieties with the disturbed people in the two groups – in Vienna and in Zurich – were likely to be different. Because of the different anxieties, the cultures of each group were likely to have different implicit and unconscious attitudes. As in the previous example it is possible, with some speculation, to trace out the anxieties, containing practices/ cultures, and the success of the containment for each culture; and then to recognise the inevitable clashes when the two groups joined.

The two groups of clinicians and researchers had already developed separately. They had had the opportunity like any other working group to form a culture and the practices to contain the two anxieties and the stress of the particular work each group faced. The previous study indicated there were different anxieties for each group, and thus each developed different containing cultures.

The Anxieties

In Vienna, Freud started weekly meetings of his Wednesday Psychological Society in 1902. It consisted of a dozen or so interested people from various backgrounds, some of whom were clinicians. Those clinicians treated ambulant out-patients who came to see the physicians in their offices, and confided their symptoms and conflicts most usually in terms of erotic tensions, the derivative symptoms and their dreams.

In contrast the Burgholzli, in Zurich, was a hospital for the confinement of seriously disturbed, mostly psychotic patients who exhibited alarming behaviour motivated by delusions and hallucinations at serious variance with reality.

The two groups were therefore challenged by quite different stresses. There were patients who lived passingly normal lives in society at large, and presented some erotic interest to the clinicians who had to contain the patients and their desires (as well as their own). In the hospital, it was different. Impulsive and unpredictable behaviour was frightening and required both physical safety and the willingness to tolerate meaningless incomprehension. In one group erotic tensions and temptations could begin to surface, and in the other, the mind-splitting headache of being infected with psychosis.

Perhaps in addition a different sense of stress arose from the means of remuneration. Those in Vienna were dependent on each other and their referral networks which required careful nurturing, whilst those in Zurich were relatively more secure, based on employment contracts of some kind.

The Cultures

The cultural practices of the two groups were consequently different (see Table 7.1). In the hospital there was a common task with a solidarity within the group facing things together, whilst the Vienna group were on the whole working individually

Table 7.1 Contrasting cultures

	Vienna	Zurich
Anxiety	Neurotic libidinal pressures on clinicians	The threatening behavioural and mental assault on the coherence of mind delivered by psychotic patients
Cultural practices	Extreme acceptance aimed to contain the anxiety of independence and inequality	The controlled quality aimed to contain the anxieties about transgression and dependence on each other
Containment achieved	Probably some containing was achieved through the relaxed individuality at the expense of authority and organisation	Anxiety was contained in a rigid defensive way that required dependence and personal conformity

with patients and problems they did not share with each other. The mutual support on offer was merely through discussion on Wednesday evenings.

These different settings offered very different opportunities for containment at the group organisational level. In Vienna with its individualism there was a free atmosphere, an 'intellectual communism' (see Gay 1988, p. 177). Views critical of Freud were accepted as well as those applying Freud's ideas as an authority to other intellectual disciplines. The freedom was in spite of the towering authority of Freud over his group. It might even have been because of Freud's singular authority that individual opinions of whatever quality could be thrown around. Perhaps the individualism of the group represented a denial of the inequality compared with Freud. This structure was it seems a containing one for the inevitable sense of isolation and individual responsibility that was characteristic of the work setting, and allowed a containment equally for rivalry and jealousy amongst the members of the group.

In contrast, in Zurich, there was no relaxed, egalitarian conviviality. Quite the reverse, its Protestant strictness demanded high standards and industry. The achievements of individuals were closely guarded possessions and could fire off quarrels. Competition extended to the sense of the international reputation of the Burgholzli itself to which they all belonged. Considering the transgressive behaviour, both physical and mental, which was the staple work, there was a strict conformity that marked a distinction from the individualism in Vienna.

At the same time a greater financial security at Burgholzli with a more formal and enduring contract of employment offered a greater security probably than in Vienna with no institution to depend on.

Relations Between the Two Centres

In 1908, these two centres joined forces to hold an International Psychoanalytic Congress in Salzburg. The disciplined nature of the Zurich group ensured they took the major share of organising the Congress, though there was a row between two Zurich members over a plagiarism accusation. Nevertheless, a journal (the *Jahrbuch*) was founded with Jung as editor. A second congress was held in Nuremburg in 1910 when the two groups formed one international one, the International Psychoanalytic Association. This caused trouble as a number of members of the well-organised Zurich group took the highest positions, and the egalitarian Viennese objected.

So, one can say that the coming together of these two groups brought issues of organisation and rivalry. The Burgholzli group operated as an efficient team, whilst the Viennese group were individualists. On both sides the ethos of the other group was not in step with their containing culture. The relaxed spirit of Vienna clashed with the organised conformity of the Zurich group, to challenge their means of coping with the fear of transgression; whilst that co-ordinated sense of efficiency from Zurich clashed with the egalitarian culture that had developed to contain the individualist rivalries and conflict in Vienna.

In the longer run the two groups were seriously affected by each other and came to an informal separation within a few years (by about 1913), but a more formal parting waited till after the end of the First World War.

Discussion

Two examples have been briefly given (expanded on elsewhere) of groups with divergent cultures coming together with some disharmony. It appeared that in each case, the cultures clashed most obviously in those features which related to the containing of anxieties that each group faced in the particular work they did.

In the examples, separate groups clashed for different reasons. Each seemed unfortunately to threaten the other. In one instance they had no choice but to continue in a debilitating mutual undermining of each other's unconscious containing functions; in the other instance, the two groups came apart again after five or six years, and have remained in rivalrous disunity ever since.

The claim is made that these clashes are inflamed unconsciously by the need embedded in the culture to contain anxieties. In both the examples the capacity for a flexible form of containing was limited, and this ensured that the culture clash was not resolved. In both cases rigid forms of container-contained led to unsatisfactory outcomes. In one instance, the NHS, the two separate professions (management and the healthcare professions) have been consigned to this inappropriate marriage on an indefinite basis, with rigid sets of attitudes that contain different anxieties in non-communicating ways. Whilst in the more voluntary association of the second example, the merger came apart quickly as the rigidity of the containing cultures failed to accommodate the characteristics of each other. If this argument is accepted, then forms of group division of labour and other intergroup working needs to be considered from the point of view of clashing modes of containment operated by the cultures and practices of each of the interacting groups. The consequence is that some attention needs to be given, however difficult, to being aware of forms of containment, to how these can be kept flexible, and to when they may be threatened by organisational restructuring.

References

Broeng, S. (2017). The impact of belonging groups in an institutional merger process. *Organizational and Social Dynamics* 17: 71–88.

Cardona, F. (2010). 'Not born to compete': Individual and organisational reluctance to compete. *Organizational and Social Dynamics* 10: 207–218.

de Grouijer, J. (2009) *The Murder in Merger: Developmental Processes of a Corporate Merger and the Struggle Between Life and Death Impulses*. London: Routledge.

Fraher, A.L. (2004) *A History of Group Study and Psychodynamic Organizations*. London: Free Association Books.

Freud, S. (1925) Negation. In *The Standard Edition of the Complete Works of Sigmund Freud* 19, pp. 235–239. London: Hogarth.

Freud, S. (1930) *Civilization and its Discontents*. In *Standard Edition of the Complete Psychological Works of Sigmund Freud* 21, pp. 59–145. London: Hogarth.

Friedman, M. (1970) The social responsibility of business is to increase its profits. *New York Times Magazine*, September 13, p. 17.

Gay, P. (1988) *Freud: A Life for Our Time*. London: Dent.

Hinshelwood, R.D. (1989) *A Dictionary of Kleinian Thought*. London: Free Association Books.

Hinshelwood, R.D. (2018) Freud and/or Jung: A group dynamic approach. In Brown, R. (Ed.) *Re-Encountering Jung: Analytical Psychology and Psychoanalysis*, pp. 20–30. London: Routledge.

Hinshelwood, R.D. and Skogstad, W. (Eds) (2000) *Observing Organisations*. London: Routledge.

Laughlin, R. and Sher, M. (2010). Developing leadership in a social care enterprise: Managing organisational and individual boundaries and anxiety: An action learning approach to leadership development. *Organizational and Social Dynamics* 10: 1–21.

Menzies Lyth, I. (1959) The functioning of social systems as a defence against anxiety: A report on a study of the nursing service of a general hospital. *Human Relations* 13 95–121. Republished in Menzies Lyth (1988) *Containing Anxiety in Institutions*. London: Free Association Books; and in Trist and Murray (eds) (1990) *The Social Engagement of Social Science*. London: Free Association Books.

Schalk, R., Heinen, J. and Freese, C. (2001) Do organizational changes impact the psychological contract and workplace attitudes? A study of a merger of two home care organizations in the Netherlands. In J. de Jonge (Ed.) *Organizational Psychology and Health Care at the Start of a New Millennium*, pp. 23–37. Munchen: Ranier, Hampp.

Part III

Applications

This section starts with the applications of containment to different contexts. Part of the success of the concept lies in the fact that its applicability has been tested in different fields, ranging from consulting to leadership, and therapeutic communities to Group Relations. The present section zooms in on some of those applications, by authors approaching different topics from this point of view. It should be noted that many contributions to this tradition predate the concept of containment, at least in its mature form devised by Bion, which can be traced back to his 1959 paper, although originally written in 1957. As such, as the traditions of consulting, group relations or therapeutic communities were already on their way, the concept starts to make its own slow appearance in the psychoanalytic literature.

The chapter "If Only We Could Contain Emotions" (Chapter 8, by Tiago Mendes) attempts to contribute to a more detailed overview of the application of containment to organisations, by revising some of the key usages of the concept in the field generally designated as systems psychodynamics. More than a critique, the intent is to detail how authors in the field draw on Bion's insights to build their work. Several areas are identified in which the concept is applied ranging from the consultant as a container, to the role of the primary task or authority in providing containment. Notwithstanding, the notion that containment is slowly drifting to become an ever-encompassing concept is signalled as a potential risk to the field, as it can become a one-size-fits-all sort of concept. One can also identify some conceptual enmeshment between containment, holding and emotional support. In a way it might be expected, as the needs from the "field" often require the use of different ideas from different schools, but the trade-off seems to be the loss of clarity regarding the conceptual building. Maybe more a concern for theoreticians than practitioners, but it is still a consideration worth taking into account. Finally, some reasons are presented for such different views, ranging from an adherence to Bion's different descriptions present in different phases of his work, to the authors using the concept to intervene in varying social contexts, to authors who simply study organisations with psychoanalytic lenses.

The chapter entitled "An Empirical Approach to Disentangle Intertwined Concepts" (Chapter 9 by Tiago Mendes) addresses the topic of social defence systems against anxiety compared with containment. Initially described by Elliott Jaques

DOI: 10.4324/9781315146416-11

(1955) and Isabel Menzies Lyth (1960), the paradigm of social defences became one of the more prominent in the field and a true theory of the role of unconscious anxiety in organisational culture (Long 2006). In fact, and crossing the bridge towards the change management field, one might state that social defences against anxiety became the paradigm for the psychoanalytic theory of resistance to change. That is, employees resist change efforts due to emotional motives and the projections they have placed in the social system which, when changed, threaten their own defences. The present chapter attempts to address such an idea and compare/contrast it with containment, since both at times appear as intertwined concepts. It should be noted that social defences share a common theoretical origin with containment and have at times been seen as preceding containment (Hinshelwood 1991). Through using a participant observation field work, that generated several vignettes of emotionally charged interactions between mental patients and their care takers, the author attempts to disentangle both concepts in the everyday life of an organisation. Surprisingly, perhaps, cultural defences and rigid modes of containment seemed to overlap in the everyday life of an institution. But the cases where a breakdown of containment was perceived were invariably followed by a secondary defensive move. Such rigid forms of containment can be seen as social defences when commonly shared between members of a culture.

Consulting to organisations has produced some of the most widely known and influential papers on the psychodynamic approach to organisations. The chapter "Organisational Research and Consulting and the Idea of Containment" (Chapter 10, by Susan Long) addresses containment through these lenses. The chapter focuses on mind as a container for emotions. But it depicts the multiple meanings that containment can take from the simplest meaning given by the Oxford Dictionary, to the more complex meaning conveyed by Bion in many circumstances. Long provides illustrations to the multiple uses of containment, arguing that we should consider that 'more important than the contained anxiety in itself, is the specific relationship entailed between container and contained'. Long argues that in organisations one should consider multiple containers: not only the person, but also the role, system and even context. On the other hand, she argues that the contained in organisations could be seen as the person in role. Armed with this framework, Long analyses cases taken from her role as coach making use of Organisational Role Analysis, as well as her consulting practice. The chapter ends by addressing the interesting topic of containers for the future, debating on how organisations can become containers for new thinking.

A Group Relations conference is a learning event that derives its core conceptual building from Bion's famous *Experiences in Groups*. It is considered that in his group period Bion's influences were quite distinct from his later Kleinian adherence. As mentioned before, his concept of containment can only be traced back to the period in which he was a Kleinian supporter and adhered to her ideas, and having creatively reviewed his group period in the light of the primitive anxieties described by Klein. At the same time, Group Relations were already ongoing starting in 1957 and drawing on Bion's work and just later on incorporating the idea of containment into a pre-existing framework. The Group Relations conferences have continued to evolve in format, events and elicited basic assumptions identified, to name but a few variables. Richard Morgan Jones' chapter "Dancing Between the Contained and the Container and Their Reciprocal Relatedness in Group Relations" (Chapter 11) addresses Group Relations through examples of the dynamics of containment encountered in a number of events. Drawing on a particular setting, a virtual event in Russia, the author elicits how the facilitator may act as a container for the different anxieties stirred up.

Leadership is a function which has also been debated in terms of containment. Be that the leaders of organisations, therapeutic communities, Group Relations events or even in terms of small group processes. Psychoanalytic Institutes and the leadership disturbances they have experienced have also been the subject of much analysis. It is not surprising that leadership is one of the topics covered in this book. The chapter "Leadership and Containment" (Chapter 12, by Stanley Gold) explores the dynamics of leadership and the implied promises they make. Gold describes the characteristics of leadership including vision, accountability and, among others, a "dash" of humility. Gold explores the always powerful dynamics of regression in leadership, and the specific relationship of the leader and the group. Drawing on Bion, the leader is always at odds with the group, attempting to fulfil the phantasy that he is some sort of magician, or has the solution to the group's problems. But the leader should be aware of the threat of breakdown latent in every change process, a threat that Gold alludes to. Drawing from a time in which he held a position of stranger in a group but with the potential for leadership, the chapter vividly describes the tension inherent between the leader and the group, and the attempt by the group to deskill the leader. Resorting to his own experience, the author argues that leadership sometimes equates to swimming with sharks and suggests a few rules on how to deal with such difficult situations.

The chapter "Father, Mother and the Guinea Pig Children" (Chapter 13, by John Diamond) delves into the context of therapeutic communities, in this particular case for children and young people. This context has a long and fertile history, with complex theoretical underpinnings, and a history of consultation which provided clearly depicted illustrations of the work and role of these organisations (Menzies Lyth 1979). Diamond's chapter addresses a terrible incident that happened at the Mulberry Bush School, reminding us of how difficult these contexts can be, and the emotional turmoil in which they exist, and survive. The therapeutic community in this context, it is argued, acted out through the actions of two children that involved uncontained aspects of a recent murder which received wide exposure in the media. The chapter describes how the director managed to help the community contain the anxieties connected with the terrible incident, without scapegoating or blaming. The chapter further argues, following from the work of OPUS, that society itself can be seen in the light of the container-contained model.

The final chapter "The Challenge of Containment: A Psychoanalytic-Systemic Approach" (Chapter 14, by Avi Nutkevich) describes a consultation to a governmental human service organisation that dealt with baby and child adoption in

Israel. The consultation describes difficult meetings and the pressure and reflective thoughts that assault the consultant in troubling times. Nutkevich argues that the challenge of containment is always under fire, and that the consultants are constantly under pressure. Furthermore, he argues that patience and security constitute the hallmark of containment in this regard. The chapter ends with Nutkevich describing his approach entitled Psychoanalytic-Systemic, which he briefly describes as placing more emphasis in the union between psychoanalytic and systemic theories, while also distinguishing it from the more common systems psychodynamics.

The different applications expressed in this final part elucidate the richness and applicability of Bion's concept, certainly one of the reasons why it has become so successful.

References

Bion, W.R. (1959) Attacks on linking. *International Journal of Psychoanalysis*, 40, pp. 308–315.

Hinshelwood, R. (1991) *A Dictionary of Kleinian Thought*. Second edition. London, Free Association Books.

Jaques, E. (1955) Social systems as a defence against persecutory and depressive anxiety. In Klein, M., Heimann, P. and Money-Kirle, R. (1955) *New Directions in Psychoanalysis*. London, Tavistock Publications.

Long, S. (2006) Organizational defenses against anxiety: What has happened since the 1955 Jaques paper? *International Journal of Applied Psychoanalytic Studies*, 3(4), pp. 279–295.

Menzies Lyth, I. (1960) The functioning of social systems as a defence against anxiety. In I. Menzies Lyth (1988), *Containing Anxiety in Institutions*. London, Free Association Books.

Menzies Lyth, I. (1979) Staff support systems: Task and anti task in adolescents in institutions. In Menzies Lyth, I. (1988) *Containing Anxiety in Institutions*. London, Free Association Books.

Chapter 8

If Only We Could Contain Emotions

A Contribution to an Overview of the Application of Containment to Organisations

Tiago Mendes

Introduction

The aim of the following chapter is to examine how containment has been used in the psychoanalytic approach to organizations. It is neither an easy nor a straightforward task, given the massive amount of literature and the importance of the concept in the growing tradition of applying psychoanalysis *outside the couch*. In light of these conditions, any overview of the theme may fall short from its objectives and, as such, this chapter simply proposes to be a contribution for what is a much wider debate. Nonetheless, it seems an important endeavour to undertake especially when its use in the literature has steadily grown in the past few years, especially within the Kleinian and Tavistock traditions as Gabriel (1999) emphasized. But it wasn't always the case. As we have seen previously, Bion's concept can only be traced back to his 1959 paper.[1] By then, interest in the psychodynamic approach to organizations was already high,[2] with the work of the Tavistock Institute and therapeutic communities blooming. Bion's work was also slowly getting traction within psychoanalysis, so it is not surprising that containment was a late addition to fields that were already well established at the time. Some of these even derived their basic tenets from outside the Kleinian tradition, such as Group Relations deriving its framework from Bion's early group work.

As psychoanalysis is an ever-evolving discipline, late additions of conceptual ideas to existing traditions is not new. When it happens, it takes time for them to be absorbed by mainstream psychoanalysis or, in this case, by the systems psychodynamics tradition. Mark Stein (2000) already pointed it out while addressing Klein's concept of envy and its absence from the psychodynamic tradition of applying it to organizations. As he noticed, envy was absent from Robert de Board's (1978) book that overviewed the developments in the field at the time. More surprisingly, containment is also absent from De Board's book, signalling it wasn't perceived as a fundamental concept in the field at the time. Nonetheless, if we venture in a quick search for "containment" in *Organizational and Social Dynamics*, a leading journal in the field, we come across the staggering number of 150 results. If we attempt

DOI: 10.4324/9781315146416-12

the same endeavour with "containing", the new search brings back 133 hits. Even if there are some colloquial uses of the term or citations from other publications, still the vast majority of the references refer to Bion's concept. Bion's concept has clearly gained a large foothold in the literature since Robert De Board's time, paralleling its growing importance in psychoanalysis in general.

Nonetheless, containment seems to be increasingly applied in the literature with a wider sense, in very different circumstances and even possibly with different meanings, becoming what could be described as a *one size fits all* concept, sometimes even being used interchangeably with other similar concepts such as holding.[3] Far from attempting to propose a correct way of applying Bion's ideas, the present chapter simply tries to review the literature and suggest how it seems to be used, highlighting what seems to be the reasons for the different applications from the authors, ranging from an increased view of containment as *containing*, to affiliation to different psychoanalytic traditions, to drawing on Bion's different usages of the concept. Nonetheless, I recognize that the success of containment implies the possibility of different and creative ways of applying and expanding it, even beyond Bion's original intentions, although one should be wary that the trade-off might be a loss of conceptual clarity.

The Application of Containment to Organizations

The Consultant as a Container

In the application of psychoanalytic knowledge to organizations, containment has become a commonly mentioned concept. Several usages have been identified and I shall briefly go over them, before attempting a critique of how they are being employed.

The most common way the concept is employed seems to be in the case descriptions of consulting projects. In this, usually the consultant is described as a container to the client, the team or the leader of a said organization dealing with a difficult task, such as caring for people, or working through a complex time in an organization, such as withstanding a change management effort (Palmer 2004). This seems to bear a direct analogy with the clinical setting where the therapist is increasingly described as being a container to the patient's emotions (Bott Spillius et al. 2011; Hinshelwood 1991; Ogden 2004). Several authors in the field have stressed the importance of organizational consultants to act as containers for their client(s) (Anderson and White 2002; Klein 2006; Nutkevitch 1998; Rosenthal and Davidoff 2000; Vansina and Vansina-Cobbaert 2008), although few give detailed accounts of what they meant by using this concept. Nutkevitch (1998) describes the role of consultant as a container for the anxiety of managers arguing that by maintaining the time boundary, it allowed the managers to perform their task in an effective and unburdened way, following from a difficult session. Rosenthal and Davidoff (2000), addressing the work of consultants also argue that they act as containers and links such a role with the importance of managing the boundaries.

Anderson and White (2002) elicit the containing function of the consultant in a manner very similar to what an analyst might do, by stating that:

> Containment occurs when the consultant takes in communications, ponders over them intuitively, and then responds to them without spilling his or her own anxieties and defences onto organizational members.
> (Anderson and White 2002, p. 505)

This description bears a striking resemblance to the clinical setting. Furthermore, they also link such capacities with managing the boundary and with clarification of the primary task, a point addressed in more detail below. Palmer (2004) also stressed the importance given to the consultant as a container for the anxieties of the client, although referring to it as temporary, while the organization is undergoing a change process. Palmer also refers to the holding environment, based on Stapley (1996), but without distinguishing between the concepts. Edward Klein (2000) has also described the consultant as a container while describing his work as a consultant with a psychiatric adolescent unit, arguing (Klein 2006) that container-contained is one of seven key concepts in the Tavistock tradition, although describing it as a *holding function*, without further clarification. David Armstrong (2005a) also describes a private consultancy to a manager who was unable to make use of the chairman as a container and instead used the consultant. In a very similar manner Hughes and Pengelly (1997), when approaching the role of supervision, argue on the importance of the supervisor to act as a container to the supervisee.[4] Although they argue for the interaction in supervision of different concepts such as authority, they seem to describe the role of the supervisor-as-container in a similar way to the relationship between analyst and patient. And in trying to connect this capacity to the task, they emphasize how the supervisor might contain the feelings of the supervisee, therefore enabling him to accomplish his task. Another very similar use of the role of consultant as a container appears in the field of group relations, although I will not go into detail on this. It suffices to say that it is usually argued that the consultant fulfils the role of container in Group Relations learning (Lawrence 2000a, 2000b; Lipgar 2003; Sher 2003; Wilke 2003).

Nonetheless, this view of the consultant as a container has been criticized by Gabriel and Carr (2002), stating "the extent to which organisational consultants may help contain the anxieties is subject to much debate" (p. 357). Notwithstanding Gabriel and Carr's affirmation, earlier in this same paper, they had assumed that their theoretical perspective, described as *Studying organisations psychoanalytically* by opposition to *Psychoanalysing organisations*, considers conflicts and anxieties present in organizational life as "virtually unavoidable within the present organisation of society" (p. 353), therefore they would necessarily have some doubts on the efficiency of organizational interventions. Stacey (2001) also criticized this view, stating that it is the group matrix that is the container for the group. The relationships in the organization – the invisible, *shadow relationships*, the liking and disliking, the covert dynamics and internal politics – are all part of the relationships of the organization's members, therefore contributing towards containment. Moreover Stacey, drawing on Bollas, argues that the consultant is an auxiliary in evoking a *new inner experience* (Stacey 2001, p. 108), not the container *per se* through an interpretative stance, as argued by Shapiro and Carr (1991).

As such, it seems that although practising consultants view their role, at least partially, as one of containing the emotions of their clients, this view is somewhat challenged by non-practitioners that study organizations psychoanalytically.

The Manager/Leader as a Container

A closely related use seemed to be the reference in the literature of the need of directors or managers of organizations to act as containers. Elizabeth Richardson (1973) was exploring such a notion already in the 60s and 70s; very much influenced by Bion's (1962) *Learning from Experience*, she attempted to apply containment to the field of teaching. Even though she did not fully develop the idea, it seems she hints that the school could have a hierarchical structure whereby students would be contained by teachers, and teachers' anxiety would be contained at the next hierarchical level. A similar design was argued by Carlyle and Evans (2005) regarding how, in organizations, the managers or persons with a role that could act as containers should also be contained, which they described as *containing containers*. Obholzer (1994c) argued that the managers have an important containment function and Nutkevitch (1998) sustained that managers are constantly confronted with anxiety, aggression and envy from the employees, due to their position of authority in the organization. Therefore they need to effectively contain such projections and act as efficient containers for their employees. James and Clark (2002) also argue that in some types of organizations the manager's role as a container for work-related emotions is crucial. Gabriel (1999), an author very much concerned with bridging psychoanalytic insights and management theory, also addressed leadership and the characteristic of a "good enough" leader, arguing that:

> The "good enough" leader relieves the followers of the burden of excessive worry. He or she wants them to ignore part of the reality, so that they can focus on their particular piece of work. He or she promises them, however, that reality will not go unattended; that he or she will bring his or her best talents and skills to the task of assessing, managing and containing the total risks the organization faces. When the leader functions in this way, we say that he or she creates a "containing" psychological space in which people feel protected enough to accomplish their piece of real work.
>
> (Gabriel 1999, p. 145)

It should be emphasized that, certainly influenced by his management background, Gabriel is one of the few authors who tries to describe how a leader should perform/ act in order to be "containing", although seeming to attempt to bridge between Bion and Winnicott. Nevertheless, his description raises interesting questions regarding when a leader should inform his followers about some "worries" since, as Cardona (1994) described, if such worries are not addressed it effectively undermines the capacity to work. In a similar vein Gutmann and Pierre (2000) argue that the leader must have the ability to perform emotional containment of the group members. In fact, they argue leadership should handle the destructive aspects of the group such as dissatisfaction, violence and frustration and that the inability to do so, or cases where there is an absence of leadership, lead to a burst of dissatisfaction, disorder and violence. Edward Klein (2006) also described the importance of leaders to act as containers for their staff and argued that by making staff feel like a family, the leader was providing containment to the staff's stress of starting a new business. Vansina and Vansina-Cobbaert (2008) also argued the importance of managers as containers, exemplifying how this might be applicable in an organization being re-structured – where rumours about lay-offs started running wild – when the general manager instead of panicking or denying the rumours instead held a meeting where he calmly explained what would happen, the number of layoffs, and what the company would do to support staff. Vansina and Vansina-Cobbaert (2008) argue that this resulted in the installation of a holding environment, but at the same time they absorbed part of the tension and anxiety and anger, transforming it, and therefore acted as a container, by not angrily attacking workers or dismissing their criticisms. They argue that at the group level it is important that the structures supposed to provide holding and containment do not become themselves a source of containment and stress. In this case we are also faced with an interchangeable use of containment and holding.

Again in this case we are faced with the idea that sources of distress inside organizations might be contained not only through colleagues and co-workers, but also by people that are in a hierarchical relationship. Gabriel even emphasizes how such a style of leadership is beneficial for organizations, in the sense that it provides the necessary capability for the people to perform the task at hand. Given his prior critique of the consultant as a container, Gabriel seems to place more importance on the role of the leader as a container of emotions.

The Organization as a Container

Another common usage of the concept seems to be referring to the role of organizations as containers. Correale and Di Leone (2004) argued that mental health institutions act as containers for the patients due to their recurrent use of primitive defence mechanisms such as splitting and projective identification, although they seem mainly concerned with how this can be a crucial technical aspect in the residential treatment of such patients. Kaës (2004) stated that institutions "have potential for containment if a work setting is sufficiently well established" (p. 122). Furthermore he adds: "The functionality of the setting as a potential container is seen as dependent upon the caregiving group's capacity to analyse the intertransferential formations that have been mobilised" (p. 122). Shapiro and Carr (1991) argue that there is a difference in mental health institutions between the containment provided by therapists, which is interpretation based, to the containment or holding offered by nurses which is physical. Also Menzies Lyth (1979) mentions containment when referring to a children's institution, arguing about the importance of staff meetings in order to provide for reverie for staff. This is an important point since the key elements that appear on the clinical description such as reverie, introjection, modification of the content or reprojection of the modified introjection are seldom addressed in the more organizational context. Furthermore, since this is a complex process, failures at some of these steps may account for failures in containment, that is, in some mal-adaptive forms. Notwithstanding, such considerations seem to be addressed in a loose manner, without much specificity, which may be connected with the aims of the authors, more concerned with depicting the successful interventions and the reasons they have discovered that account for such successes.

> The function of reverie is important also for staff in children's institutions. It can be reverie in the individual staff member or it can be something analogous to reverie in group situations, staff talking things through in an intuitive way together. The communications on which staff must work are often massive and very disturbing and staff in turn need support of the kind I have mentioned. Like the ordinary devoted mother (Winnicott, 1958) they need themselves to be contained in a system of meaningful attachments if they are to contain the children effectively.
>
> (Menzies Lyth 1979, pp. 253–254)

But the idea that organizations may act as containers for society has also been argued in the literature, the main argument being that some organizations fulfil a specific role for society, such as religious organizations. This approach, even though it considers the importance of the organization as a container, focuses on the relation between society and the organization. Stokes (1994) argues that "our public institutions need to provide a reliable and stable container for the nation, helping to manage issues concerning inequality, sickness and disorder" (p. 125). Obholzer (1994b) also argued that public institutions of large social systems fulfil the role of containing certain aspects of society, such as education or health systems. This view is also sustained by Shapiro and Carr (1991) regarding religious organizations, arguing that these organizations act as containers for society by marking the transitions of life in a contextualized and ritual way, through baptisms to mark births, or marriages.

This view seems derived from Bion's own description of the mystic and the establishment and, in this case, the authors have assumed that by analogy the same idea could be understood to mean society as a whole. I argue that in these cases, different authors resort to different aspects of Bion's work when referring to containment. Drawing on such different descriptions by Bion might account for such differences.

Other Links

A further reference has appeared in the literature regarding how a clearly defined primary task is important in "containing" anxiety. Nutkevitch (1998) argued that clarity and ongoing discussion about the primary task, together with efficient boundary management, are crucial in creating a safety net where containment can occur. Fraher (2004) also seems to sustain this idea. Nonetheless, clarity about the primary task is not an *a priori* element. In fact, Stacey (2001), though stressing the importance of clarity regarding the primary task for the Tavistock approach, states that when workers in an organization are clear about the task, then creativity does not come into play. He argues that if too much anxiety regarding the task is destructive and harmful, knowing exactly what to do leads to an almost rigid dynamic. The ideal situation would be working "on the edge", that is, trying to figure it out without being too overwhelmed with anxiety.

A further employment of containment is connected with authority, a crucial concept in the Tavistock model (Obholzer 1994a; Obholzer and Miller 2004). Connections between the two concepts seem implicit in a paper by Long et al. (2000) when stating that a steering committee needed authority in order to perform a containing function for an action research project. Rules and procedures, structural elements, also seem to be emphasized in connection with containment. For instance, Wiltshire and Parker (1996) argue that the most important thing regarding handover meetings in nursing is their structure, and that this structure provides containment. It might be considered that these elements are much more relevant in organizations than when one considers containment as solely an interpersonal phenomenon. James and Clark (2002) also argued that in some types of organizations rules and procedures inherent to the organization are in themselves a source of containment. Nevertheless it seems hard to separate, if one takes up this idea, what is containment and what is defensive in this case. It might then be argued that in Menzies Lyth's paper (1960) the nurses were contained by the task list system they needed to perform, instead of defending themselves from establishing a true relationship. A similar use connects with the role of training and professional development, referred to by James and Clark (2002) as a source of containment for anxiety among the employees of service-providing organizations who need to make decisions and have discretion in their roles. Similarly Vansina and Vansina-Cobbaert (2008) also mention the importance of training in organizations in order to contain the anxiety of its members. While addressing containment and holding and providing the example of a surgical team, Vansina-Cobbaert argues that each member has been trained to handle difficult situations and that this has a containing quality.

Other authors have argued that the group should be seen as a container for individuals. When studying the relation of groups and organizations to enemies, Erlich (2001) sustains that several individuals in group act as paranoid, even though individually they would never be clinically considered paranoid or psychotic. According to Erlich this is so "precisely because their paranoia is contained and supported by a group that gives it consensual validation and political respectability of sorts" (Erlich 2001, p. 116). But this might be more of a description of a failed or fragmented container, an important distinction to be made when it comes to organizations. While describing the relationship between the group facilitator and the group, besides arguing for a containing style of facilitation, Wilke (2003) also systematically refers to the need for the group to become containing. In a sense, he argues that the facilitator acts as container until the group itself can perform such a function.

In an introduction to Part V of his compilation of Tavistock Institute contributions to organizational psychology, which was dedicated to the psychoanalytic view of organizations, Eric Miller (1999) argued for a link between providing boundary conditions and providing the individuals with a sense of safety and containment.

> Second, it is in fact difficult to see a direct connection between this perspective and job design. The influence is more indirect, through attending such conditions as assigning a "whole task" and providing the boundary conditions that can enable the group to be self-managing and also give it safety and containment.
>
> (Miller 1999, p. 3)

Goodwin (1997) also described how the members of a mental health team were contained by the rigid boundary which they established during the assessment of the patients' treatment plans. This boundary acted as *protective barrier* clearly seeming to maintain a split between staff and patients. In this sense Goodwin seems to use containment as in the sense of rigid protection from becoming overwhelmed, rather than with the intention of modifying anxiety. It is important to notice that the rigid form of containment, as we have seen in Part I of this book, is a failed form of containment. In this sense there is no modification of anxiety, since the container and contained do not mutually adapt. As we will see in the next chapter it usually leads to a phenomenon know as task drift, or anti-task. The rigid form of container, by not allowing anxieties to be worked through, in the end also intensifies the anxiety.

From Different Forms of Containment to Containment Seen as a *One Size Fits All* Concept

As can be seen from the literature review, containment seems to be used in the most disparate of ways and even in connection with the majority of the concepts in the Tavistock tradition ranging from authority to boundary, and even to the role of training. Such usage seems excessive, to say the least, being indiscriminately applied in different contexts, at different levels, regarding different concepts. It is worth noticing that some use containment with the meaning of "containing" (Bott Spillius et al. 2011), while others use two maladaptive forms (rigid and fragmented) and one adaptive (flexible).[5] Lipgar (2003) also criticized such an excessive use of the term containment applied to groups, and in fact the broad use of the term makes it lose the complex myriad of transformations and projections involved which were present in Bion's original description.

> Often the term "container" itself, so identified with Bion, does not connote the kind of active participation and interaction, the processing and modifying of the projected part-objects which he shows is required of leaders who would contribute to developmental psychological work in groups. The term is often taken in a more static sense, not conveying a sense of the kind of subjective activity, the stressful experiences entailed in working creatively with internalizations and projective identifications.
>
> (Lipgar 2003, p. 42)

Nonetheless, authors who argue against such excessive usage sometimes fall in the trap of excessively using the concept to apply to every phenomenon (Hughes and Pengelly 1997). Furthermore the distinction between emotional support and containment seems very blurred. For instance when it comes to funerals, Jaques' (1955) and Shapiro and Carr's (1991) description might have different connotations. While for Jaques it clearly has a defensive purpose, for Shapiro and Carr a funeral can be seen as designed ritual, created in a holding environment. In this sense, Shapiro and Carr also argue that "the social task of religious institutions is to enable individuals to face the connections between dependency and irrationality by providing a managed and contained context for both" (p. 159). Obviously a ritualized ceremony, such as a religious funeral, provides support regarding the anxiety caused by the death of a loved one. But the question arises of whether we can consider this ceremony as a demonstration that social organizations have a defensive purpose or, in contrast, if they provide containment and support at crucial moments. Obholzer (1994c) also states the importance of staff support systems, which he tries to describe by stating that in a way the problems should have a group quality to them. Furthermore, Menzies Lyth's (1960) description provides examples of how staff support each other emotionally, although the adaptive form of containment of anxieties seems absent, since her description shows how staff members support the rigid defences employed and that are maintained culturally as the way things are done.

It seems there is a case here for refinement of the concept and its application. A first aspect concerns the fact that there seem to exist different views based on different phases of Bion's work, that is, containment in some cases is used as "containing", while in others it is used in its three-dimensional model – rigid, fragmented and flexible – and at other times it references Bion's description of the mystic/establishment. Furthermore, there is an excessive use of the concept and it seems widely seen as synonymous with holding and emotional support, and is possibly equated somehow with a successful intervention by practitioners. That is, a successful intervention implies that at a given moment in the process, anxieties were elaborated, contained and worked through. Another aspect concerns the different aims of the authors when applying the concept, which might also account for such different usages, since many are practitioners. It is worth noticing the particular type of organizations being described, which may also account for an increasing presence of containment in the literature. The initial descriptions of the Tavistock tradition projects with the Glaciar Metal Company, and the Ahmedabad experience detail interventions with organizations whose primary task was not concerned with the care or direct work with people. Those organizations lay within the profit sector. As opposed to many descriptions of successful interventions where containment plays a main role in care-providing organizations, or organizations whose throughput are people, such as schools transforming uneducated children into educated children, healthcare organizations or structures operating in the non-profit sector. Despite anxieties being rife in both the profit and non-profit sector, one might argue that the specific type of organizations under analysis, and the impact on staff of providing care for clients, certainly makes containment an appropriate concept to make sense of the intervention. Maybe herein lies some of the reasons why containment has grown so importantly while describing successful consulting interventions within care and social organizations. Of course this does not mean that containing anxiety is not a key part of working in other types of organizations. Anxieties connected with threats to one's self are highly present in organizations that work in *up or out* systems where you are either promoted or invited to leave. One can only imagine the anxiety inherent in working in weapons factories, or even the anxieties faced by the pharmaceutical company's staff working on vaccines for COVID. Still, an over usage of the term may devoid it of meaning and fail to convey the dynamic nature of the relationship Bion struggled to describe.

Containment Versus Holding

A further point concerns the relation between containment and holding. In the literature there clearly seems to be some interchangeability between holding and containment (James and Clark 2002; Palmer 2004; Richardson 1973). In other cases the concepts appear as distinct, though interrelated in some sense (Klein 2000, 2006; Shapiro and Carr 1991). Shapiro and Carr (1991), for instance, described what they call the holding environment as having two fundamental characteristics: "empathic interpretations and containment of aggression and sexuality" (pp. 35–36). They describe containment in the sense of "bearing painful affect" (p. 49). Afterwards they describe the holding environment as a complex construction where several concepts are intertwined, one of which is containment. Long, Newton and Dalgleish (2000) also connect the two concepts and describe a "'facilitating' or 'holding' environment" (Long et al. 2000, p. 168), which they argue must be present in collaborative work and which "could allow and contain negative as well as positive aspects of the collaboration so that these could be understood, learned from, and worked with alongside the primary work of the project" (Long et al. 2000, p. 168). It seems these authors also try to make a connection between a holding environment and containment, thus differentiating between them. As in the case of Shapiro and Carr, described above, Long et al. also consider containment of painful feelings and experiences as a facet or correlate of a good holding environment. Still, a clear distinction between both concepts seems to require further attention.

One is left with the impression that when it comes to consultancy there is a need for a clearer distinction between *holding* and *containment*, as both concepts seem to be used sometimes indistinctly and other times complementarily. Such an endeavour is important to prevent confusion and enmeshment between the two concepts in the field. It must be noted that Winnicott's concept implies a passive role whereby there is an illusion of omnipotence from the good mother that promotes development. In Bion's case we see more of the reality principle in operation, modifying the anxiety through the use of someone else as an auxiliary ego. In a way, regulating one's emotions, as seems to be the case when Klein (2006) states that the container-contained[6] "is a holding function occurring in groups and organizations that can facilitate effective work in stressful situations" (2006, p. 12). And, in fact, the above quoted examples serve to highlight a common misuse of both concepts as being interchangeable, as if they refer to the same thing. However, as stated in Chapter 3, these concepts are different, not only theoretically, but also in practice, highlighting different aspects of psychic reality.

Authors who try to view them as interrelated focus on holding being more connected with the external environment, while suggesting that containment is more relational and occurs within the interrelational domain. Although such a view allows both concepts to be connected, it does so at the expense of conceptual unity. That is, when concepts from different schools of psychoanalysis are utilized to explain the same phenomena, the trade-off is a loss of conceptual rigour. But possibly that is a small price to pay for practitioners in the field, who pursue and expand their thinking and practice based on client's requests, which may be different from more scholarly aims. Maybe the challenge is for Kleinians to expand their conceptual framework in such a way that accommodates the needs of practitioners in the field.

Related with containment and holding, another concept that seems hard to disentangle is that of emotional support for staff, whose importance is argued by several authors from different fields (Biran 2003; Obholzer 1994c; Wilson 2003). This also seems hard to separate from containment and holding, although Hughes and Pengelly (1997) separate containment from emotional support in supervision by stating that the supervisor (container) is more than supportive and tries to acquire meaning from the supervisee's feelings. Wiltshire and Parker (1996) argue that, regarding handover meetings in nursing, containment results from good boundary management of such meetings, and not necessarily from giving emotional support. As one can see, even when different authors attempt to distinguish such concepts, they do so in different ways.

And in fact, these three concepts which are used interchangeably may in fact be quite different. As Thomas Ogden (2004) has already argued with regard to the clinical aspect, holding and containment are in fact very different. Furthermore, emotional support, a rather elusive concept, may also be of a completely different kind. In a sense it can mean support of individual defences to evade anxiety, but it can also mean supporting for instance staff members to face their anxieties. In fact, Menzies Lyth's (1960) description of the defensive techniques employed by the nurses mentioned how the nurses received support for their individual defences from the group. And, in fact the nurses can feel emotionally supported by their peers when they all project despair, inadequacy and aggression into less powerful groups in an organization, such as the auxiliary staff.[7] This is especially the case when individual nurses struggle to cope with strong feelings of disempowerment and with being unable to help difficult patients, as well as with their own aggression towards patients. The same feeling of emotional support can be experienced by all the members of an organization while in competition against other organizations, as in an example taken from consultancy (Roberts 1994). Nevertheless, this does not mean that they are in touch with their own difficult feelings, though if one asked them they might state that they had emotional support from the team. Therefore emotional support does not necessarily mean the same as containment or holding. And job satisfaction might not necessarily be connected with the previous concepts, nor for that matter might effectiveness at task performance. But these questions fall outside of the scope of this chapter. However, with regard to the psychoanalytic approach to organizations, there is a strong case that holding, containment and emotional support should be disentangled. If not, the risk is that the concepts will become so broadly and indistinctly used that they lose their meaning and cannot communicate precise ideas to other theoreticians and practitioners.

Different Backgrounds – Different Views?

When it comes to the different usages of containment in the literature, it seems that these differences seem, at least partially, to be connected with different approaches regarding the application of psychoanalysis, as emphasized by Gabriel and Carr (2002). These authors argue that it is different to make sense of organizations, as a product of human society, through the use of psychoanalytic insights, which seems closer to Freud's own writings on social aspects such as in *Totem and Taboo* (Freud 1913–1914), whose work Gabriel and Carr seem to consider genealogically closer to their own stance, from trying to "improve" organizations using psychoanalytic tools.[8] In this sense, it seems that the use of containment made by external consultants regarding their own work would probably be different from that of researchers or scholars who would use it with other aims. Obviously when one speaks about containment from one's own experience of consultancy, that is quite different from speaking of group containment through the use of observation or another methodology.

Another aspect has to do with whether the authors come from a management or a therapeutic background. The background of the authors writing about containment and organizations seems to have an added explanatory power in separating not only the differences in the language employed, but also the different usages of containment. Authors connected with management (Gabriel 1999; Gabriel and Carr 2002; James and Clark 2002; James and Hunfington 2004) seem to look for sources of anxiety reduction that allow workers to perform their task. Authors coming from therapeutic settings, mainly mental health institutions (Correale and Di Leone 2004; Kaës 2004; Shapiro and Carr 1991), tend to consider the institution as a whole as a potential projective arena for patients, therefore seeing its potential for containing the patient's self. It adds that care organizations are quite different from other types of organizations, a point Isabel Menzies had already made when addressing the problems arising when the technological and the social systems reside in the mind of the same individual (Menzies Lyth 1979). This certainly had an impact in the work of any author.

Following from this description, I argue that although the usage of containment has increased steadily over time, it has been indiscriminately applied to every organizational phenomenon. Moreover, there has been increasing use of containment with the meaning of successful organizational intervention or as an argument for the need for support structures for organizational members. Thus, there is an urgent need of conceptual clarification regarding its application to organizations, since there is a risk that containment becomes such an over-generalized concept that it eventually loses its precise meaning.

Notes

1 See chapters in Part I for a more detailed view on containment and its origins.
2 See Chapter 4 of this book.
3 See Chapter 3 for a comparison between both concepts.
4 Although it is outside the aim of this chapter to discuss the differences between consultation and supervision, in the literature on the topics there is a clear differentiation between them on the basis of the accountability of each model. In supervision the supervisee is accountable to the supervisor who has authority over him, while in the consultation the hierarchical relationship is absent. Such differences are debated in detail by Wilson (2003).
5 See Chapter 2 of this book for a more detailed description.
6 Italics in the original.
7 Example taken from my own work.
8 The latter approach can also be divided according to the psychoanalytic theoretical model employed (object relations, ego psychology and so on) and according to the genealogical line followed (The Tavistock model, Levinson's approach, etc.). Gabriel and Carr (2002) already noticed the different approaches from the Tavistock and the North America paradigm (Levinson, Diamond) and noticed that several authors tried to bring together these different approaches (see Hirschhorn 1988). For the theoretical differences between important authors in the field see Anderson and White (2002).

References

Anderson, D. and White, J. (2002) Psychoanalytic organizational theory: Comparative perspectives. *Free Associations*, Vol. 9(52): 500–525.
Armstrong, D. (2005) *The analytic object in organizational work.* In Armstrong, D. (2005) *Organization in the Mind*, pp 44–54. London, Karnac Books.
Bion, W.R. (1959) Attacks on linking. *International Journal of Psychoanalysis*, Vol. 40: 308–315.

Bion, W. (1962) *Learning from Experience*. London, Tavistock Publications.

Biran, H. (2003) *"Attacks on linking" and "Alpha function" as two opposite elements in the life of organizations*. In Lipgar, R. and Pines, M. (2003) *Building on Bion: Branches*, pp. 164–181. London, Jessica Kingsley.

Bott Spillius, E., Milton, J., Garvey, P., Couve, C. and Steiner, D. (2011) *The New Dictionary of Kleinian Thought*. Hove, Routledge.

Cardona, F. (1994) *Facing an uncertain future*. In Obholzer, A. and Roberts, V. (eds) (1994) *The Unconscious at Work*, pp. 139–146. London, Routledge.

Carlyle, J. and Evans, C. (2005) Containing containers: Attention to the "innerface" and "outerface" of groups in secure institutions. *Group-Analysis*, Vol. 38(3): 395.

Correale, A. and Di Leone, G. (2004) *Contributions from Italy: Psychoanalytical approches to the study of institutions in Italy*. In Hinshelwood, R. and Chiesa, M. (eds) (2004) *Organisations, Anxieties and Defences*. London, Whurr.

De Board, R. (1978) *The Psychoanalysis of Organisations: A Psychoanalytic Approach to Groups and Organizations*. London, Routledge.

Erlich, S. (2001) *Enemies within and without: Paranoia and regression in groups and organizations*. In Gould, L., Stapley, L. and Stein, M. (eds) (2001) *The Systems Psychodynamics of Organizations*. London, Karnac Books.

Fraher, A. (2004) *A History of Group Study*. London, Free Association Books.

Freud, S. (1913–1914) *Totem and Taboo*. In *The Standard Edition of the Complete Psychological Works of Sigmund Freud*, Vol. XIII, pp. vii–162. London, Hogarth.

Gabriel, Y. (1999) *Organizations in Depth*. London, Karnac Books.

Gabriel, Y. and Carr, A. (2002) Organizations, management and psychoanalysis: An overview. *Journal of Managerial Psychology* 17(5): 348–365.

Goodwin, S. (1997) *Comparative Mental Health Policy: from Institutional to Community Care*. London, Sage.

Gutmann, D. and Pierre, R. (2000) *Consultation and transformation: Between shared management and generative leadership*. In Klein, E., Gabelnick, F. and Herr, P. (eds) (2000) *Dynamic consultation in a changing workplace*, pp. 3–31. Madison, WI, Psychosocial Press.

Hinshelwood, R. (1991) *A Dictionary of Kleinian Thought*. 2nd ed. London, Free Association Books.

Hirschhorn, L. (1988) *The Workplace Within*. Cambridge, MIT Press.

Hughes, L. and Pengelly, P. (1997) *Staff Supervision in a Turbulent Environment: Managing Process and Task in Front-Line Services*. London, Jessica Kingsley.

James, K. and Clark, G. (2002) Service organisations: Issues in transition and anxiety containment. *Journal of Managerial Psychology* 17(5): 394–407.

James, K. and Hunfington, C. (2004) Containment of anxiety in organizational change: A case example of changing organizational boundaries. *Organizational and Social Dynamics*, Vol. 4: 212–233.

Jaques, E. (1955) *Social systems as a defence against persecutory and depressive anxiety*. In Klein, M., Heimann, P. and Money-Kirle, R. (1955) *New Directions in Psychoanalysis*. London, Tavistock Publications.

Kaës, R. (2004) *Contributions from France: Psychoanalysis and institutions in France*. In Hinshelwood, R. and Chiesa, M. (eds) (2004) *Organisations, Anxieties and Defences*, pp. 97–124. London, Whurr.

Klein, E. (2000) *The consultant as container*. In Klein, E., Gabelnick, F. and Herr, P. (eds) (2000) *Dynamic Consultation in a Changing Workplace*, pp. 193–208. Madison, WI, Psychosocial Press.

Klein, E. (2006) *Applying systems psychodynamics in an organizational consultation*. In Klein, E. and Pritchard, I. (eds) (2006) *Relatedness in a Global Economy*, pp. 11–30. London, Karnac Books.

Lawrence, W.G. (2000a) *Signals of transcendence*. In Lawrence, W.G. (2000) *Tongued with Fire: Groups in Experience*, pp. 74–91. London, Karnac Books.

Lawrence, W.G. (2000b) *Emergent themes in group relations in chaotic times*. In Lawrence, W.G. (2000) *Tongued with Fire: Groups in Experience*, pp. 146–164. London, Karnac Books.

Lipgar, R. (2003) *Re-discovering Bion's experiences in groups: Notes and commentary in theory and practice*. In Lipgar, R. and Pines, M. (eds) (2003) *Building on Bion: Roots*, pp. 29–58. London, Jessica Kingsley.

Long, S., Newton, J. and Dalgleish, J. (2000) *In the presence of the other: Developing working relations for organizational learning*. In Klein, E., Gabelnick, F. and Herr, P. (eds) (2000) *Dynamic Consultation in a Changing Workplace*, pp. 161–192. Madison, WI, Psychosocial Press.

Menzies Lyth, I. (1960) *The functioning of social systems as a defence against anxiety*. In Menzies Lyth, I. (1988) *Containing Anxiety in Institutions*. London, Free Association Books.

Menzies Lyth, I. (1979) *Staff support systems: Task and anti task in adolescents in institutions*. In Menzies Lyth, I. (1988) *Containing Anxiety in Institutions*. London, Free Association Books.

Miller, E. (1999) *Introduction to Part V*. In Miller, E. (1999) *The Tavistock Institute Contribution to Job and Organizational Design*, Vol. II, pp. 3–6. Aldershot, Dartmouth Publishing.

Nutkevitch, A. (1998) The container and its containment: A meeting space for psychoanalytic and open systems theories. 15th Annual Meeting of the International Society for the Psychoanalytic Study of Organizations ISPSO, Jerusalem, Israel, June 14.

Obholzer, A. (1994a) *Authority, power and leadership: Contributions from group relations training*. In Obholzer, A. and Roberts, V. (1994) *The Unconscious at Work*, pp. 39–47. London, Routledge.

Obholzer, A. (1994b) *Managing social anxieties in public sector organisations*. In Obholzer, A. and Roberts, V. (1994) *The Unconscious at Work*, pp. 169–178. London, Routledge.

Obholzer, A. (1994c) *Afterword*. In Obholzer, A. and Roberts, V. (1994) *The Unconscious at Work*, pp. 206–210. London, Routledge.

Obholzer, A. and Miller, S. (2004) *Leadership, followership and facilitating the creative workplace*. In Huffington, C., Armstrong, D., Halton, W., Hoyle, L. and Pooley, J. (2004) *Working Below the Surface*, pp. 33–48. London, Karnac Books.

Ogden, T. (2004) On holding and containing, being and dreaming. *International Journal of Psychoanalysis*, Vol. 85: 1349–1364.

Palmer, B. (2004) The Tavistock Paradigm: Inside, Outside and Beyond. *Organisations, Anxieties and Defences*: pp. 158–182 London, Whurr.

Richardson, E. (1973) *The Teacher, the School and the Task of Management*. London, Heinemann.

Roberts, V. (1994) *The organization of work: Contributions from open systems theory*. In Obholzer, A. and Roberts, V. (eds) (1994) *The Unconscious at Work*, pp. 28–38. London, Routledge.

Rosenthal, J. and Davidoff, D. (2000) *The consultant's use of inner dialogue in family business consultation*. In Klein, E., Gabelnick, F. and Herr, P. (eds) (2000) *Dynamic Consultation in a Changing Workplace*, pp. 113–132. Madison, WI, Psychosocial Press.

Shapiro, E. and Carr, A. (1991) *Lost in Familiar Places*. New Haven and London, Yale University Press.

Sher, M. (2003) *From groups to group relations: Bion's contribution to the Tavistock "Leicester" conferences*. In Lipgar, R. and Pines, M. (2003) *Building on Bion: Branches*, pp. 109–144. London, Jessica Kingsley.

Stacey, R. (2001) *Complexity at the "edge" of the basic assumption group*. In Gould, L., Stapley, L. and Stein, M. (eds) (2001) *The Systems Psychodynamics of Organizations*. London, Karnac Books.

Stapley, L. (1996) *The Personality of the Organization: A Psycho-Dynamic Explanation of Culture and Change*. London, Free Association Books.

Stein, M. (2000) After Eden: Envy and defences against anxiety paradigm. *Human Relations* Vol. 53(2): 193–211.

Stokes, J. (1994) *Institutional chaos and personal stress*. In Obholzer, A. and Roberts, V. (eds) (1994) *The Unconscious at Work*, pp. 121–128. London, Routledge.

Vansina, L. and Vansina-Cobbaert, M.-J. (2008) *Psychodynamics for Consultants and Managers*. Chichester, Wiley-Blackwell.

Wilke, G. (2003) *The large group and its conductor*. In Lipgar, R. and Pines, M. (2003) *Building on Bion: Branches*, pp. 70–105. London, Jessica Kingsley.

Wilson, P. (2003) *Consultation and supervision*. In Ward, A., Kasinski, K., Pooley, J. and Worthington, A. (2003) *Therapeutic communities for children and young people*, pp. 220–232. London, Jessica Kingsley.

Wiltshire, J. and Parker, J. (1996) Containing abjection in nursing: The end of shift handover as a site of containment. *Nursing Inquiry*, Vol. 3(1): 23–29.

Chapter 9

An Empirical Approach to Disentangle Intertwined Concepts

Tiago Mendes

Introduction

Containment and social defences against anxiety are hallmarks of the psychoanalytic tradition, having withstood the test of time and continuing to be widely used today (Long 2006; Lopéz-Corvo 2005; Sandler 2005; Bott Spillius et al. 2011; Armstrong and Rustin 2015; Stein 2000). Although both trace their origins to Klein's projective identification (Bion 1959, 1962; Jaques 1955; Hinshelwood 1991), they have evolved differently, with the first stemming from the clinical context (Bion 1959, 1962) and the latter derived from an action research project with the Glacier Metal Company (Jaques 1955). Nonetheless, the links between such concepts are not firmly established in the literature. In fact, social organisations are sometimes seen as either containing the anxiety of their members or promoting defensive attitudes towards the primary task, thus conjoining both concepts as two opposites on a continuum. On other occasions, social defences are interpreted as simply a distraught form of containment. Whilst different attempts at addressing the concepts emerged, these views in most cases fail to convey all the richness of Bion's idea,[1] whilst not considering potential empirical overlaps. Assessing the empirical links of both concepts was the aim of my PhD thesis (Mendes 2013), drawing from Bion's notion of vertices (Bion 1965), and the present chapter addresses the main findings of such research, while attempting to disentangle what is perceived as two intertwined concepts which, to a certain extent, is expected given both have similar (conceptual) origins.

Why Vertices?

The starting point for this chapter is one of Bion's lesser known or, for that matter, applied contributions. Initially presented in *Transformations* (Bion 1965) as an analytical tool, the notion of vertices is a way of addressing a problem from different angles, each enlightening a part of the problem since *O*, what really happened in the analytic session, is unattainable. And, in fact, it does seem that at this stage in his clinical practice Bion was very interested in the phenomenology of the clinical

DOI: 10.4324/9781315146416-13

session. Bion argued that the importance of vertices lies in providing a different take on a problem and therefore contributing to a solution that might not be visible from simply using one vertex to address the problem. As Grotstein argued, Bion seemed to be exploring with ideas, standing them "on their heads and observ[ing] them from different angles, which he is later to call 'vertices'" (Grotstein 2003, p. 22). I argue that to clarify the links between containment and social defences, one must first and foremost resort to vertices (Bion 1965), since both concepts can be seen as different vertices, each "looking" at the same phenomenon in a different light. I shall expand further in this chapter what I consider to be the vertices of each concept.

Methodological Questions

After clarifying my approach to the conceptual entanglement, I shall now address the methodological approach used. The psychoanalytic framework is deeply rooted in clinical practice (Dreher 2000; Rustin 2001; Wolff 1996), nonetheless attempting to reproduce the clinical approach to the understanding of groups and organizations falls short from understanding the multiple factors involved in these, as has been previously argued.[2] The many vivid descriptions of social defences systems are in most of the cases drawn from action-research projects where participant observation played a key role. In this respect, Isabel Menzies Lyth seemed to be a keen observer, as was also Elliott Jaques, and in this they followed in Melanie Klein's footsteps, who was not only a very acute observer in the analytical setting, but also very compelling in her detailed descriptions of analytic sessions (Klein 1935, 1940, 1946; Hinshelwood 1994).

To discern between both concepts, I collected observational data from the life of mental health institutions in Portugal, resorting to a well-known method in the field, the *Observing Organisations* methodology devised by Hinshelwood (Hinshelwood and Skogstad 2000).[3] Two institutions were observed, although the data presented in this chapter comes mostly from one. The culture in this regard is more institutional, concerned with control, although attempts to have activity programmes do exist. And, to be fair to staff, the general culture in the Portuguese national health service is concerned more with the care of the dependency needs of patients. Once the data collection process was complete, comprised of detailed accounts of the observations as well as the observers' emotional experience, I restricted the full amount of data to the essential observational vignettes which could be analysed in depth. It was considered that the records of the observations needed to be sufficiently detailed to be able to infer from them that an emotional interaction, or at least anxiety, was present. As such, included are only vignettes in which something emotional might be inferred from the observed behaviour of patients or staff, or from the subjective emotional experience of the observer, or, furthermore, from the previous observations whereby patients were observed as stirring up anxiety in staff. It was helpful to this part of Bick's (1964) idea of patterns as well as Michael Rustin's argumentation regarding infant observation that the "key evidence in this work will be the samples of observational material, just as the main evidence in clinical work is samples of psychotherapeutic discourse and clinical observation" (1997, p. 63). Although one must be careful not to cherry-pick the observations that suit one's argument. What we considered evidence was every observation of moments of high, visible or perceived emotion.

What Do I See When I Observe

The next logical step was to devise criteria for both concepts that could be applied to the vignettes and, most of all, could be meaningful for other practitioners in the field. Not an easy task, especially given the fact previous approaches had focused on presenting an aggregate view of their findings on defensive cultures, as opposed to detailed observational records, which is understandable given the action-research nature of said presentations, some of which may have derived from client reports, as in Menzies Lyth's published papers (Menzies Lyth 1988, 1989). In this I was influenced by Betty Joseph's (1988) description of projective identification from clinical examples and, as such, the criteria were elicited from vignettes where containment and social defences were deemed to be present. The inferences on the data were made from both the description of what was seen and heard, but also from the experience of the observer. The presentation of these criteria, albeit somewhat dense, is deemed important so that readers can grasp the key differences and similarities between the concepts – at least that was the aim.

1.   Criteria for Containment

In devising criteria for containment I considered both its adaptive form (flexible) as well as its two mal-adaptive forms (rigid and fragmented). Furthermore, Bion's (1959) sharp and thorough description of a patient who attempted to project his fears of dying into the analyst is thoroughly used as a model, due to its clearly depicted description.[4] The following set of criteria was defined as indicative, extrapolating from data where containment was considered to be present. A vignette taken from the data records illustrates how the criteria were extrapolated from the data.

A patient with headphones goes to a nurse. [Before he can speak] the nurse asks him to let her hear the headphones, since the patients sometimes put the music too loud. An auxiliary staff comes from behind and touches the patient's headphones, to take them away. The patient, playing, raises his arms to touch the auxiliary, who backs away. The patient, still kidding, continues trying to touch her. She avoids him one more time, before grabbing his arms and saying loudly and emphatically "Stop, Stop!" being visibly upset.

(Vignette 1)

At first glance, the above vignette possibly seems just stereotypical of the daily interactions in a mental health facility. Nonetheless, I argue that a more detailed look in fact elicits a more complex interaction, strikingly resembling Bion's (1959) description of his patient, albeit in a social context. This statement requires a more detailed explanation: In Bion's (1959) description we have a patient that attempts to communicate with the analyst resorting to a primitive mechanism of splitting and projecting his feelings into the analyst with a communicative intent. Nonetheless, the patient felt that the analyst had evacuated them so quickly that the feelings were not modified but had in fact become more painful (Bion 1959, p. 312). As in the case of Bion's analysand, we see that the attempts to communicate by the patient at the institution seem to bounce back, instead of reposing in the container, in this case the nurse in the ward. Bion's analysand seems to have become distressed with Bion's apparent refusal of the patient's "attempts to force them into me [the analyst] with increased desperation and violence" (Bion 1959, p. 312). This also seems to be the case in the vignette from the institution, where the patient repeatedly tries to touch the auxiliary, as if attempting to get inside of her, until she grabs his arms telling him to stop. Bion argued that in the case of his analysand the violence of his attempts to force his feelings into the analyst was in fact a reaction to the hostile defensiveness he perceived from the analyst. Thus Bion separates his analysand's reaction from the violent form of projective identification designed to control the object (Bott Spillius et al. 2011; Hinshelwood 1991). Bion will also conceptualise from this analysand that he probably experienced a mother who was dutiful and was not very available emotionally to her child, which was expressed in her impatience regarding what he did. Though not mentioned by Bion, his description also seems to entail the idea that the mother's impatience also had in it an element of irritation. All these qualities seem to be present in the vignette, wherein the nurse and the auxiliary seem to be emotionally unavailable and also have, at least in the case of the auxiliary, that quality of impatience and irritation regarding the patient's attempts at communicating, as if to say "I don't know what is wrong with this patient". Bion's description of his analysand seems to run parallel with the situation observed, although with some differences. In Bion's description the whole sequence occurs between analysand and analyst, a one-on-one situation. However, in the vignette the patient's forceful attempts to play, which the staff seem to equate in their phantasy as forceful attacks, are directed toward the auxiliary rather than the nurse, who prevented him from communicating in the first place. This difference concerns the fact that this vignette was taken from a social setting, rather than from a clinical setting.

From this example, I hope a clearer view is possible. **Criterion 1** emphasises that the interaction starts with an attempt by a person to interact with another. This might be a patient attempting to address a staff member either individually or in a group, as in the case of Bion's (1959) description of his patient. The approach might be of a very different kind, from directly walking towards a staff member or by expressing feelings of disgust close to a staff member. **Criterion 2** emphasises the reaction from that staff member, which can be one of attending and transforming anxiety (adaptive form of containment), one of preventing the patient from projecting his feelings (mal-adaptive containment of a rigid form) or by becoming prey to the emotion (mal-adaptive containment of a fragmented form). **Criterion 3** refers to the emotional aspect of that relationship. Containment was inferred not only as an observable phenomenon (outbursts of emotion, stammering in moments of tension, etc.) but also through the emotional reaction of the observer.

1. **Moment of approach** – There is a moment when there is an approach by an individual to another individual/group.
2. **Reaction** – There is a reaction towards that approach, either by effectively attending to the communication; by blocking it and denuding it of meaning; or by being distressed and becoming a prey to the emotion.
3. **Emotional interaction** – The above described situations are desperately emotional, which can be inferred.

While said criteria may be subject to criticism, they try to convey and, to a certain extent, expand Bion's notion of a social setting where social interactions deeply rooted in emotional experiences are present and, I argue, observable.

2. Criteria for Social Systems as a Defence

Menzies Lyth (1960) described as a fundamental characteristic of social defence systems the avoidance of the experience of anxiety, guilt, doubt or uncertainty by staff. Such emotional experiences were triggered by work situations due to the similarity such situations have with the phantasies of staff. Therefore, such work situations were defended against in a mal-adaptive manner, instead of the emotional experience that they triggered being worked through. The criteria try to capture this element from Menzies Lyth' description, which can be seen in the vignette below taken from the weekly observations of a mental health facility.

> I hear him saying to another patient "You need to speak about that with a nurse" and as I hear this I have the distinct impression that I am observing in fact a nurse.
>
> (Vignette 2)

This present vignette is taken from one of the last observations of lunch time. The psychologist is dressed in a white gown, an unusual way of dressing for psychologists, but the common outfit of a nurse. A patient approached him complaining about food delays, which seemed to be very distressing to patients. The patients were getting increasingly anxious regarding the delays and when they approached staff members this usually seemed to leave them quite anxious. As soon as he hears the patient's request he replies that the patient needs to speak about it with a nurse, ending the dialogue. The attempt by the patient to approach the staff seemed to stir up anxiety and uncertainty, probably regarding his role and responsibility regarding the patient's distress. Doubts, uncertainty, anxiety and possibly guilt over the increasing distress the patients were suffering due to the lunch delays seemed to be present, and in fact I was also increasingly feeling guilty when observing the patients' distress. In this difficult moment, the psychologist seemed to assign responsibility for the matter to a nurse, a staff member from another professional group, while diminishing his own responsibility for that situation, but also diminishing his guilt regarding the delays of the food and, possibly, regarding his own autonomy regarding the food. This reaction seemed in fact to reduce the impact of responsibility by delegating it to another staff group. It was the group of nurses who had the responsibility to attend to the patients' distress. This was a culturally shared defensive technique where, in moments of stress, the staff seemed to collusively assign responsibility for what went wrong to other staff groups and, at the same time, diminish their own responsibility at a phantasy level. Such complex interplays of distribution of responsibility across the hierarchy as a defensive technique were described by Isabel Menzies Lyth (1960). In the present vignette this was activated when a patient approached a staff member. As a consequence the psychologist did not need to acknowledge the patient's distress or attempt to help him, since now in his phantasy it had become a concern of the nurses. As this was a defensive manoeuvre no reality-based action was attempted such as leading the patient to a nurse, or informing a nurse of the patient's distress. Furthermore, there was a purposeful obscurity in attributing the patient to another staff group, to which the psychologist did not belong, instead of referring him to a specific colleague. The end result was that the patient was left to cope on his own with his emotional distress, thus caring for the emotional distress of this patient was in fact diverted into caring for the potential emotional distress of the psychologist. Finally, there is a moment of perceived anxiety in the psychologist when the patient approaches him.

Criterion 1 stresses this aspect and, in fact, staff members were observed in several work situations to act defensively and those defences were culturally shared. It is the fact that they are part of the culture that transforms individual defences in social defence systems. A strong emphasis on obsessive control was observable at times, especially control of patients' interactions, following situations which stirred paranoid anxieties. Menzies Lyth described how distorting the task could also be a defensive manoeuvre against anxiety (1979). **Criterion 2** emphasises the task. Defensive techniques in fact impact on the overall task of caring for patients. Menzies Lyth (1960) was very poignant is this respect when she demonstrated how such defensive techniques denied the importance of emotional proximity in the task of caring for patients, or how the primary task of an organisation might be transformed into something else, termed an anti-task, due to unconscious pressures (Menzies Lyth 1979). As such, the performance of the overall task of the institution is affected by the activation of such techniques and this might be observable either by transforming the task into something else, for instance drifting from caring for the patients to controlling the patients, or by denuding it of any emotional aspect, for instance, focusing on caring for chores instead of people, thus denying the emotional component of the primary task of the institution. **Criterion 3** stresses the importance of anxiety as a key trigger for the culturally activated defensive techniques. Anxiety could be inferred due to the emotional experience of the observer, or as present in the data due to the behaviour of the staff or patients.

1. **Culturally activated defensive technique** – This means that there are culturally shared defensive techniques which are activated in critical moments.
2. **Impact on the task** – When these culturally activated attitudes or techniques are activated, there is a change in the way the task is performed.
3. **Anxiety** – The two previous criteria coincide with a moment of perceived anxiety.

Analysing the Data

I shall now provide examples of the flexible rigid and fragmented forms of containment and the presence or absence of social defences, before commenting more deeply on the interaction of both concepts. It must be noted that the following examples solely serve the purpose of illustrating the analysis conducted.

1. Flexible Containment

I shall exemplify flexible containment with an example which requires some contextualisation. It was observed in a completely different emotional atmosphere in the canteen. Everyone seemed anxious, staff and patients alike. A general trend had emerged after the first observations, that the patients were becoming more restless, anxious and angry regarding lunch delays, for which the staff were not responsible.[5] There was a general sense of hungriness and a demand for oral gratification which, when not attended to, had caused some fiery responses by staff to the demands of the patients. A general neediness and frustration seemed to be ever-present.

> Today the mood seemed to be different, much more agitated. [...] One of the kitchen staff seemed to be in a very good mood. A patient said to her that she was fat causing her to reply, "Fat? Are you calling me fat? This is strength, I am strong!" in a cheerful way. [...] the lunch seemed to start smoothly.
>
> (Vignette 3)

It is in this emotional context that a patient seemingly anxious and upset with the delay of the lunch makes a comment to the auxiliary cook which might be considered insulting (**1. moment of approach**). On similar occasions, the same sort of remarks by patients had been ignored or anxiously rebuffed, with staff apparently feeling over-burdened. The auxiliary cook's reaction was one whereby the remark was noticed and humorously responded to (**2. reaction**), allowing the lunch to start smoothly. The situation was deeply emotional due to the particular emotional atmosphere of that day (**3. emotional interaction**). And in fact, after the lunch starts, several distressing events will ensue even to the point where the patient's demands are angrily responded to and dismissed by the kitchen staff. But on this occasion the auxiliary cook was able to accept the comment without being distressed or responding in a dismissive way or violently rebuffing it. The interaction created a shared feeling of safety allowing lunch to continue smoothly. Humour in this case was used as a way of creating a safe space where joking comments could be made regarding someone else, instead of as a way of belittling the other. The cook was able to relate to the patient without diverting from the topic at the same time as being able to construct a shared sense of safety where the comments of the patient were transformed and tolerated and not seen as violent attacks on the kitchen staff and her body image. A further important point connects with the result of the interaction, which seem to transform to some extent, albeit temporarily, the general mood in the canteen.

From a task vertex, a striking characteristic of this vignette is the use of humour in a situation where the emotional atmosphere (Hinshelwood and Skogstad 2000) is tense. Humour was in fact used on several occasions as a manic defence characterised by denial, triumph and contempt for the object (Bott Spillius et al. 2011; Klein 1935, 1940, 1946; Hinshelwood 1991, 1994; Segal 1957), and was designed to protect the staff from anxiety. However in this particular situation, what characterised the other interactions was not present. The cook did not belittle the patient, nor did she mock him to diminish him, triumph over him and finally control him. Furthermore, there was no visible negative impact on the task. On the contrary, it seemed to continue smoothly and lunch, which seemed to be very important for the patients, also ran smoothly. Though there was a tense emotional atmosphere (**3. Anxiety**), there was no evidence of humour being used as a defensive technique nor of a constraint on the primary task, hence the criteria of Culturally activated defence and Impact on the task seem absent from this vignette. This example illustrates how in the case of the presence of flexible containment, no defensive manoeuvres were observable in the social interaction.

2.   Rigid Containment

As the nurse is speaking, the patient that usually sits on my right walks up towards her and plants a big kiss on her cheek, which seemed to surprise and upset her, but she said in a controlled way "Control yourself, be calm!" and continued to speak.

(Vignette 4)

This situation was observed when the patients were receiving some information regarding the outside. The patients are listening to the nurse when one of the patients, apparently seeming pleased with what is happening, approaches the nurse and kisses her cheek, with what seems a mix of gratitude and joy (**1. moment of approach**). The nurse, though apparently surprised and upset with his behaviour, possibly also anxious, quickly says in a controlled and un-emotional way to the patient that he needs to control himself and to calm down (**2. reaction**). The contact by the patient seemed to distress the nurse, and probably leaves her anxious as well as surprised and upset (**3. emotional interaction**). The nurse's response seems to suppress the emotional aspect of the communication and deplete his communication of the meaning he was conveying, as if an emotional display of gratitude had no place in the institution and emotions should be under control. The nurse seemed to become upset, but the emotions and meaning were suppressed, and the nurse tried to continue speaking as if nothing had happened. Thus, this seems to bear the characteristic un-emotional contact and superficial dialogue characteristic of rigid containment.

From a social defences vertex the approach by the patient seemed to make the nurse feel anxious and upset, maybe through the threat of a sexual contact, and also possibly guilty by feeling upset regarding a patient. The nurse seems to attempt to control the interaction, as an attempt to control her own feelings as Klein (1940) argued, at the same time denying her own personal feelings regarding the incident, a point already made by Menzies Lyth (1960) (**1. Culturally activated defence**). The nurse seemed to perceive the patient's approach not as a sign of joy and gratitude, but with the unconscious phantasy that liveliness is a threat that will lead to an uncontrollable outbreak of madness, a common unconscious phantasy in mental health care settings and which has already been described by Flavia Donati (2000; Hinshelwood and Skogstad 2000). The nurse's perception of her task as one of controlling outbreaks of madness coincided with a perceived experience of anxiety on her part. In fact the nurse seemed quite anxious due to the patient approaching and kissing her on the cheek. Her anxiety, which seemed connected with the fear that the patient's contact might cross her personal boundaries, appeared to be intense, and a fear was also experienced by the observer, though not necessarily anxiety (**3. Anxiety**). Nevertheless, the threat did not seem to be a real one as, on the contrary, the patient seemed to want to express joy. But the staff member's reaction was based not on reality, but on the phantasy that the patient's approach was a violent one and that their task was to prevent the patient from interacting. This attitude had an impact on the task, since the patient rarely seemed to have moments of liveliness, as previously observed, and this seemed a missed opportunity. The task of caring for mentally ill patients was diverted to a simpler one of controlling possible outbreaks of madness from the patient's actions, thus missing an invaluable opportunity to engage with a patient who seldom seemed responsive to staff (**2. Impact on the task**). Also, a feeling of lack of spontaneity seems present in this vignette, although the feelings of the nurse of anger were certainly experienced by her as difficult to bear. In these cases, there was an overlap observed between the rigid form of containment and the defensive techniques.

3. Fragmented Containment

The next vignette has several different characteristics to the previous one, and was a situation observed on several occasions.

> Then an auxiliary, who I also had never seen before, walks in, seeming very resolute. She looks at a patient, who looked at her, and says out of the blue "Today you are forbidden to speak with me. Forbidden!" in a very harsh and aggressive tone.
>
> (Vignette 5)

This vignette is quite a disturbing one, but was quite typical of the life of the institution, where staff seemed to become very distressed by contact with patients. Looking from an emotional maturation vertex, we have a patient looking at an auxiliary, who previously looked at him (**1. moment of approach**). His intention is not quite clear but its effect causes the auxiliary to shout, hastily forbidding him to speak (**2. reaction**). The shout echoed through the canteen since it was very loud, and one could see how the staff member seemed to be very distressed by the patient's stare, as were the rest of the people present in the canteen, including staff and the observer (**3. emotional interaction**). The contact by the patient seemed to have had such an impact that the auxiliary seemed to become filled with anxiety and her reply was inappropriate to the situation. It reveals that the auxiliary seemed to be overfilled with emotion which spilled everywhere in the way she shouted. This seems to bear some resemblance to Bion's patient who stammered and where words did not seem able to contain emotion. In this circumstance, however, the staff member does not stammer, the violence of his response indicates that the patient's stare was highly distressing and she was unable to contain inside herself the powerful emotions. She seemed to be quite distressed and during the rest of this observation several distressing moments were observed. On this occasion, it seemed that more than the explosive quality of the patient's stare, it was the container that seemed to be too fragile to contain it, Just as the requests from a normal baby for milk and comfort to a mother might feel too overwhelming if she is depressed.

From a task vertex, the auxiliary did not seem to see her task at that moment as one of caring for patients, but one of caring for her own emotional needs, the need for emotional survival, as it were. She seemed to act in order to protect herself from the emotional impact of the patient's stare (**3. Anxiety**), though clearly this was detrimental to the task of caring (**2. Impact on the task**). Furthermore, she seemed to resort to very primitive mechanisms of projective identification, attempting to intrude on the patient and later on the observer by staring at me in a way that caused me to look away and made me feel quite vulnerable and intruded upon. Rather than the shared cultural attitudes where detachment, depersonalisation, control and splitting the staff/patient relationship were more evident, on this occasion it seemed that a more primitive defensive mechanism was at play. Furthermore, it seemed to have that primitive quality of very intense projection, which seemed absent from culturally shared attitudes. My experience of intrusion and vulnerability seems to be what she felt when the patient stared at her and she needed to evacuate her feelings onto me in order to cope with the lunch time. Although, as mentioned, this seemed more an individual defence than a culturally shared one.

Conclusion

One aspect of my observations was the positive impact that interactions where flexible containment was present seemed to have on patients, though in some cases this was limited in time. This seems an important point, though not a new one, but which seems to highlight that an ability to promote transformation in the patients has a positive outcome. After these interactions the patients seemed to become calmer and even able to interact in more appropriate manners. Some vignettes provide striking examples of this aspect, regarding patients that, although very distressed, after such interactions with staff were able to relate to the researcher and resume conversations or were able to sit closer to me. Another feature that it is important to highlight is what can be described as the characteristic of genuineness present in these vignettes, and how working on the task of caring for patients and being able to be in a state of *reverie*, thus giving meaning to the communications of the patients, did in fact overlap in daily practice. As a final point, it seems important to state if social defence systems and flexible containment are, in effect, two vertices of the same phenomenon. And the answer seems to be "No". Although it is always harder to prove that something is absent than it is to prove its presence, it is argued that in the group of vignettes where the adaptive form of containment is present there is no evidence of the two main criteria for social defence systems, that is, Culturally activated defence and Impact on the task. On the contrary, the data suggest that in the cases where the adaptive form of containment is present, there is no evidence of culturally shared defensive techniques.

While the flexible form of containment seemed to have a positive impact on the patients, rigid containment seemed to have a negative impact. An observable pattern (Rustin 2002) seemed present whereby a situation of intense distress in patients, connected with frustration, seemed to lead the patients to seek support from the staff. However, the emotional and physical detachment of the staff invariably led the patients to have to deal with their distress alone. In some extreme cases, this meant that the patients ended up delusional.

Another important point concerns the staff's manner of interacting with patients which seemed to lack authenticity. These seemed to correspond to what Klein described as a marked artificiality and lack of spontaneity (1946, p. 104) regarding schizoid object relations. And in fact the omnipotent use of denial and splitting are characteristic schizoid mechanisms. Furthermore, such artificiality seems to correspond to the unavailability and lack of understanding of the dutiful mother described by Bion (1959). A further point is the fact that the majority of the vignettes correspond to group situations. Thus, a question arises regarding the importance of the group in the maintenance of such defensive ways of coping with personal anxiety stemming from the task. One striking vignette appears to answer this question, which I will briefly summarise here due to its size. When a patient approached a group of staff, he was immediately prevented from talking, and engaged through the use of humour as a manic defence. Although, as the interaction continued, an auxiliary seemed to interact with him in a more genuine manner regarding the French fries. Nonetheless, a nurse immediately prevented her from continuing by resorting again to making fun of the patient, and triumphing over him. This seems to illustrate that the social systems are not only used to reinforce individual defensive mechanisms, but there is also an active pressure for individuals to conform to the shared defensive techniques. The final point is the question of whether social defence systems and the rigid form of containment can be seen as two vertices of the same phenomenon. And, in fact, the data from this group of vignettes suggest that social defence systems and the rigid form of mal-adaptive containment appear as the same phenomenon. That is, in the group of vignettes where the rigid form of containment was present, the staff invariably dealt with anxieties arising from the task through the use of culturally shared defensive techniques, which had an impact on the task. As such, one might state that both concepts overlap in this vignette and social defence systems maybe be described as a rigid form of containing personal anxiety in organisations.

Finally, regarding fragmented containment, it seemed that these interactions had quite a negative impact on patients, although the data is scarce. Although somewhat speculative, it could be suggested that this was also quite detrimental for the patients. Furthermore, the capacity of the patients to shatter the staff with their violent contents might also bring with it the added anxiety that they are stuck in a terrible, dreaded, internal world full of persecutors, and that there is no hope of internalising an object that might mitigate such an internal state, thus resorting to powerful defensive mechanisms that end up depleting the ego, which is the only viable alternative for patients. Furthermore, these interactions did not have that marked artificiality which was so poignant. It was very painful to observe, and a general feeling of danger seemed to be present, a sense that things might in fact explode. The staff seemed to feel burned and they seemed to feel that contact with patients was "too much to handle". In regard to the interaction between social defence systems and fragmented containment, this did not seem to overlap; instead it seemed that one followed the other. In fact, after a moment of fragmented containment was perceived, it was followed by a defensive way of dealing with anxiety. The moment of fragmented containment occurred, in some interactions, immediately after a defensive technique failed in its purpose of keeping anxiety at bay. While in other cases the only thing that could be observed was a staff member falling prey to emotion, as Bion might have stated. In both situations, the moment of fragmented containment is followed by a more primitive mode of defence, such as a massive projective identification of an omnipotent kind. One might therefore state that such a distressing event appeared as a consequence of a failure in either the culturally shared defensive techniques, or a failure of a person's personal capacity to manage anxiety. Thus, from the perspective from two vertices, social defence systems in this case may be seen as a failed container.

It is worth mentioning, as an end note, that social defences seem to be about a particular form of failed containment, the rigid type of containment. As such, containment and social defences can be seen as different concepts, each highlighting a different point of view.

Notes

1 See the chapters in Part I of this book.
2 See Chapter 6 in this book.
3 The method is comprised of weekly observations followed by detailed recordings of the observations including the emotional experience of the observer, that are discussed in weekly seminars of 3–5 members with a supervisor (see Hinshelwood and Skogstad 2000 for a detailed description of the method and its roots in Bick's observational method).
4 For a more in-depth description of Bion's containment, see Chapter 2 of this book.
5 For unclear reasons, the food delivery arrived increasingly late and the staff were not the ones responsible, since they also complained about the delays.

References

Armstrong, D. & Rustin, M. (2015) Social Defences Against Anxiety: Explorations in a Paradigm. London, Karnac Books.

Bick, E. (1964). *Notes on infant observation in psycho-analytic training.* International Journal of Psychoanalysis, 45, 558–566. Reprinted In Briggs, A. (2002) Surviving Space: Papers on Infant Observation, pp. 37–54. London, Karnac Books.

Bion, W. (1959) *Attacks on linking.* International Journal of Psychoanalysis, 40, 308–315.

Bion, W. (1962) Learning from Experience. London, Tavistock Publications.

Bion, W. (1965) Transformations. London, Karnac Books.

Bott Spillius, E., Milton, J., Garvey, P., Couve, C. and Steiner, D. (2011) The New Dictionary of Kleinian Thought. Hove, Routledge.

Donati, F. (2000) *Madness and morale: A chronic psychiatric ward.* In Hinshelwood, R. and Skogstad, W. (eds) (2000) Observing Organisations, pp. 29–43. London, Routledge.

Dreher, A. (2000) Foundations for Conceptual Research in Psychoanalysis. London, Karnac Books.

Grotstein, J. (2003) *Introduction: Early Bion.* In Lipgar, R. and Pines, M. (2003) Building on Bion: Roots, pp. 9–25. London, Jessica Kingsley.

Hinshelwood, R. (1991) A Dictionary of Kleinian Thought. 2nd ed. London, Free Association Books.

Hinshelwood, R.D. (1994) Clinical Klein: From Theory to Practice. Free Association Books, London.

Hinshelwood, R.D. and Skogstad, W. (2000) Observing Organisations. London, Routledge.

Jaques, E. (1955) *Social systems as a defence against persecutory and depressive anxiety.* In Klein, M., Heimann, P. and Money-Kirle, R. (eds) (1955) New Directions in Psychoanalysis. London, Tavistock Publications.

Joseph, B. (1988) *Projective identification: Clinical aspects.* In Spillius, E. (ed.) (1988) Melanie Klein Today, Vol. 1, pp. 138–150. London, Routledge.

Klein, M. (1935) *A contribution to the psychogenesis of manic-depressive states.* International Journal of Psychoanalysis, 16, 145–174.

Klein, M. (1940) *Mourning and its relation to manic-depressive states.* International Journal of Psychoanalysis, 21, 125–153.

Klein, M. (1946) *Notes on some schizoid mechanisms*. International Journal of Psychoanalysis, 27, 99–110.

Long, S. (2006) *Organizational defenses against anxiety: What has happened since the 1955 Jaques paper?* International Journal of Applied Psychoanalytic Studies, 3(4), 279–295.

Lopéz-Corvo, R. (2005) The work of W.R. Bion. London, Karnac Books.

Mendes, T. (2013) Tasks, Emotions and Emotional Tasks: A Study on the Interconnection Between Social Defence Systems and Containment in Organisations. PhD Thesis, University of Essex.

Menzies Lyth, I. (1960) *The functioning of social systems as a defence against anxiety*. In Menzies Lyth, I. (1988) Containing Anxiety in Institutions. London, Free Association Books.

Menzies Lyth, I. (1979) *Staff support systems: Task and anti-task in adolescents in institutions*. In Menzies Lyth, I. (1988) Containing Anxiety in Institutions. London, Free Association Books.

Menzies Lyth, I. (1988) Containing Anxiety in Institutions. Selected Papers, Vol. 1. London, Free Association Books.

Menzies Lyth, I. (1989) The Dynamics of the Social. Selected Essays, Vol. 2. London, Free Association Books.

Rustin, M. (1997) *What do we see in the nursery? Infant observation as laboratory work*. In Rustin, M. (2001a) Reason and Unreason: Psychoanalysis, Science and Politics, pp. 52–68. London, Continuum.

Rustin, M. (2001) Reason and Unreason: Psychoanalysis, Science and Politics. London, Continuum.

Rustin, M. (2002) *Looking in the right place: Complexity theory, psychoanalysis, and infant observation*. In Briggs, A. (2002) Surviving Space: Papers on Infant Observation, pp. 256–278. London, Karnac Books.

Sandler, P.C. (2005) The Language of Bion. London, Karnac Books.

Segal, H. (1957) *Notes on symbol-formation*. International Journal of Psycho-Analysis, 38, 391–397.

Stein, M. (2000) *After Eden: Envy and defences against anxiety paradigm*. Human Relations, 53(2), 193–211.

Wolff, P. (1996) *The irrelevance of infant observations for psychoanalysis*. Journal of the American Psychoanalytic Association, 44, 369–392.

Chapter 10

Organisational Research and Consulting and the Idea of Containment

Susan Long

This chapter will explore the idea of psychological containment and its relevance to organisational research and consultation. I will be drawing on psychoanalytic and socioanalytic thinking and experience. I will argue, following Bion (1970), that psychological containment concerns the emergence and development, problems and creativity of the mind. It is mind that creates perceptual, emotional and cognitive boundaries and attendant psychological containment in a world of flux and continuous evolution (Chattopadhyay 2019; Bohm 1980; Morgan 1986). For Bion, the mind has a capacity for thinking thoughts that may be present consciously or unconsciously in a community. His theory of thinking traces the manner in which the mind develops as a container for this purpose.

I argue that mind is a social phenomenon and depends on group and social processes for its vitality (Harre 1984, 1993). Mind is an emergent, psychic phenomenon, linked to the physical body and brain but not equivalent to them. It is a phenomenon to be studied in itself (Long 1996). In this chapter my focus will be on mind as a container.

First, I will give some thoughts about containment more broadly. There are many ways of using the term containment. A container is generally thought about as an object for holding or transporting something as per the meaning given in the Oxford Dictionary. It might refer to a physical process such as a room containing objects and people, or the skin containing other organs. A more specialised idea sees containment as the provision of boundaries that hold some thing or activity *inside* those boundaries. The container may be an object – a box, a house, or some rules or values that constrain the contained. It might refer to a symbolic function such as a word or speech containing a meaning, or a mother containing the distress of her infant. It might refer to a group process such as a leader containing the impulses of their followers, or an institution containing the values, purposes, anticipations and memories of a culture. It is the relation of the container to what is contained that is essential to the idea of containment rather than any specific content or context.

Bion (1967, 1970) takes up the ideas of container and contained as part of his theory of thinking. His meaning sees the container and contained in a

DOI: 10.4324/9781315146416-14

relationship where both affect each other. He gives the example, for instance, of the following:

> A man wishing to communicate his annoyance is so overcome by emotion that he stammers and becomes incoherent... the forms of speech that the man uses to convey his meaning: these I regard as being intended to 'contain' what he has to say... the annoyance he strives to communicate I regard as being what should be 'contained' in his speech.
>
> (Bion 1970, p. 95)

The words, explains Bion, cannot contain the emotion. The emotions overcome the capacity of his words and incoherence is the result. If he could become coherent – that is if his mental development allowed for the emotions to be held or contained, then his emotions could be communicated by words.

For Bion, a mind provides a container for thoughts and may have the capacity to think those thoughts. Alternatively, the mind may eject thoughts or pre-conceptions or may eject what he calls beta-elements which are emotional experiences that cannot be tolerated. Containment described in this way is an internal psychological phenomenon.

I am using containment to straddle across these meanings, but predominantly I refer to psychological rather than physical containment although both meanings are related to one another. Being 'held-in-mind' by another person can feel like being contained psychologically, and so can being physically held when distressed. In the following I will give examples of different kinds of containment and their properties.

1. Containers are *constraining*. Prisons, for example, contain inmates who are constrained in their movements and activities and prevented from escaping into the community. While the constraint here is physical, it is also an example of a social/psychological container because a prison is an idea in the minds of those who legislate for and build prisons. The physical prison is a realisation of an idea contained in a society. So, it is with all boundaries. They begin in the mind.

   In terms of the individual, we can consciously constrain our behaviours to fit appropriately into a variety of contexts – or not. And what we think and feel can be constrained unconsciously by personal repressions, drugs, biological capacity, technological capabilities and social norms. Constraint is necessary and comes from the development of boundaries. Without psychological boundaries distinctions would not be possible. But constraints can sometimes be constrictions so that systems become over-bound (Alderfer 1980). An organisational example would be over-regulation such that organisation members are unable to make changes to their work when a situation demands them to do so. In another example, a consultant might jump to conclusions about an organisational issue and constrain their thinking so that a pre-emptive solution is given, and new data is missed.

2. Containers can *hold* their contents. A mother may hold her infant so he feels safe and does not fear falling or falling apart. Winnicott called this a holding environment. While holding environments appear to be wholly external (Symington and Symington 1996), again they have their origins in the contained idea of that environment. A speaker may hold her audience so their attention is focused and they can think about what she is saying. Container in this sense allows for creativity and growth. The relation between the container and the contained is one of mutual advantage. Bion named this as a symbiotic relation (Bion 1970, p. 95). Containers and contained, when the holding is psychologically done with care and thoughtfulness, grow together. Winnicott (1996) refers to this type of container as a holding environment). Biologically, our skin grows as do its contents. So does our psychological skin grow, or not grow to contain our growing emotional capacities (Bick 1988).

3. Containers may be 'leaky'. An organisation may have unclear policies together with a laissez-faire culture or lax leadership so that employees feel conflicted and unable to gain authority for their work thus increasing the risk of mistakes in the work. A leader may make promises that they cannot keep. In Alderfer's terms, an organisation might be under-bound (Alderfer 1980). If under-bound and also punitive, organisation members will become quite stressed without direction and yet blamed for consequent mistakes. In such a culture, a consultant may well be blamed for managements' mistakes.

4. A container may be destructive to what is contained. A company may defraud its customers and hence the relation between container and contained may be considered a parasitic relation – consciously or unconsciously – where the container grows due to the disadvantage of the contained (Bion 1970, p. 95). The banking Royal Commission in Australia, for instance, in 2018 found some banks to be defrauding through charging fees from accounts and estates of people who had died, in one case for more than a decade (www.theguardian.com/australia-news/2018/apr/19/commonwealth-bank-charged-fees-to-dead-clients-royal-commission-hears). Such cases are perverse (Long 2008) or corrupt. When working as a consultant to perverse organisations, the consultant must be careful not to be seduced into the perversion (Long 2008; Chapman and Long 2009; Chapman 2021).

5. Containers may become the contained and the contained may become the container. A thinker may hold a thought, but a thought might 'possess' a thinker. Long Term Capital Management were possessed by the idea that they could make money from the many small discrepancies in international exchanges that would make them inviolable (Long 2008). They were eventually destroyed by this idea as it led them into extremely poor decisions. A government might constrain its people, but the people might constrain its government. It is important for the researcher or consultant to understand what they are containing for the organisation and what in the organisation is containing them.

6. Containers and contained may grow disproportionately to each other. An idea may grow beyond the capacity of a culture to contain it so the culture must develop, change or be destroyed. Bion refers to this as an abortive container (see Bion 1970, p. 40). Computer records, for example, handle information much faster and more efficiently than paper records. The information contained becomes too vast to handle manually. Many an organisation has had to adapt to new technologies lest they become financially unviable.

7. Some psychological phenomena may be uncontainable. A psychotic process lacks a conception of container for projections. There is no internalisation of a containing function or there is intolerance of its constraints (Bergstein 2015). An infant may not be able to contain some emotions or experiences so projects into mother for containment, yet unconsciously retains the experiences for later processing. When untested assumptions or projections between groups or nations cannot be held, constrained or worked through, when there is no process or function to act as a container, then hostilities and war may result. Some thoughts are unthinkable. Quite often a consultant may come to an organisation and, in holding a 'not knowing' stance (that is, a stance of negative capability; Simpson and French 2006) is able to think thoughts that the organisation members cannot. How to introduce such ideas is then a skill that the consultant must learn, lest they be rejected along with the thought.

8. A group can contain all the thoughts, emotions, behaviours, memories and anticipations of its members. It contains them as objects or processes. Group processes can allow these to be available and shared, or may shut down and constrain such sharing. Constraints and boundaries can be positive or negative in the growth of the group.

9. Mind is a container of thoughts, memories, anticipations and processes such as perception, cognition, intention and memory, as well as containing unconscious and defensive processes such as repression, suppression, projection, introjection, displacement and rationalisation. Mind is what makes human intention possible. It forms associations and links between its contents, and it forms anticipations of what might come.

10. Containment allows new meaning to emerge through the provision of semi-permeable boundaries between the container and what is contained. A new organisational project, for example, has the potential to create new meaning for the organisation by containing people, thoughts, processes and technology that have not previously been bound together and can traverse old exclusionary boundaries. Mind is interrogative – it asks questions and is curious: unconsciously it asks for that which is as yet unthought but is unconsciously available. 'The pressure of a question is driven by some unthought knowledge' (Bollas 2018, p. 148).

Organisational Research and Consulting Using Psychoanalytic and Socioanalytic Methods and Processes

Organisations are made up of people making decisions about the work they do. They may have buildings and other material assets, but the recent global Covid-19 pandemic has shown us how many organisations can operate with people working from their homes, remotely. They have structures – businesses, departments, hierarchies and roles. These are filled with people who make decisions about purposes and tasks, and then who realise those decisions. The interactivity of those decisions, their realisation and their place in a wider environment of suppliers, customers, politics, social change and technology form a complex system. Those organisations that survive and are prosperous are able to adapt to the complexities in their environments and their internal cultures and can continue to fulfil their purposes. Containment is a large part of this capacity.

Organisational research and consultancy using socioanalytic or systems psychodynamic approaches work with complexity. The approach is one of understanding that the complexity involves dynamics many of which are unconscious to the organisational players. Such dynamics are uncovered through methods that discover unconscious systemic patterns in the behaviours and decision-making processes of the groups contained in the organisation and the contexts within which the organisation is contained. Some of these are defensive patterns aimed at reducing the anxieties and other difficult emotions attendant upon the nature of the work done and the human relations and relationships that emerge during the work. These defensive patterns may also be unconsciously destructive to the work (Armstrong and Rustin 2015). Organisation structure, culture, authority and accountability aid or impede complex group dynamics, including unconscious dynamics and the development of collaborative roles and relations. In taking a systemic socioanalytic perspective the importance of displacement as a dynamic is recognised, where problems in one part of the system may appear as symptoms elsewhere (Long 2000; Long and Harding 2013; Long 2018).

A model is put forward by Ruch (2007) who proposes that organisations should consider three kinds of containment: emotional; organisational; and epistemological. Writing from a social work perspective, this author argues for workplace reflective practices that provide emotional containment for individuals and their relationships; for organisational practices, such as workloads, appraisals and guidance; and for learning that integrates technical, experiential and formal learning. This model termed 'wholistic containment' emphasises a need for organisation members to make sense of their experiences. Beyond such a model are those that look to unconscious processes.

One such framework for systems psychodynamic consultancy is the Transforming Experience Framework. This framework, developed through the then Grubb Institute in London, regards human experience as coming through different lenses or sets of conditions. The framework focuses on experience gained through i) being a person, ii) being in a role, iii) being in a system, iv) being in a broader context, and v) experience from a source (source being that which gives ultimate purpose). I have described this framework more thoroughly elsewhere (Long 2016). But here it is worth thinking about experience as being gained through the **containers** of person (individual mind and body), role, system, context and source. We can think of the contained in an organisation as being the person in role, in a system, in a context, in a purpose, making decisions and carrying out tasks. I believe that each of these containers calls or invokes the organisational player to make decisions.

Sometimes the different containers require the person to make different decisions so that the person experiences conflict. For example, a university (the system) may require that a certain percentage of students pass their examinations at different levels, while a teacher (in role) may not hold to these percentages because their purpose is not to decide on percentages but on the merit of the student. But the contained may also be a group, in a system, in a context, in a purpose. So, the group needs collectively to discern its own patterns of behaviour. Or the contained may be a system in a context and so on. Each of these categories of person, role, system, context and source is a container and also the contained. We might understand each of these containers to hold different experiences and unconscious memories or anticipations such that they each throw forward different questions (Bollas 2008) or call forward different expectations (Grotstein 2000) and hence provide conflicting answers or behaviours.

The systems psychodynamic consultant or collaborative researcher aids the organisation as a whole and through its members to understand its own patterns of behaviours and to decide when these are helpful to purpose or not. Distinctively, this way of working considers unconscious dynamics as well as those consciously observable. These dynamics are hypothesised through their effects and are discerned through specific methods (Long 2013; Stamenova and Hinshelwood 2018; Sher 2013).

In the following vignettes of research and consulting issues, I hope to show how the researcher, consultant or consulting team uncovers patterns of behaviour for the organisation members through the consultants' acting as containers for dynamics at a person, role, system, context or source level. This process sits alongside other methods for uncovering patterns both conscious and unconscious.

An Initial Situation

One of my professional roles is as a coach to managers, leaders and others in organisational settings. I do this through organisational role analysis using the Transforming Experience Framework and other socioanalytic approaches (see Long 2013). Carol was a senior manager in a government organisation who was unsure about her next career step. In one session she came with a story about her manager, who she said continued to take her (Carol's) ideas and not acknowledge them. While she recognised that this was common practice up the hierarchy of government, and was justified by a system where managers had to gather the ideas of their 'subordinates' and present them in a unified way to their own 'superiors', she felt robbed and unrecognised, especially as her manager did not openly thank her for her contributions. In this story Carol's manager had rejected Carol's idea that a particular project be prioritised in the department's budget because, as Carol had argued, this project met more of the department's objectives as set out in their operational strategy than another project that was a contender for prioritisation. Carol's arguments were dismissed because the manager argued that critical stakeholders in the second project would be offended and they needed these stakeholders 'on side'. But in a later meeting, her manager brought these same arguments prioritising the first project forward as if they were her own ideas, in a document under 'Future Plans'. Carol said she was dumbstruck and didn't voice her feelings because she felt they would appear as petty in front of others. Although this was just one incident, Carol saw this as a pattern and believed that her chances for promotion were lessened because of this. She confronted her manager in a private meeting, describing her feelings in an angry tone. The manager replied that she was surprised – she thought all was going well and that she had simply taken the ideas of many of the team and put them into her own document. She was sorry that it seemed as if Carol's ideas were stolen. Carol felt betrayed not only by her manager, but by her own inability to contain her feelings, and suspicious – was the manager genuinely surprised or was she duplicitous? Carol left the meeting and went to her own office to cry, feeling angry, ashamed and betrayed.

In this fairly simple example several questions about containment arise:

1. How are the emotions of the players contained or not contained – Carol said she was unable to contain her emotions and this made her ashamed? Who or what was the container? Her manager said she was surprised; was the container of her ideas about how she worked and produced her document suddenly changed?
2. What are the mechanisms of containment for these players? Suppression? Repression? Fear? Shame? Mechanisms of containment and the existence of containers need not be simply personal, but may be what the organisational culture or the society have available.
3. How does the organisational hierarchy contain the ideas that arise within it?
4. If Carol's ideas arose in the course of her work – to whom do they belong?
5. In what ways might the consultant contain Carol in her role?

These questions are best tackled if we understand the nature of containment at group and societal levels.

Bion's (1970) formulations of containment encompass his thinking about both individuals and groups, in terms of container and contained. The mind of the individual (the container) may contain thoughts. That is, people entertain and think thoughts which may appear as discrete entities (for example, the thought 'I have to tell my partner that I will do the shopping today' and the relationship between them. 'If I tell my partner that I will do the shopping maybe he will cook the dinner tonight'. We can think, in terms of Bion's formulations, that a person may entertain an idea (contain the idea) so that we imagine the idea is *in* the mind and can thus be thought about rather than defended against, repressed or extruded. Or we may understand that the idea may contain the individual, that is, hold the individual – perhaps in a positive and supportive way, as when the idea of a cure may ameliorate anxiety in a suffering person. Alternatively, a thought may dominate thinking as when a scientist is pursuing a particular outcome; or even possess the individual – as sometimes a lie may possess the thinker it needs for its expression (Armstrong 2005). So, when I say psychological containment is all about the mind, I mean that the mind must have both containing functions and itself be contained. It may contain thoughts and be able to process those thoughts through thinking; but it also needs itself to be contained with boundaries and constraints, lest it is lost – the colloquial term of 'losing one's mind' testifies to this. 'The psychotic individual lacks a conception of container for projections' (Bergstein 2015, p. 9) either because there is no containing function or the constraints imposed by a container cannot be borne.

And then there are groups. A group may contain its members. That is, the group has members who are part of the group because they have a common purpose. Each member identifies with the leading idea or purpose of the group as they see it, and consequently members have affiliations and identifications with one another (Freud 1921; Long, 1992). In simpler terms, the members of a hiking group, for example, each (more or less) believe in and hold to the purpose and values of the group and share camaraderie in so doing. Similarly, with members of political groups, sporting groups, work groups and others.

But also, members contain the group. This means that they each have an internal image of the group (a group or institution-in-the-mind – or an internal team – Long 2002) that guides their own purposes and roles within the group. Containing the group means that a member can think about the group and can act on behalf of the group. We can speak of the group as giving authority to members in their roles to act on its behalf. This occurs when, for example, a member of staff represents their organisation or a diplomat, their country. To take up such representation successfully so that the group is faithfully represented requires the person, in their role, to contain the group; to hold it in mind and stay in tune with its purposes and tasks. Otherwise, such representation may be false.

In the above examples, containers are not absolutes, but depend upon a function. The mind may be container or contained. Similarly, the group may be container or contained. These are not absolute entities, but functions.

So, to return to Carol:

1. How are the emotions of the players contained or not contained – Carol said she was unable to contain her emotions and this made her ashamed? Who or what was the container? Her manager said she was surprised; was the container of her ideas about how she worked and produced her document suddenly changed?

    Both Carol and her manager have different ideas about how documents in an organisational hierarchy are produced. A discussion in the whole team about this might help so that a mutual understanding is reached. Carol says she understands the process and would be happy with more recognition from her manager, even if that were not formally in the document. It would at least be recognised in the team. This seems crucial. People require recognition for the ideas that they are able to think and communicate (Benjamin 1988). The work of thinking, whether theoretically or in very practical terms, is central to a person's identity. Just the thinking of one's name demonstrates this. Positive containment would be to find a supportive environment in which to have the team discussion.

2. What are the mechanisms of containment for these players? Suppression? Repression? Fear? Shame? Mechanisms of containment and the existence of containers need not be simply personal, but may be what the organisational culture or the society have available.

The government organisation where Carol and her manager work has particular ways of doing tasks, of thinking about tasks and even of how people should react and feel when doing tasks. This is part of the organisational culture. Being 'professional' is important there: meaning that they believe emotions should be held in check and communications should not be personalised. But Carol's experience was coloured by her belief that her manager's behaviour *was* personalised and driven by the manager's own need for recognition or envy of Carol. She may have been right. But then again, the manager may have been acting within general cultural norms, regardless of her own motivations and believing that Carol would conform to those cultural norms. There was little space in the organisation to work through the different perceptions about the way things were done and how in fact, despite the rhetoric, this affected people personally. Shame was certainly available as a constraint on questioning the norms.

An extreme form of such a dynamic comes when atrocities are committed 'under orders' and the container (an army for instance) constrains or even obliterates the use of personal ethics.

3. How does the organisational hierarchy contain the ideas that arise within it?

The hierarchy here had a way of gathering reports such that the higher up the chain of authority, the more deidentified the ideas became. Reports tend to be identified by the name of the manager on the report. This could be seen as an efficient way of managing a multiplicity of different ideas, AND as a defence against challenges to hierarchy and authority. Personal 'ownership of ideas' is discouraged. Yet although the organisational hierarchy has an established way of working, ideas can enter the organisation from anywhere. Bion talks of an establishment as having the purpose of taking a new idea, making it accessible to the group and preventing disruption, but it does this in a dogmatic way; while the purpose of the new idea is to challenge the establishment – perhaps destroy it so a new order can emerge. He describes the containment or non-containment of the new idea by the establishment as two forces containing each other as in a military situation (Bion 1970, pp. 112–114). Is the new idea or the establishment destroyed in the process?

4. If Carol's ideas arose in the course of her work – to whom do they belong?

Organisations manage this consciously through intellectual property policies. Ideas within the organisation are contained in this way, which defends against chaos and against the anxieties of senior management. If we think from the perspective of the group mind, it can be said that ideas arising in the workplace 'belong' to the organisation. That is the basis of intellectual property rights. If we think from the perspective of the individual who may have thoughts that come from a variety of contexts, or different containers in terms of the TEF, then the ideas might be seen to 'belong' to the person from within a wider culture. In such instances as this, ownership of ideas becomes problematic. 'Ownership' as a concept becomes the container for such disputes and for the emotions that surround the production of ideas. In this case, the word is the container of meaning.

5. In what ways might the consultant contain Carol in her role?

In the first instance I already had a relationship with Carol and she understood my way of working. I had contracted with her about the work – that it would be a collaborative endeavour working towards understanding her role in her organisational system; the pulls and pressures of the system on the role; her own capacities and valencies in role; and that together we might understand the patterns in the ways she took up her role and develop working hypotheses about the meaning of her role in the system at conscious and unconscious levels. She understood that I was not taking an 'expert role' in the sense that I would provide answers to her issues, but that I would work with her in making sense of her role, the system and its context. This would free her to make more informed decisions about the way she worked. This contracting and understanding, of course, did not prevent that from time to time she expected me to provide answers and would try to get me to take on that role. But the contracting provided an explanation of our task together, to which we could return when confusions entered. It provided containment for the work.

Second, I listened to Carol's story, only asking questions for clarification attempting to make sure she felt that I had heard what she wanted to convey. I listened to the content of her story and I also listened for the meaning of the story beyond face value. While doing this, I paid attention to how she was feeling.

Third, I paid attention to my own feelings and thoughts as I listened. What were the pulls for me in the story? What might Carol hope I would think and feel? Did she want me as an ally in condemning her manager? Did she want me to see that although this could be understood as a systemic issue – the way the organisational hierarchy worked – she also wanted me to see how she, in role, felt personally about this aspect of the organisational culture? I know that I was thinking fairly dispassionately about this. I was uncertain about whether or not the manager was deliberately undermining her feelings or if the manager herself was too caught in the systemic process to see its effects on the staff. I could listen and accept Carol's anger, but also help her to see the situation in its greater complexity. Carol, I think, had wanted me to hold her rational self, while she went through an emotional process. Together we worked on thinking through a process where she might bring her dilemma forward not as a personal hurt, but as a group dynamic within the organisational culture.

Institutional Examples

Inter-organisational consortia where members from different organisations work together on specific issues and projects require collaborative processes that can work across organisational differences in purpose, task and culture. Moreover, the issues addressed by such consortia and projects can often be described as 'wicked problems' because they cannot be solely addressed by one organisation with its specialised approaches and skills, but need multiple approaches. These are issues such as racism, poverty, drug use, climate change and global pandemics, e.g., the recent Covid-19 pandemic; issues that affect a broad diversity of communities and are global in their effects.

I have worked on several projects involving inter-organisational and cross-disciplinary collaborative efforts in the areas of justice, health and climate change. The inter-organisational efforts to work on these issues require various forms of containment. The need is to develop a mind that can contain work across different organisations and disciplines, such that staff can internalise a collaborative mindset.

Leadership

In these inter-organisations there is no single leadership and sometimes unclear lines of authority for tasks that cross the boundaries of the organisations involved. Prins (2006) says, for example, 'A particular challenge of collaborative work is how to define leadership in an organizational context where hierarchy is not a valid organizing principle. Often, there is no formal leader, authority relations are ambiguous, and the consensual nature of collaborative work inhibits the emergence of overt leadership' (p. 336). Leadership is one of the central containing influences on a group, institution or society. The leadership needed in a consortium is necessarily collaborative because other forms of hierarchy are not available. This is not to say that all leadership comes from an establishment hierarchy; it may be evidenced at any formal organisational level. As discussed earlier, new ideas can come from anywhere as can other leadership functions.

Cross Organisational Understanding

From a systems perspective the development of inter-departmental or inter-organisational memoranda of understanding, where senior leaders in each of the stakeholder groups arrive at a shared understanding of the way they work together, supports and contains staff in their attempts to design and implement processes that respect the differences within, and reap the benefits of the multidisciplinary teams involved. Without such agreements staff become conflicted about the nature of their roles, their reporting commitments and their purposes. Strong agreements between leaders provide stable holding containment in inter-organisational and multiparty contexts so long as these agreements are able to include the experiences of the staff who actually do the work. Having their experiences recognised – both the difficult experiences and their successes – gives staff members at all levels of a hierarchy and across groupings security and stability in their roles and personal lives.

Avoidance of Destructive Group Dynamics and Social Defences

Group dynamics always affect collaborative efforts (Prins 2010). Skills in recognising group dynamics need to be developed, such as: when the group is 'off task'; when roles are confused or undeveloped; when sub-groups become 'locked into' intractable positions and the whole group becomes polarised; when issues are avoided due to fears and anxieties; when the leader dominates rather than facilitates discussion. Sometimes expert consultation is required, but the group members need to recognise these dynamics and either manage them themselves or seek help. The worst outcome is if these dynamics predominate and are only discussed in subgroups behind closed doors.

Good communication across the different organisations and groupings is necessary to avoid mistrust, ill-informed myths about the work and lack of co-ordination of efforts. Good work group practices with clear purpose, task and role definition are needed for collaborative work.

An example

The example here involves different disciplines from different organisations working together in a law court setting. It is provided as an example of the containment needs of a complex multidisciplinary work environment.

The law as a social institution provides a container for social behaviour in terms of its constraints and freedoms. It is also a container for many of the emotions people have in conjunction with that behaviour. The old example of the wisdom of Solomon illustrates this. Two women claimed a baby as their own. The anxiety of one woman was for the potential loss of her child; the envy of the other woman was that she didn't have a child. These emotions were strong and uncontainable by the women. Solomon's judgement not only found the true mother, because her love for the child meant the child should not die, but also showed how the law, as embodied in Solomon, could contain and process the women's emotions to enable a just solution.

A court contains in many ways. It has a physical presence that can be intimidating. Legal professionals wear wigs and gowns, furnishings are often sombre and formal rituals and proceedings are instituted. Increasingly minor courts can be far more informal with no wigs and gowns, modern furnishings, and a judge who addresses the defendant in more personal ways. While formal rituals and proceedings are still maintained, together with a presence of judicial authority, the atmosphere is less overtly intimidating.

Beyond the physical containment of the court, because of the power and authority of the judicial system, behaviours and emotions are held strictly in check. Court ritual and procedure is subject to a long history of precedent. It is the behaviour between the various players, each within prescribed roles and within a strict set of purposes, that provides for emotional, behavioural and cognitive containment. As well as overt containment, there is psychological containment at a social level. The emotions stirred by the issues involved and by the court process are projected into the court (as an institution), processed by the court and re-introjected by the parties involved – even where the decisions reached are disappointing or hated.

A therapeutic jurisprudence court attempts to fit an informal model. Such courts may be family violence courts, juvenile justice, indigenous courts and drug courts. This example is of a drug court. The first drug court was instituted in Miami USA in 1989. There are now three and a half thousand drug courts in the USA and in 20 other countries, including Australia. They are based on the idea of therapeutic jurisprudence and the belief that imprisonment is not the answer to drug-related crime.

The Drug Court of Victoria (DCV) began as a pilot programme in 2002 and was approved three years later. It was established to provide sentencing and supervision of the treatment of offenders with a drug and alcohol problem whose offences would normally warrant a custodial sentence of two years or less. It is an alternative to the normal penalties that may be imposed by legislation for the particular offence committed. Participants are placed on a Drug Treatment Order (DTO) which integrates alcohol and other drug treatment strategies with the coercive aspects of the criminal justice system. It emphasises the rehabilitation of the participant (Winick and Wexler, 2015) to reduce recidivism and integrate participants back into the community, thereby protecting the community.

In order to manage this successfully, the court requires the collaboration of several departments and professional roles in the process of convicting and treating the offender. These include: magistrates; police prosecutors; court administration; corrections case managers; the court clinical advisors; drug and alcohol counsellors from agencies outside the court itself; defence lawyers; and housing officers. Each of these roles has a reporting line directly within the court and a reporting line back to their 'home' organisations – each of which were established with quite different purposes.

In 2017, the Drug Court of Victoria, Australia was extended to the Melbourne Magistrates Court where two new courts have been established. Future plans include the provision of Drug Court services in regional areas. Managing regional teams from a central location creates an additional layer of complexity, making it even more important to understand and work with the issues of collaboration across the multidisciplinary teams.

This example draws upon collaborative action research that has many parallels with collaborative action learning consultancy. This research was aimed at examining and supporting collaborative capability between the different professional groups through a collaborative action research process. It was an enquiry into the way that the different disciplines work together in a collaborative rather than the adversarial manner typical in most court settings. This required police prosecutors and corrections officers, for example, to work with drug and alcohol counsellors, where each of these professional roles has different and sometimes conflicting task ideas. The drug court requires them to make the shift from their organisational roles in their 'home' departments or organisations (e.g., police-force, corrections organisation or counselling service) to a role on the drug court team during case conferences for each participant on a DTO, during court appearances and throughout all the background work needed in dealing with cases.

We (Susan Long and Nuala Dent from the National Institute of Organisation Dynamics Australia) did extensive interviews and observations.[1] In addition, we conducted reflective practice sessions and ran role-play workshops with court staff. These helped us as researchers and the staff members to deepen the ways that they understood and internalised the various tasks and roles involved across the whole court. The research outcomes informed the drug court as an organisation and court systems at an institutional level.

Containment at these organisational and institutional levels can be seen from the perspectives of person, role, system and context (see Long 2016 for more on the Transforming Experience Framework that underpins these different domain perspectives). Containment in this instance primarily means support for clarity of purpose, role, task, procedures and forums for staff to discuss these in an open manner. Lack of containment within specified boundaries will result in confusion and consequent mistrust between team members. Following the outcomes of the research we found ways in which therapeutic courts support collaborative endeavours across multidisciplinary teams. The following points are indicative of the ways in which the therapeutic courts might operate for maximum effectiveness. They do not indicate problems found in the courts under study but are agreed upon outcomes about good practice.

1. From a systems perspective the development of inter-departmental memoranda of understanding, where senior leaders in each of the court stakeholder departments arrive at a shared understanding of the way the departments work together, supports and contains staff to design and implement processes that respect the differences within and reap the benefits of the multidisciplinary team. Without such agreements staff would become conflicted about the nature of their roles, their reporting commitments and their purposes. Strong agreements between leaders provide stable holding containment in inter-organisational and multi-party contexts (Prins 2006), where these agreements include the experiences of the staff who actually do the work. Having their experiences recognised – both the difficult experiences and their successes – gives staff members at all levels of a hierarchy security and stability in their roles and personal lives.

2. From a role perspective staff need clarity about gaps between old ways of working and the new ways needed in a new court setting. This indicates the need for work processes to have established algorithms and guidelines especially in those areas where discretion in decision-making is needed. For example, clear agreements are needed about requests that come from outside the formal reporting lines across the team to all roles. Important is a thorough induction for new staff members to the new court and its purposes. Forums for team building and sharing different perspectives by all players outside of decision-making meetings and ongoing training and reflective practice sessions to aid staff with complex issues are highly beneficial.

3. From a contextual perspective there is a need for the broader judicial system and the community to understand and support the role of therapeutic jurisprudence

as a different way of approaching crime. People who work in these courts often feel undervalued by their peers in other courts and by the community at large. Some participants on a DTO, for instance, may well, because of their histories and current conditions, breach their order conditions. If in the eyes of other government departments or the broader community this reflects negatively on the work of the courts, then their positive work is undermined, and staff capacity is less contained than it might be.

At a broader contextual level, the cause of drug crime often rests in poor societal conditions for users who end up on a DTO.

4. In terms of person, a therapeutic court gives hope to many who, if incarcerated would not have the opportunities for reform that the court offers. There are strict conditions to be fulfilled, for example, on a DTO that include containment through giving the offender regular commitments, the chance to detox, counselling and living support, and if these are successfully achieved, the person is more likely to achieve a crime-free existence.

A drug court is an important societal container for the minimisation of drug-related crime. The whole judicial system is a container for that court. The shift from adversarial to therapeutic approaches in sectors of that system is a challenging move for both the system and the society (Winick and Wexler, 2015).

The Consulting Team

Some organisations are large and extremely complex. A consulting team is required. I like to work with other consultants where possible even in small organisations because the team becomes a container for many of the dynamics that occur in the consulting project. I mean by this that the team is able to take in and examine different aspects of the organisation through its different members. In simple terms, multiple perspectives are gained from emotional as well as cognitive dimensions.

It is natural to think of mind as an individual phenomenon. By ourselves, we think, ruminate, imagine, experience emotionally, anticipate, remember – all the functions that we understand as pertaining to the mind.

However, my interest is predominantly with the mind of the group-as-a–whole, taking a systemic perspective; that is, where the whole is greater than the sum of its parts. It means, in this case, that a group mind is a phenomenon in itself, not just the amalgamation of individual minds. As an extension of this idea, I argue that the individual mind is a representational part of a wider mind – that wider mind being a systemic collection of assumptions, myths, beliefs, values and other cultural phenomena mostly articulated in language, but also in art, music and mathematics and other significations. Individual minds are thinking muscles that can do the work of thinking about the contents of that wider system as they become available within various constraints, biological, personal and societal. This thinking work involves understanding some of the implications, risks and possibilities of the thoughts and ideas present or available to the wider system, group, organisation or society.

The consulting team is available to do this thinking work and from there encourage the organisation members to also do such work. The idea behind the teamwork is not simply that there are more people to do interviews, observations and to collect data. The idea is also that each member of the consulting team will observe different things and will introject different aspects of the organisation. These observations and introjections will then be available for study in the dynamics of the consulting team. Here consulting team members must be willing to examine their own thoughts and feelings in the work even when these are painful or anxiety provoking. Understanding that the thoughts and feelings that one contains as part of the project belong not to one personally but to the organisation is not only enlightening but personally helpful to the consulting team members. This is not easy work, because often feelings are stirred up that pertain to other team members and the danger that the dynamics become personalised is ever present.

Most of my organisational consulting is done in the form of collaborative action learning projects where the organisation wishes to learn more about some aspects of its own structure, culture or work processes and may wish to change or transform itself in light of internal challenges or contextual pressures. Fundamentally, the consultant(s) works together with the organisation on an identified issue. The consulting team take an issue identified by the client organisation. This 'presenting issue' may not be the problem that needs the work, it may simply identify a symptom of the 'real' problem. Action research may work in a similar way, but the issue might be one that the researcher wishes to investigate and the organisation will then be a willing partner in the investigation. The ways in which a team of consultants work can parallel action research but there are differences. Importantly, there are questions of ownership and authority. This chapter will not explore the differences; such an exploration is for another time.

An action learning approach to consulting requires not only a team of two or more consultants, but also a group that oversees the project made up of the consulting team and members of the organisation, and as much as possible has support from the senior management or governance body. This group gets called, variously, a steering group; a governance group; or an action learning project group. Its task is to advise the consultants, to aid with gathering information from throughout the organisation; to understand and interpret deidentified data collected by the consultants and to integrate the learning from the consultancy into the organisation. The formation of this group means:

1. The organisation takes on responsibility for and ownership of the project and its outcomes, hence the project becomes *fully contained* within the organisation/system.
2. Organisation members become engaged with the project, and have a more personal stake.
3. The data from the investigative aspects of the project may be validated against the experiences of group members if the group contains representatives from different parts of the organisation.

4. The interpretation and implementation of outcomes is done within the language and culture of the organisation and hence more easily taken up, even though the project will, as a part of the organisation, modify that language and culture as it progresses.
5. Additionally, the consultants can work closely with group members to aid them and then the organisation to 'see' aspects that had not previously been seen.
6. Having such a group allows the consultancy to proceed in an iterative and organic way, rather than leaving the organisation with a report at the end of a process which then must be digested in its entirety.
7. Having such a group aids integration of the project, its processes and outcomes, into the organisation.

We can think of the process of an organisational collaborative research or consultancy as a temporary part of the organisation. Working collaboratively in this temporary container through action learning requires the development of many skills in the participants. These include holding ambiguity and uncertainty about what might be discovered; tolerating and even welcoming different perspectives about the organisation and its work; a willingness to examine one's own part in the issues presented and to recognise the differing experiences of different roles – often there is no right or wrong, just difference and a willingness to understand the meaning of those differences.

In a project with a cardiac unit in a hospital, action learning explored the many skills of teams of staff from different disciplines: cardiologists, cardiac fellows, radiologists, nurses, secretaries, administrators and receptionists (Long et al. 2010). Working together through action learning explored these skills as they emerged in real-life, real-time situations. The collaborative work involved meetings with a steering group, whole department meetings and team meetings as well as the independent cultural analysis conducted by the research team as an action research project.

The whole project which also involved role analysis, open space learning and times when the research team explored their own dynamics provided a container for departmental members to explore their thinking about the issues they faced and their emotional reactions and team dynamics during the exploration. The problems faced by the department were primarily due to the differing needs of the different staff roles in relation to patients and the fact that there were few forums where these could be explored. The focus initially was on the work with patients, with little time for seeing how the current culture affected this. The organisational researchers provided well-bound places and times, so that trust between staff developed and day-to-day problems with their work could be solved together.

Containers for the Future

How might our organisations in the future become containers for new thinking? It may be helpful for leaders and managers to think about the design of good holding containers for work. This is beyond the design of the physical environment, although that is important. It is beyond the design of organisational structures such as departments, work groups and roles, although clarity around structure is important. It involves the building of work cultures that hold rather than unnecessarily constrain; that provide clarity, including clarity about authority and accountability at the edge of, rather than in chaos; that allow for collaborative effort rather than command and control, and that nurture enquiring minds. It involves the provision of spaces where difficult group dynamics and communications can be safely explored and the perspectives from different roles considered. Such dynamics will always occur because of the complex and difficult tasks that organisations face; some of which may be necessary but hated tasks (Menzies-Lyth 1951; Armstrong and Rustin 2015; Chapman 2003). Without the places and skills to hold such discussions, work may be perverted or corrupted (Long 2008; Chapman 2003; Chapman and Long 2009).

Psychodynamic consultants can aid this through not only providing containment for the consulting process and the organisation during the project, but also through action learning methods aiding organisation members to be better containers of their own experiences; to aid systems to see how they might be better holding containers for staff, rather than unnecessarily restrictive or leaky; to aid organisations to understand how they are held, or not held by wider systems of stakeholders and how they in turn might better hold their stakeholders.

Increasingly, organisations at global and local levels are subject to the problems of our social systems. These include global warming, the divide between the employed and the unemployed, racism, gender inequity, poverty, population displacement and more recently the Covid-19 pandemic. These organisations – private, government and not-for-profit – have these issues inside their systems and in their contexts. How they contain them affects the possibility of *thinking about* them rather than dismissing these issues as not relevant or too hard to deal with.

Note

1 The research was conducted through the National Institute for Organisation Dynamics Australia (NIODA) by Prof. Susan Long and Dr Nuala Dent, with a governance group made up of researchers, a Judge of the Drug Court of Victoria, a Senior Manager at Corrections Victoria and the CEO of the Judicial College of Victoria. It was funded by Corrections Victoria.

References

Alderfer, C.P. (1980) 'The methodology of organizational diagnosis'. *Professional Psychology*, 11, 459–468.

Armstrong, D. and Rustin, M. (eds.) (2015) *Social Defences Against Anxiety: Explorations in a paradigm*. Routledge: London.

Armstrong, D. (2005) 'Names, thoughts, and lies: The relevance of Bion's later writing for understanding experiences in groups', in R. French (ed.) *Organisation in the Mind*. Routledge: London.

Benjamin, J. (1988) *The Bonds of Love: Psychoanalysis, Feminism and the Problem of Domination*. Pantheon: New York.

Bergstein, A. (2015) 'Attacks on thinking or a drive to communicate: Tolerating the paradox'. *Psychoanalytic Quarterly*, 84(4), 921–942.

Bick, E. (1988) 'The experience of the skin in early object relations', in E. Spillius (ed.) *Melanie Klein Today*, Vol. 1: *Mainly Theory: Developments in Theory and Practice*. Routledge: London.

Bion, W.R. (1967) *Elements of Psychoanalysis*. Tavistock Publications: London.

Bion, W.R. (1970) *Attention and Interpretation*. Tavistock Publication: London.

Bohm, D. (1980) *Wholeness and the Implicate Order*. Routledge: London.

Bollas, C. (2008) *The Infinite Question*. Routledge: London.

Bollas, C. (2018) *The Shadow of the Object: Psychoanalysis of the Unthought Known*. 20th Anniversary Edition. Routledge: London.

Chapman, J. (2003) 'Hatred and corruption of task'. *Organisational and Social Dynamics*, 1, 40–60.

Chapman, J. (2021) 'Guarding against corruption'. *Socioanalysis*, 21, 35–53.

Chapman, J. and Long, S.D. (2009) 'Role contamination: Is the poison in the person or the bottle?' *Socioanalysis*, 11.

Chattopadhyay, G. (2019) 'The sixth basic assumption baPu (basic assumption purity/pollution)'. *Socioanalysis*, 21, 17–34.

Freud, S. (1921) *Group Psychology and the Analysis of the Ego. S.E.* Vol. XVIII, 65–144. London, Hogarth.

Grotstein, J.S. (2000) *Who Is the Dreamer. Who Dreams the Dream? A Study of Psychic Presences*. Routledge: New York.

Harre, R. (1984) 'Social elements as mind'. *British Journal of Medical Psychology*, 57, 127–135.

Harre, R. (1993) *Social Being*. Wiley-Blackwell: London.

Long, S.D. (2002) 'The internal team: A discussion of the socio-emotional dynamics of team (work)', in R. Weisner and B. Millett (eds.) *Human Resource Management: Contemporary Challenges and Future Direction*. An interactive digital book on CD-ROM. Wiley.

Long, S.D. (1992) *A Structural Analysis of Small Groups*. Routledge: London.

Long, S.D. (1996) 'Psychoanalysis, discourse and strange lists: These are a few of my favourite things'. Paper given at ISPSO Annual Meeting 1996.

Long, S.D. (2000) 'Conflict and co-operation: Two sides of the same coin', in R. Wiesner and B. Millet (eds.) *Current Issues in Organizational Behaviour*. Wiley.

Long, S.D. (2008) *The Perverse Organisation and its Deadly Sins*. Karnac: London.

Long, S.D. (ed.) (2013) *Socioanalytic Methods: Discovering the Hidden in Organisations and Social Systems*. Karnac: London.

Long, S.D. (ed.) (2016) *Transforming Experience in Organisations: A Framework for Organisational Research and Consultancy*. Karnac: London.

Long, S.D. (2018) 'The socioanalytic interview', in K. Stamenova and R. Hinshelwood (eds.) *Methods of Research into the Unconscious*. Routledge: London, pp. 43–54.

Long, S.D. and Harding, W. (2013) 'Socioanalytic interviewing', in S. Long (ed.) *Socioanalytic Methods*. Karnac: London, pp. 91–106.

Long, S.D., Penny, D., Gold, S. and Harding, W. (2010) 'A shared vision: Using action research for work culture change in a cardiology department', in J. Braithwaite, P. Hyde and C. Pope (eds.) *Culture and Climate in Healthcare Organizations*, pp. 163–173. Palgrave McMillan: London.

Menzies-Lyth, I.E.P. (1951) 'A case-study in the functioning of social systems as a defence against anxiety: A report on the study of the nursing service of a general hospital'. *Human Relations*, 13(2), 75–96.

Morgan, G. (1986) *Images of Organization*. Sage Publications: Thousand Oaks, CA.

Prins, S. (2006) 'The psychodynamic perspective in organizational research: Making sense of the dynamics of direction setting in emergent collaborative processes'. *Journal of Occupational and Organizational Psychology*, 79, 335–355.

Prins, S. (2010) 'From competition to collaboration: Critical challenges and dynamics in multiparty collaboration'. *The Journal of Applied Behavioral Science*, 46(3), 281–231.

Ruch, G. (2007) 'Reflective practice in contemporary child-care social work: The role of containment'. *The British Journal of Social Work*, 37(4), 659–680.

Sher, M. (2013) *The Dynamics of Change: Tavistock Approaches to Improving Social Systems*. Routledge: London.

Simpson, P. and French, R. (2006) 'Negative capability and the capacity to think in the present moment: Some implications for leadership practice'. *Leadership*, 2(2), 245–255.

Stamenova, K. and Hinshelwood, R. (eds.) (2018) *Methods of Research into the Unconscious*. Routledge: London

Symington, J. and Symington, N. (1996) *The Clinical Thinking of Wilfred Bion*. Routledge: London.

Winick, B. and Wexler, D. (2015) 'Drug treatment court: Therapeutic jurisprudence applied'. *Touro Law Review*, 18(3), Article 6.

Winnicott, D.W. (1996) *Through Pediatrics to Psychoanalysis: Collected Papers*. Routledge: London.

Chapter 11

Dancing Between the Contained and the Container and Their Reciprocal Relatedness in Group Relations

Richard Morgan-Jones

My Initiation into Group Relations Work

Example 1

I was introduced to group relations as a 16-year-old signing up for a weekly Tavistock group studying its own dynamics from experience. It ran weekly for a year during term time at an all-boys school. The group was an intervention to provide something humanising in a largely institutionalised world, shaped not least by the colonial and post-war legacy that middle class boys should become leaders of institutions at home and abroad. This cultural context carried all the risks of failures in emotional intelligence later described across political, governmental and commercial leadership and now connected with failures in emotional intelligence described as "Boarding School Syndrome" (Khaleelee, 2016, Schavarein, 2015). This experience opened up for me new possibilities for the emotional experience of belonging with others. It also placed me at odds with the cultural context in which I had been raised.

The effect of this group experience was life and career changing. It was also challenging. Who was I to dare to hold opinions when I dared to voice them? Deepening group inter-actions and the dance between mistrust and trust were transcended by something far more mysterious through the rise and fall of personal and collective authority being discovered and tested. I, along with others in the group, discovered what we were like in the minds of others, how we did and did not attract and impress. This opened up a whole new world of confiding and honest relating that was like finding a new country with a new language.

In this chapter, I am using the metaphor of a dance, because it represents movement along with others, contained by music that speaks through emerging bodily movements and improvisation. The music is larger than the people moving with or against each other. It was this mystery in the group that fascinated me – not least the rhythm of it, as we moved from sharing experiences, into fear and defensiveness and then heart-felt surprises. Vague sensations and then emotions arrived from somewhere, got expressed through words and stories. But then they moved on restlessly searching for deeper experience and meanings.

DOI: 10.4324/9781315146416-15

Later I discovered that such a metaphor could also be used to describe experience in psychoanalysis:

> INTERSPACE: "[I]n the happiest moments of analysis, one also plays with adults. By not worrying about generating meanings, there remains only one – but maybe the most important one of all – meaning without meaning, that of dance. A dance of colourful words. As Pound wrote, in order to be effective, poetry should be music and music – dance."
>
> (Civitarese, G., 2019: 57–58)

I later discovered through Bion's writing his description of the experience of belonging in a turbulent sea of emotions, which echoed my first group learning experience (Bion, 1997). These were alternately frightening, thrilling, deeply touching, anger inducing and alongside them the group provided a safety net where one could move between hiding and engaging, digesting and encountering. These moves evoked the sense of belonging to something much bigger than could be described as limited to myself. This was the heart of the dance of group relations experience. It was larger than us yet inside us. We chose what we contributed and yet something deeper and wider spoke through us that could move rapidly between the emotions of torment, joy and sorrow. Bion describes this not so much as insight but something deeper to be apprehended through intuition, namely, the drive for emotional truth about group relations, becoming, ultimate reality and the origin of things, for shorthand "O" (Bion, 1970).

Many future experiences in groups revealed that what seeks containment feels impossibly and forbiddingly bigger than any container of meanings that can be found. But then one is found. It provides a resting place of containing insight. However, this too proves to be transient, as insight becomes a familiar and easily outworn sort of knowing. So new avenues of risk and adventure must be sought, new experiences of deeper and wider truths. It is this reciprocity between the interpretation of collective transferences of emotion, and projective identification towards an eventually containing group and group consultant, that this chapter explores.

In sum, my first group experience provided four key learnings:

1) The possibility of finding words to express emotional experience in relation to others. Words could contain meanings which contained emotions. In the unfolding group, its members, including me, could speak words to describe what had been hitherto unconscious, that were so close to the experience of others, it was as if they had been "taken out of my mouth".

2) Similarly, the roles that people took in the group as leaders and led, initiators and followers, among many other roles, could be described and thought about. This could reflect particular group dynamics as well as revealing truths about how each of us was drawn emotionally to take or avoid such roles.

3) We began to dare questioning taken for granted contextual institutional dynamics and their impact on shared assumptions that could be understood and challenged.
4) The setting of the group itself, the room, the timings marked by the predictable arrival and departure of the consultant and the closed group membership. Each provided something conscious and planned, but also an unconscious and subliminal container of attention, for what was awaiting us.

Each of these as well as their inter-lacing insights opened the door to deeper experience that Bion described as transformations in knowledge T(K) (Bion, 1965). What propelled us forward as a group and indeed what had led me to sign up was the potential for encountering what was as yet unknowable. This was the unfathomable music I describe as shaping the dance of the group. It is this dance with its enveloping, yet detectable silent music that I suggest points towards working with what Bion describes as "Transformations in Ultimate Reality" T(O). Such an approach makes use of his guiding principle of negative capability, "…a capacity for staying in 'uncertainties, mysteries and doubts' and deferring attempts at logical or discursive sense-making" (Snell, 2013: 1, Bion, 1965, 1962, 1970).

Origins of Containment in Group Relations

The development of the study of group dynamics and in particular leadership, followership and authority, in wider organisations began with the Tavistock Institute for Human Relations' first Leicester University "Working Conference" in 1957. In its report, the idea of the need to contain tensions within a group is very clear. Writing about the deep emotional attachments to the Small Study Group and the challenges of moving to Application Groups, the authors of the conference report describe specific tensions:

> The Application Groups did not begin well. Conference members had become attached to their Study Groups and to the individuals with whom they had shared this engrossing, if stressful, experience… Such difficulties had been anticipated. They were, in fact, the kinds of stress which the Application Groups had been designed to mitigate. There are obvious advantages if such tensions can be contained and dealt with in a conference, rather than be left to arise later.
> (Trist & Sofer, 1957: 22)

Before Bion developed his thinking about the nature of psychotic experience and how it emerges in psychoanalytic consulting, he was pre-occupied with seeking to understand the primitive emotional dynamics across many life roles and experiences. These included his role as a leader and soldier in the First World War, an Army Psychiatrist and adviser in the selection of leaders in the Second World War, and a therapeutic community pioneer (Bion, 1982, 1985, 1991, Bion & Bion, 1997). This work culminates in his *Experiences in Groups* (Bion, 1961), where he explores the oscillation between effective working groups and basic assumption group life. Basic assumption dynamics explore the way groups seek to survive by clustering their emotionality around shared norms and behaviour. He observed how this dynamic detracted from individuals making their resources available to the practical tasks of collaboration in what he described as the work group, whereas basic assumption behaviour also involved members in losing their own capacity to think clearly (Morgan-Jones, 2022a).

To study group dynamics, Bion initiated leaderless groups to which he offered observations and consultation. This effectively allowed him to study how members could lose their minds to herd mentality (Trotter, 1916) and groupthink where mindless obedience to unspoken norms takes over the capacity of individuals to think for themselves (Tuckett, 2011). This work was initiated at the Tavistock Clinic, and later developed a tradition through the Tavistock Institute of Human Relations and other institutions internationally. The use of this model sought to help individuals to learn the dynamics of small and large groups, relations between groups, and of organisations as a whole in relation to wider societal forces.

The range of experiences from these different settings can foster learning about leadership and understanding what it means to take up a role. This includes discovering internal and external sources of authority for both leaders and followers. It means coming to realise the tendencies to be mobilised by peer pressure, or to volunteer unconsciously, for formal or informal roles, which may be either constructive or destructive. Within this 60-year-old field of developing practice and thinking, the idea of learning how we, and others, tend to construe situations we participate in demands emotional containment of the anxieties that underly them.

Learning Contextual Dynamics Through Failed Containment

Example 2

A key aspect of an initial Group Relations Conference, within an organisation in Russia, is the inter-group exercise. Using a translator in my role as director, I introduce the framework of the exercise, the rooms available, the way staff were distributed to consult to those who chose to come to a particular room. I describe the task of the event: "to offer the chance to learn about inter-group relations between the groups that members themselves formed in the event". It was also suggested that this could mean briefing different kinds of representatives authorised by the group to represent them and communicate across the boundaries of each group that formed. Such representatives might be messengers, observers or carry fuller authorisation, like plenipotentiaries used in diplomatic relations, with full powers to represent their group more freely and fully.

This outline was to most members a strange and vulnerable-making situation, with little similarity with working situations in Russia, where leaders are expected to dictate instructions rather than explore collaboration with more democratic negotiated representation. This had been anticipated to some extent, however encountering the emotional turmoil evoked by it had not. The introduction of this key group relations method created anxiety and a lot of urgent questions. Rather than work with these questions and their underlying anxiety, I as director responded to some, but then told the large group I felt they were beginning to work at the task and needed to do so with each other rather than with me, and that I was going to leave the room to go to the room in which I was to consult, leaving two colleagues to continue consulting to the membership as had been outlined.

This left some chaos, confusion and tensions. Some had experienced similar events before and wished to show their leadership ability by seeking some discussion about what groupings and themes could cluster people, whereas others were seeking answers to questions from a now absent authority in me as director, leading to them fleeing the room in search of a safer base.

The truth of the matter was that in my role as director, I was experienced as abandoning members to deal with these conflicts. In part this was not just about translation of words like authority and group meeting and representative, but whether it was allowed to speak of such things in a culture where authority meant doing what the government or business leaders said, not taking it for yourself or sharing it in negotiated ways with others. It took the rest of this event for these cultural differences to crystallise and be addressed, and for me as director to realise the depth of emotional abandonment where imposing leadership was absent, that was familiar in Russia. By enacting this abandonment and later in being able to recognise and own it in the final review session of the experience, it was possible to meet the deeper anxieties belonging to the wider cultural context that intruded under the skin of the conference and embedded itself in me as director.

By articulating this dynamic with the help and protest of members, it began to be possible to explore the challenges of the aspiration to invite Western group relations "experts" into the Russian context, but also to explore how those so-called experts needed educating by immersion to discover how learning about group dynamics could begin to be managed. This experience was a painful and confusing one, but also an educating experience for the director, staff and members.

Through such an experience the consultant becomes implicated in the experience in ways that reveal the vulnerability of all in the encounter. For Ed Shapiro, this becomes the hallmark of authority relations in creating learning opportunities, a key idea in group relations consulting:

> …authority is not just a feared boundary to be avoided, but also a longed-for boundary with inevitable vulnerability on both sides. The mutual vulnerability of the authority boundary, a deepening of the… theme of interdependency,

[with…] the wish of the next generation to take up the reins, the wish of the elders to pass on what they have learned, the shared anxiety about death, the embarrassment of needing, the rage about dependency, and the envy and longing in both directions all factored into this vulnerability.

(Shapiro, 2020, p. 79)

The question that now arises is: what moves can be developed in the mutual bond of difference in a way that can become generative?

Range of Reciprocity Across Container-Contained and Beyond

The container/contained model as a theoretical description is a constant companion in seeking for interpretation, sense and meaning. And yet it is also totally inadequate in describing the larger field of the "dance-floor" and the music within which it coheres. It was this experience that led me later to explore what Bion himself described using the analogy of a spectrum. He suggested that the visible nature of container and contained was available for words to describe across the spectrum of visible colouring of familiar interpretations, but in no way did justice to the infrared and ultra-violet ends of the wavelength beyond visible colours (Bion, 1977).

This is what led me to explore two wider and deeper dimensions of "contained/container", upstream from the focus on group dynamics:

1) At one end of the spectrum, part of transcendent experience Bion explored (see Bion, 1961, Ch. 5) included truths about shared political, organisational and social context. It might also include history, beliefs and culture. These dimensions add not just metaphors, characters and identifications, but links to the wider fields in which people are unconsciously players. These are at the heart of roles in the community inspired by group relations work, that after a conference experience, members might apply themselves to or innovate. It was with this focus that Turquet prepared his group relations conference staff.

2) At the other end, truth was to be found at the level of sensation bound embodiment. Such experience of sensations that have not yet become clear emotions could be overwhelming without the support of staff with whom to think it through exercising the patience of negative capability. Bion first described this sensational overwhelm as stemming from the protomental matrix where "what is physical and what mental cannot be distinguished" (Bion, 1962: 102; see also Morgan-Jones, 2010). Initially for Bion (1961) this was a group phenomenon, where the sense of belonging to an emotionally supported group dynamics to which a person was drawn he described as like a chemical valency. In later writing he described sensation-bound experience as proto-emotional beta-elements, seeking maternal reverie and attention and eventual understanding through verbal formulations he described as a containing alpha function accessed through reverie (Bion, 1963).

Moving across these dimensions as resources for learning from experience, as well as including the dimension of the context shaping experience demands, focused the need to isolate each of these elements and only then to see how they might connect. In order to explore this aspect of what I have described as a dance, I now want to describe a practical design to develop understandings across three distinct domains while being open to reflecting on experience and what shapes it, within a complex force field.

The Trilogy Matrix

To reflect on such dynamics in a group relations conference, I developed whole conference plenary reflection sessions where three sub-groups, meeting in con-centric circles, each reflect on their experience at different levels. Each circle, observed by the others, works one at a time. The inner circle focuses on the experiences of moving between sensations to feeling to social roles observed or taken during the conference. The second reflects on group and system dynamics they were part of. The third associates to wider cultural or political dynamics revealed across conference dynamics. People are asked to make links between what is voiced by each circle and to note the force field pressures from one circle upon another.

This "trilogy matrix" provides a resource for investigating the dynamics of a conference setting as well as in other organisational engagement in learning from experience. It provides a framework for thinking about present time consultations within self-study groups that seek to move with the dance between these differ-ent dimensions (Morgan-Jones, 2022a). Its three perspectives also echo the tripar-tite dimensions of group-analysis described by Carla Penna and Earl Hopper and others as: personal, inter-personal and trans-personal (Hopper & Weinberg, 2021; Morgan-Jones, 2023; Penna, 2023).

The following example illustrates the way interpretations of the aggressive and sexualised nature of a shared basic assumption provide containment as a defence against the pain of intrusive suffering embodied in Russian women's experience of traumatic loss, down the generations. Its loud and defensive sexualised/aggressive rhythms are followed by quieter music.

Example 3

The group unfolded through what appeared to be friendly but competitive aggres-sion between pairs, often cross-gender. Once a speaker began, they would not give way to the person singled out to address. This partner would then seize the lead and give a similarly lengthy speech, seeming unwilling to let go of holding the floor. On one occasion a male member just screamed across the room to gain impact and shut the other up. This expression of aggression and competition across difference conceals the confusing experience of being confronted with the threat of anarchy resulting from there being no overt management leadership. Meanwhile the challenge of the task remained, to learn from this experience.

As consultant I intervened, seeking to provide a container for wilder emotions and sensations before any reflective thinking could occur. I suggested that people seem to talk at each other and not much listening and linking to each other; I then suggest that the silenced members might have a better idea what was going on from their passive observations and that these divided off sub-groups represented missed opportunities and a resource for learning.

One younger female member expressed her pain, through her tears, of feeling bombarded by noise. She had seemed particularly attentive, picking up everything, and at last the group was able to listen to deeper sensations and feelings, not so far represented in the exchanges. She had been providing the sensation based and emotional container for the suffering of failed dependency within the group. Her intervention and the silent respectful attention of the group seem to change the emotional group culture for a while with more reflective contributions. One key learning was about the contrast between the "noise" of competitive leading-seeking-recognition versus listening to painful words about the experience of being dominated and silenced. The consultant refers to the traumatising masculine Russian history and Russian leadership styles and the suffering of women passed down the generations. Meanwhile absent men had been lost to war or deported to camps through the trauma of the Gulags and the Patriotic War (1939–1945) whose privations and losses were carried down the generations by often silenced women.

The sensation-bound noise awaiting transformation into emotion and suffering became a key first step towards containment and learning. This enabled the subsequent step of finding meaning through the uncontained sensation of "noise" seeking a container. This eventually led to understanding external forces of trauma and impingement that had been unconsciously introjected and embodied in the group dynamic. In describing this interplay between the group that is patient and analyst, Ogden describes how:

> Debussy felt that the music was the space between the notes... Between the notes of the spoken words constituting the analytic dialogue are the reveries of the analyst and the analysand. It is in this space occupied by the interplay of reveries that one finds the music of psychoanalysis.
>
> (Ogden, 1997)

In group relations, this could be described as a two-step model of containment. First, embodied emotion is expressed and attended to so that feelings that lie beyond sensation can be expressed. Second, the emotion and its pain can be understood as not just an expression of the group dynamic, but an enactment of something larger from the context of societal history and culture. This theme was also revealed during the online Russian small study group during the Covid-19 pandemic.

Example 4

Despite the growing familiarity of members with online working, the group is disrupted by occasional technical difficulties as well as by intrusions from other family in home-base settings necessitated by the pandemic. The effort of concentrating and the subliminal anxiety familiar to online screen working makes cueing and turn taking a constant challenge and adds to feelings of discontinuity, disaffection and exclusion. Members speak of not knowing whether they are seen looking at others as would normally happen in exchanges of glances in a meeting in a room. This adds to the dynamics of managing the domestic privacy boundary to which members are exposed working from home and along with it a group feeling of being disembodied.

This disembodied element exacerbates the dynamics of exhibitionism and voyeurism that are an ordinary aspect of the narcissistic trauma of group membership. Turquet wrote about the struggle of being in a large group where to gain a feeling of belonging, individuality has to be sacrificed in becoming a Membership Individual (Turquet, 1975). By contrast he suggested that retaining personal authority while taking up a role of leadership that makes a difference means becoming an Individual Member. Increasingly and especially in online study groups, I believe this large group dynamic creeps into smaller groups. In this sense one can oscillate between being very important to others and of feeling excluded and of no significance in a very short time. It is as if this small study group is expressing dynamics usually belonging to large group experience.

These dynamics add the fear of uncertainty due to the pandemic in the Russian context due to lack of trust about the accuracy, reporting and management of health issues. One meeting coincides with the referendum about constitutional changes that will extend the Russian presidential term indefinitely. The group is divided between those vehemently against it and others, outsiders, represented by in-laws, wanting the secure leadership that such continuity promises. Such a view is characterised as providing a defence against the fears of anarchy that appears as the alternative Russians have experienced since the 1989 collapse of the USSR.

The consultant points to the displacement onto political leadership of uncontained frustrations with the management of this event with its distancing of intimacy and trust building. Could this consultant be like the President inflicting omnipotently a context that is disruptive and power seeking through studying group dynamics online?

These contextual dynamics of mistrust in political leadership cross the skin of the group from its political context, along with fears around the pandemic and uncertainty about whether and when any "normal" life will return.

One member switches rooms at home which moves his image to a new position on members' screens. This creates sudden instability and a perception of the physical setting being radically disrupted creating what one member described as hallucination. This she communicates excitedly speaking Russian rather than the English in which the group has been working. The emotional thrill of aliveness and fear is eventually translated, but not before the consultant has picked up the excitement of transgression in establishing a Russian speaking group culture as an act of rebellion against what is felt to be the dominating leadership of the group consultant from a foreign culture and language. This became the focus for a consultation and seemed to open up more sober reflection on the anxieties colliding at this moment.

The Dance Between Container and Contained: Transcending the Caesura Beyond Negative Capability

A caesura is the beat between notes in a piece of music. It is the pause as breath is emptied, before the lungs are once again filled. It is comparable to Winnicott's urging of the importance for feeding mothers of hesitating before a feed to ensure the feed is not an over stimulating impingement, but rather related to the timing of the growing hunger of the baby to enhance their sense of their own need and instinct (Winnicott, 1941).

The hallmark of the metaphor of the caesura for Bion was birth as a liminal moment between life within the womb and without. For him this becomes the metaphor for giving birth to new and wild thoughts searching for a thinker to give them life. It is this idea that is the fulfilment of his earlier notion of negative capability, which through waiting patiently for meaning and sense to cohere provides the means of creativity. It is with his development of this idea into the caesura that his method of working takes on a new lease of life.

Caesura is his term to describe the in-betweenness across the terms he chooses to use. Whether it is container/contained, conscious/unconscious, dream-life/waking-life, pre-/post-natal, it is the "/" that interests him most:

> Can any method of communication be sufficiently "penetrating" to pass the caesura in the direction from post-natal conscious thought back to the pre-mental in which thoughts and ideas have their counterpart in "times" or "levels" of mind where they are not thoughts or ideas? That penetration has to be effective in either direction.
>
> (Bion, 1977, p. 45)

A Group Pauses to Take Breath

Example 5

An online Small Study Group meet to learn group dynamics from present time experience. The online setting, and group membership, is drawn from consultants aspiring to become more effective with their own clients. The early period of the group includes many projections of expectation upon the group consultant whom they fear will be judging them both personally and professionally. This phantasy is elaborated: that I am like a Russian president controlling them with invisible judgements or even sanctions; that I have a hidden curriculum of standards they have to demonstrate; or that I will condemn them for their acting out through one member's delinquent drug taking; or else for failing to find a private place in their households from which to join the group. Eventually, this series of phantasies appears to subside.

There is a pause in the hitherto continuous stream of contributions and exchanges. Across a single session, one member puts her head on her hands on her desk in front of her laptop screen; one is joined by a child in nappies seeking, or maybe giving comfort, while another moves rooms between sessions to seek better privacy and comfort. The exchanges stop for a moment and it is as if the group has given a deep intake of breath and sighs it out. These observations, I suggest to the group, are a regression at the relief at not having to try so hard to please a demanding judge or intrusive political regime. Later I point to the anxiety that the group does not know how to find a new set of rules beyond the imagined fear-ridden dependency they have been living under as a familiar establishment or order.

In consequence, a member of the group feels able to trust the group with her experience in a war zone in another country, determined not to die underground in a bomb shelter but to face the risk in the open. Her vulnerability and openness to risk transforms the emotional atmosphere in the group and elicits other more personal emotional responses giving the possibility of vitality to the lived experience of being in the group beyond the fear of being shamed to death.

This could be seen as an "In-between moment". The confiding member chose life over dying with her un-lived life unborn, entombed in the womb of the shelter. It could also be seen as the moment when the group knew it had been born and could live independently in its own skin, with members becoming able to take authority for shaping the group through their own initiatives, through aspects of their own painful and joyful lived stories and through reflection on roles taken and evoked by the group interaction. To that extent this group moment was analogous of the first breath taken as the baby emerges from the womb and therefore as a moment of psychological and emotional birth (Mahler, Pine & Bergman, 1975). This echoes what Bion wished to explore with his concept of the caesura between pre- and post-natal experience in his work on the caesura represented through characters in conversation in his autobiographical *Memoir of the Future* (Bion, 1991). The recovered memory moved the group emotionally and can be seen to represent the development of a shared authority for seizing life and developing one's own meaning and imperative rather than suffering under that of others.

For Bion's commentator Giuseppe Civitarese, such in-betweenness is at the heart of Bion's method: "'Transcending' the caesuras that redraw the boundaries of settled thought is the only truly general, conscious and strategic criterion... that inspires Bion's thought" (Civitarese, 2013).

Concluding Implications for Group Relations Practice

How Can Group Relations Practice Be Stretched?

Learning from group relations experience has the potential for the reciprocity of the relationship between contained and container to be extended further in three important directions:

1) In one direction it is possible to explore what Bion described as the protomental matrix beneath basic assumption activity and from which it arises. Containment of sensations and rhythms becoming emotions needs to come prior to group-as-a-whole interpretations of basic assumptions.
2) In another direction, it is possible to explore the way the context and socio-political environment impinges, shapes and makes its presence felt across the external skin (Anzieu, 1989).
3) Exploring where these wider and deeper projective forces in the field meet in group dynamics and how emerging emotional containment for them can be innovated in a well-paced rhythm is the task of consulting to groups. These I have described along with a methodology for exploring such unconscious fields as a trilogy matrix.

Opportunities and Limitations of the Online Container for Group Relations Work?

Review of experiences of online experiential learning with participants suggests that while such events create many possibilities for learning, there are limitations in comparison to face-to-face events.

Online work enables international meetings at less cost financially and to the environment. The possibilities for learning and development include members using the experience to express and develop phantasies about the group, the consultant, and the wider context, to explore the taking of roles in leadership and followership and in sharing moments of profound personal experience in the here and now that evoke genuine and group-shaping emotional engagement that enhance learning about authority relations.

However, limitations include vital elements worth further exploration. One ethical question is: "Is it safe?" Experience of running online self-study groups suggests that the regressions that are part of deep conference learning and personal and collective transformation cannot be contained by a wider system without face-to-face contact and engagement where non-verbal cues are more naturally available and provide visual containment not available on screen. This limitation in being able to work with the emergence of embodied protomental experience restricts learning about group dynamics at deeper levels and risks failing to provide emotional containment for any regressions that might be provoked. My provisional conclusion is that the defences of dissociation and the network of pre-existing professional networks therefore have to carry the burden of this containing and regulating dimension as a means of inhibiting the risk of emotional casualties.

In Sum

In this chapter I have argued that for such work to be developed, the consultant has to listen to and search with deepening intuition for the call of unknown and unknowable dimensions of present time experience coalescing in emotional embodiment from multiple directions. I have described it as the dance between the reciprocity of the contained seeking a container accompanied by unheard rhythms and music. This search and the exploration of the dance between contained and container and their accompanying music is caught in Eliot's Four Quartets (1942).

This chapter has benefited from the suggestions by the editors of this book as well as by Megan Kolano, Angela Foster, Gerard van Reekum, Robert Snell and Jolita Buzaityte-Kasalyniene. I am also grateful to members of the conferences, workshops and study groups in Moscow and beyond who have contributed so much to this chapter and my thinking, and prior to them Brian J. Thorne who took the first Bion group in which I participated and so launched my career.

References

Anzieu, D. (1989). *The Skin Ego*. New York: Yale University Press.
Bion, W.R. (1961). *Experiences in Groups*. London: Tavistock.
Bion, W.R. (1962). *Learning from Experience*. London: Karnac (1984).
Bion, W.R. (1963). *Elements of Psychoanalysis*. London: Karnac (1984).
Bion, W.R. (1965). *Transformations*. London: Karnac (1984).
Bion, W.R. (1970). *Attention and Interpretation*. London: Karnac (1986).
Bion, W.R. (1977). *Two Papers: The Grid and the Caesura*. London: Karnac (1989).
Bion, W.R. (1982). *The Long Week-End, 1897–1919: Part of a Life*. Abingdon: Fleetwood Press.
Bion, W.R. (1985). *All My Sins Remembered: Another Part of a Life and the Other Side of Genius: Family Letters*. London: Karnac.
Bion, W.R. (1991). *A Memoir of the Future*. London: Karnac.
Bion, W.R. (1997). *Taming Wild Thoughts*. London: Karnac.
Bion, W.R. & Bion, F. (eds) (1997). *War Memoirs: 1917–1919*. London: Karnac.
Civitarese, G. (2013). *The Violence of Emotions Bion and Post-Bionian Psychoanalysis* (The New Library of Psychoanalysis). London: Routledge.
Civitarese, G. (2019). *An Apocryphal Dictionary of Psychoanalysis*. London: Routledge.
Eliot, T.S. (1942). Burnt Norton: The Four Quartets. In *The Complete Poems and Plays of T.S. Eliot*. London: Faber & Faber (1969).
Hopper, E. & Weinberg, H. (2021). *The Social Unconscious in Persons, Groups and Societies: Clinical Implications*, Vol. 4. London: Routledge.
Khaleelee, O. (2016). Boarding school, Brexit, and our leaders' judgement. *Organ. Soc. Dyn.*, 16(2): 271–276.
Mahler, M.S., Pine, F. and Bergman, A. (1975). *The Psychological Birth of the Human Infant: Symbiosis and Individuation*. London: Hutchinson.
Morgan-Jones, R.J. (2010). *The Body of the Organisation and Its Health*. London: Karnac.

Morgan-Jones, R.J. (2022a). Ranging across Tavistock approaches to consulting with teams and organisations: A history, an inventory of key concepts, and links to key organisations. *Organisational & Social Dynamics*, 22(2), 187–204.

Morgan-Jones, R.J. (2022b). The trilogy matrix event: A new practice for the study of group and organisational dynamics. *Socioanalysis*, 23: 41–60.

Morgan-Jones, R.J. (2023). The Trilogy Matrix Event (TME): A setting for collective reflection on social system dynamics of the tripartite matrix. In E. Hopper (Ed.), *The Tripartite Matrix in Developing Theory and Expanding Practice of Group Analysis: The Social Unconscious in Persons, Groups and Societies*. London: Routledge.

Ogden, T. (1997). *Reverie and Interpretation*. London: Karnac.

Penna, C. (2023). *From Crowd Psychology to the Dynamics of Large Groups: Historical, Theoretical and Practical Considerations*. London: Routledge.

Schavarein, J. (2015). *Boarding School Syndrome: The Psychological Trauma of the "Privileged" Child*. New York: Routledge.

Shapiro, E.R. (2020). *Finding a Place to Stand: Developing Self-reflective Institutions, Leaders and Citizens*. Bicester: Phoenix.

Snell, R. (2013). *Uncertainties, Mysteries and Doubts: Romanticism and the Analytic Attitude*. London: Routledge.

Trist, E.L. & Sofer, C. (1957). *Exploration in Group Relations*. Leicester: Leicester University Press.

Trotter, W. (1916). *Instincts of the Herd in Peace and War*. London: T. Fisher Unwin.

Tuckett, D. (2011). *Minding the Markets: An Emotional Finance View of the Financial Markets*. London: Palgrave.

Turquet, P. (1975). Threats to identity in the large group. In L. Kreeger (Ed.), *The Large Group: Dynamics and Therapy*. London: Constable.

Winnicott, D.W. (1941). Observation of infants in the set situation. *IJPA*, 22: 229.

Chapter 12

Leadership and Containment

Stanley Gold

Introduction

What constitutes leadership?

> La reponse est le malheur de la question. The answer is the misfortune or disease of curiosity – it kills it.
>
> (Maurice Blanchot/Bion 1978, pp. 21–22)

To move first, as it were, into the "real" world, what are the qualities of leadership and the relationship to the quality of containment? There are some more qualified to say, especially those who have made a study of it (Kernberg 1979; Krantz 1990; Hirschorn 1990; Alford 2001; Amado & Elsner 2007; Simpson & French 2005; Stein & Allcorn 2014). It does seem however, that apart from individual qualities, context is important, at least in terms of personal experience and a history of past success in the current or related fields. This is despite the fact that he/she might move from the CEO of a telecommunications company and reappear at the helm of a bank or hospital.

Krantz (2015, p. 8) points to the vast industry which has grown up, "funding, training, developing, and supporting leaders", with business schools centred on turning out leaders via endless seminars, speeches and books offered by "experts". Despite this, he concludes that "no personality nor personal traits exist that can reliably predict who will become an effective leader" (Krantz 2015, pp. 9–10). However "a key learning function", is the leadership capacity, at all levels, to "contain" anxiety, "which erodes the capacity for creative action" (Krantz 2015, p. 21). Containment which keeps in mind the complexities, the connection of work to larger purposes, and by retaining the task in mind and in helping co-workers to remain connected to it (Krantz 2020).

A leader cannot be appropriately criticised unless he/she has not delivered what was promised by them, rather than expected by others, in the same way that psychoanalysis cannot be criticised for not being scientific, any more than that it is not religious or not artistic. The question is, as Bion suggests, is it psychoanalysis? (1970, p. 62). The issue here becomes, has the leader delivered what they said

DOI: 10.4324/9781315146416-16

they would? This is despite the current practice of awarding performance bonuses even in the absence of performance. In the context of this chapter, and as Krantz describes, what is highly relevant is whether or not there is also a capacity for containment and an understanding of its link to performance.

So I am attracted to a more general description. The qualities might include accountability and perhaps responsibility depending on the degree of "hands on" activities. Vision, resilience, integrity and even a dash of humility. Inspirational perhaps, in the capacity to lead others to engage in tasks that they have thought beyond them. Whilst a drive to succeed may be as much a danger as an asset, there is the ineffable quality of "charisma". I am drawn to Bion's description of the Genius, akin to madness perhaps, but, as he proposes, if there are "psychotic" mechanisms, there is "the capacity to manipulate them in a manner which promotes growth or life" (1970, p. 63). Whatever else may be involved, leadership must include containment. But what are its qualities?

What Is a Container?

"The essential thing is to give as much help as you can, because they are the people who don't know what they are up to" (Bion 1978, p. 12). Bion is, I believe, referring to the central role of unconscious processes.

To my mind, a capacity to "manage" unconscious processes is the central quality. That capacity is, as I see it, central to Bion's (1961) understanding of the development of thinking, and of the group, both of which are nascent but where the consequences of enactment are perhaps not yet fully understood or practiced (Bridger, 2005). Bion (1961) describes the inability of the establishment to tolerate his changes, and Bridger's account chronicles Bion's apparent inability take their inability into account. Containment was mutually lacking.

There can be little argument that Bion's early work (1961) has had a far-reaching influence on our understanding of small and large group behaviour. But can we do the same with his more complex findings on the development of thought, it's mode of transmission and the vicissitudes which accompany it. This carries with it the assertion that his theoretical framework, essentially aimed at the psychoanalyst and about the psychoanalytic process, can be extrapolated to other situations and roles.

Can this apply in the present context? I believe it can, and Bion would seem to agree. "I am sick and tired of hearing psycho-Analytic theories – if they don't remind me of real life, they are no use to me" (Bion 1978, p. 44).

The Group in the Leader

As Hinshelwood has cautioned, "having a mind is not easy and his [Bion's] contributions add considerably to the debate about what it is to have a mind" To this he adds "the problem (is) of having a mind that is aware of minds" (Hinchelwood, 2003, p. 181). Having a mind, he later comments, "implies dealing in meanings, not information" (p. 184).

To complicate matters further, to focus on the individual leader may be an over-simplification. As Norman Brown (1966, pp. 146–147) comments, "The existence of the 'let's pretend' boundary does not prevent the continuance of the real traffic across it. Projection and introjection, the process whereby the 'self', as distinct from the other is constituted, is not past history… but a present process of continuous creation… there is a continuous unconscious wandering of other personalities into ourselves."

Jean Paul Sartre (1943) in his philosophical work, *Being and Nothingness*, writes in his chapter on the first attitude towards others, "Everything which may be said of me and my relations with the other applies to him as well. While I attempt to free myself from the hold of the other, the other seeks to enslave me. We are by no means dealing with unilateral relations with an object in itself, but with reciprocal and moving relations". Later he goes on to say, "I am possessed by the other. The other's look fashions my body in its nakedness, causes it to be born, sculpture it, produces it as it is, sees it as I shall never see it. The other holds a secret – the secret of what I am" (pp. 471–774).

Anticipating Klein's (1946) concept of projective identification by some three years, these very insightful philosophical problems are inherent in all consultant work, the consultant as "leader", challenged to maintain the integrity of his or her own personality, whilst absorbing himself in the structure and function of the organisation which has arranged his/her presence.

Regression in the Leader

The effectiveness and sanity of the individual resides in their capacity to know the difference between what is going on inside of them, and their perception of the structure, function and influence of the outside world upon them. No less important is the capacity to have a clear view of the boundary between the two experiences (Rosenfeld, 1965). The use of projection blurs this boundary and distorts reality, allowing pathological internal processes to remain unchanged.

The particular problem faced in leadership is that of knowing and retaining one's own identity while attempting to enter into constructive relationship with the group. This task requires a limitation in the extent to which the "self" is disturbed by stimuli from the external world and the internal feelings that they arouse, whilst retaining a relationship with the group, a task which requires retaining constant interaction with it. As the group increases in size, the possibility of having a shared internal picture of relationships within the group diminishes.

Main (1975) implies that regression in leaders of any kind may activate the intra-psychic object relations in the subsequent interpersonal relations of the staff, i.e. the existing staff. The leader may induce in his social field the re-enactment of the conflict which is initiated within his own intra-psychic world. Who is the recipient of whose projections? Bion (2018, p. 87) asks: "Is it possible that we can organise ourselves into communities… institutions in order to defend ourselves against the invasion of ideas which come from outer space, and also from inner space?"

Although, as mentioned above, most of Bion's influential papers and presentations were directed toward the psychoanalyst and the psychoanalytic process itself, I feel it is legitimate to transpose many of his propositions to the role of containing leader experienced as maternal object, with all of the pressure to understand and perform in a manner which enhances both the growth of the individual(s) in his/her care, and also the family/group/organisation for which he has been made responsible.

As for Bion himself, the leader/container, based on the maternal object, must remain highly sensitive to and receptive of any thoughts and ideas "looking for a mind to lodge in… however familiar he might think he was with previous experience" (Bion 1981, p. 1). It underlines the crucial role of curiosity in leadership, and links to the difference between transformations in K, knowing "about" something, a kind of intellectual knowledge, and "transformations in O, the experience of deep change, mental growth and insight" (Bion 1970, pp. 26–40). The difference in leadership style, development and results is self-evident. As is the capacity to judge the confluence or otherwise of L (love), H (hate) and K (knowledge) in any communications, with the emphasis on the latter (Sandler 2003).

This moves it beyond Lawrence's view that "the leader is pushed into a Totalitarian way of thinking, because he is there to take care of the anxiety feelings of the employees by sure and decisive leadership" (Lawrence 2005, p. 61).

We are in the area of the importance of the epistemophilic instinct of Klein (1931), and the "engagement with the not already known" (Fairbairn 1943). Otherwise, as Bion asks, "If there are not two very frightened people in the room, why are we spending so much time discovering what we already know?" (Bion 1990, p. 5). He is not, I believe, dismissing the value of past experience, any more than he dismisses the relevance of past memory, but is emphasising the originality and danger of the future. In this, as Segal has identified, There "should be a constant oscillation between normal, paranoid/schizoid position… a state of patience… similar to maternal reverie – and that of the depressive position, in which elements cohere and give a state which he calls security" (Segal 1981, p. 10). Or to put it another way, leaders should have some narcissism and paranoia, but not too much of either (Kernberg 1971, personal communication).

Leadership, Containment and the Capacity for Thought

I will take two of Bion's original thoughts, emphasised by Grotstein (2003). First that "schizophrenics, as infants were deprived of the experience of having a mother who was willing and able to tolerate (contain) her infant's experience of dread" (Grotstein 2003, p. 11) and "there is… a necessity for the infant to tolerate frustration long enough to be able to encode his/her raw sense impressions into alpha thoughts. In the meanwhile, the infant's mother must employ her alpha function to accept, tolerate, and 'translate' (into meaning) her infant's raw sense impressions". Later on he observes that he/she "becomes a 'thinker' once they can project their wild thoughts into this now internalised maternal container" (p. 11). Bion emphasises the centrality of the above, with his "pictorial" representations of the mother/child relationship and the emergence of thought or its alternative, projective identification (Bion 2013, p. 36). The leader as maternal container? Perhaps not too wild a thought.

Thus, a capacity for containment and the conjunction between container and contained sits at the very centre of Bion's understanding of the development of the capacity for thinking and the relationships both between individuals and within groups. The paradigm he adopts, which fits well with a leadership role, incorporates the infant's connection to the maternal object, either adequate, fostering the development of an apparatus fostering thoughts available for thinking and dreaming, or inadequate, due to the absence of "reverie" in the Mother and fostering the only alternative, protective identification, a vehicle certainly of communication, but also of control and suitable only for a forced evacuation of unwanted aspects of the self (Bion 1967, p. 116). I am talking here of scapegoating (Gold 2014), with all of it's internal, organisational and national examples, with ramifications internationally (Gold 2016).

The Leader and the Group

Bion emphasises that the individual, including the "leader" cannot "help being a member of a group... at war, both with the group and with those aspects of his personality that constitute his 'groupishness'" (Bion 1961, p. 131). The responsibility of the leader therefore includes managing the dynamic of the group as such, whilst acknowledging that "a collection of people in a room, adds nothing to the individual... it merely reveals something that is not otherwise visible" (Bion 1961, p. 134).

To the question, Does the answer lie in the group? Bion responded, "I think it is a convenient idea because it restricts the area of search". To the question, Do you believe that a group has an unconscious? Bion responded, "I wouldn't want to abandon that idea; nor would I want it to obscure the discovery of what else the group has" (Bion 1978, pp. 22/23).

One has only to read Bion's *Experiences in Groups*, to understand that he is, above all else, describing the leader's experience, particularly of the defence against learning from experience, and the temptation to fulfil the phantasy that he is a magician or should "act like one" (p. 84). But as Meltzer suggests, what is needed from an experienced officer is one who is afraid of neither the hatred nor the love of his troops (Meltzer 1981, p. 18).

R.D. Laing (1970, p. 1) wrote:

They are playing a game. They are playing at not playing a game. If I show them I see they are, I shall break the rules and they will punish me. I must play their game, of not seeing I see the game.

(p. 1)

What is this game? I believe it is the politics of survival in small and particularly large group settings. There is a significant correspondence between the mental content of psychotic patients and the unconscious content and process of groups and organisations composed of "normals" (Skolnik 1998).

Organisations and large groups of any kind, by their very nature and their primary task, arouse fears of catastrophic change. "They fear for their survival, organisationally and individually. As they experience a radical break or cleavage from all that is past" (Lawrence & Armstrong 1998, p. 62). The new leader, the new idea, "always disruptive of accepted routines or assumptions threatens, as I see it, the return of chaos, the return of the repressed, of breakdown, of the myths and experiences that are transmitted trans-generationally or genetically. The chaos of remembered primitive individual, familial or tribal life" (Gold 2006, p. 91). The breakdown which has already occurred (Winnicott 1974). All of which revives the view that "Bion was wrong to abandon instinct as an influence" (Miller 1998, p. 40). He goes on to say that "there are good arguments to support the bio-genetic explanations of groupishness, which would have implications to the very theory of group, organisational and even societal behavior. The reformulation in no way diminishes but even broadens the significance and relevance of Bion's discoveries".

It follows that leadership must include a recognition of the threat of breakdown and particularly of that associated with change in the group (Bion 1977). Change which may or may not be destructive of existing rules, relationships, conventions and culture, or of the intra-group functioning and liaisons, but which is always disruptive of them, reflected in a commensal, symbiotic or parasitic focus of the relationship (Bion 1970, p. 78). Coming closer to the responsibilities of leadership, Grinberg (1975) summarised the vicissitudes of catastrophic change, the term used by Bion (1970), in connection with any new idea that contains a potentially disruptive force that violates to a greater or lesser extent the field in which it occurs. The leader as container of catastrophic anxieties associated with change. Certainly a challenge of leadership, and perhaps one that involves not containment so much as holding.

Bion's development of the concept of the work group and its alternatives, dependency, pairing and flight/fight (1961, pp. 144–151), names first that the group "is met in order to be sustained by a leader on whom it depends for nourishment... and protection" (1961, p. 147). But accepting this role may call on the leader to manage the feeling of being manipulated so as to be playing a part... in someone else's phantasy" (p. 149). He advises that the analyst/leader must develop the capacity to "shake oneself out of the numbing feeling of reality" (p. 149). Perhaps the most dangerous temptation is to feed the idea that the group has met to fight something or to run away from it – the fight-flight group, where the leader's demands on the group provide incentive for fight or aggression. Whilst there may be a distinction then between basic assumption and task leadership, the instinctive nature of this and other basic assumption groups, instantaneous and sudden, demands containment. Bion's own musings that the three states of mind have resemblances to each other, that led him to suppose that they may not be fundamental phenomena, is a concept which I have also explored (Gold 2006).

At what stage and at what level is there a need for the leader to abrogate him/herself to the needs of the "other", the led, ensuring confidence and growth, and when is the leader influenced by a deeper, more unconscious and basic crisis in the organisation? This may include the positive and developmental role of ruthlessness in the infant/mother dyad (Winnicott 1989). The "legitimate" use, including the ruthless exploitation of the other. Seen from the vertex of development, ruthlessness is within the norm. This necessitates a leader who can tolerate (contain) the experience. If not, the "led" can only hide his ruthless self/need, fearing disintegration, abandonment or becoming the subject of such attacks himself. It is surely a dilemma for the leader. To contain the attacks, criticism, complaints and clear competition in order to encourage the developmental needs of the "other".

The containing task for the leader in such circumstances lies in his recognition of survival mechanisms. The "going on being" of the group which, with change, is threatened with extinction. A constant struggle between development and destruction and the anxieties which accompany it and which must be recognised and contained.

The Leader as Mystic

Bion remarked that "An emotional experience cannot be conceived in isolation from a relationship" (Bion 1962, p. 42). Winnicott agreed, that "there is no such thing as a baby. If you set out to describe a baby, you will find you are describing a baby and someone else" (1987, p. 85). In the present context it can meaningfully be reversed. That is, a relationship cannot be conceived in isolation from an emotional experience. That might well include the messianic hope that an idea or a person who holds that idea "will save the group from its feelings of hatred, destructiveness or despair" (Grinberg 1975, p. 17).

Bion sets the tone. "The group needs to preserve its coherence and identity; efforts to do so are manifested in conventions, laws, culture, and language. It also needs the exceptional individual and therefore needs to make provision for the exceptional individual" (Bion 1970, p. 63). The "exceptional individual", as Bion says, may be genius, messiah or mystic and in his contract and behaviour, may declare him/herself to be essentially a revolutionary "or he may claim that his function is to fulfil the laws, conventions and destiny of his group" (Bion 1970, p. 64).

Declaring oneself may be expected and even necessary for the group, but limits the leader's capacity to grasp, and contain, the coincident anxieties of the group, represented in concretised expectations to allay them (Menzies Lyth, 1970). It also negates the need – perhaps one among many, but nevertheless – of the group to examine the health of the community as such (Hinshelwood 1979).

How to manage the expectations of the group and of oneself, in short to put aside "Memory and Desire" from both vertices, may be the single most daunting task of containment for the (new) leader. As Bion puts it, "memory is a dwelling on the unimportant to the exclusion of the important. Similarly 'desire' is an intrusion into the 'analyst's' [leader's] state of mind which covers up, disguises and blinds him to, the point at issue" (Bion 1970, p. 69). I will be exploring this further in my clinical example, which follows.

In clarifying the relationship between mystic and group, Bion's alternatives of commensal, one essentially of co-existence and of symbiotic involving confrontation and difficult but essentially growth promoting, may be acceptable in the former and worth the trauma in the latter. Both are preferable to a parasitic, perhaps one might say competitive, relationship which he sums up as, "an explosive force which tries to contain it... and takes place between the 'mystic genius' and the 'Establishment' with its function of containing, expressing and institutionalising the new idea provided by him and of protecting the group from the destructive power of this idea" (Grinberg 1988, p. 188). Main (1975) and Kernberg (1976) made it abundantly noticeable that healthy and even well-trained individuals were not immune from primitive emotional responses in the context of large groups.

The Establishment and the Stranger

Bion (1959) points out that projective identification is the mode of client therapist interaction in the clinical setting, as well as groups. While such a mechanism is developmentally appropriate in children, and also in empathy, its utilisation in group contexts as a thoughtfulness response is a sign of regression. However, what is the purpose of such regression?

It might be argued that an unconscious policy that encourages the use of splitting and pathological projective identification is present. It might further be speculated that it disguises, in a defensive manner, primitive aspects of the self, in this case, the establishment self. This technique would involve the establishment as the ones that know, as opposed to the capacity for not knowing, Bion's negative capability (Bion 1970).

The complex issue lies in the recognition of the projective identifications which aim to attack the object and the projective identification with a communicative intent. Like in the clinical setting, within the organisational context the projection may arise from the group's omnipotence, which sometimes is in syntony with the new leader's wish to be experienced as the messiah or genius. It entails, nonetheless, the experience of a delusional transference.

If the leader does not accept such projections, it all goes well. But there is a challenge to behave as an auxiliary ego, interpreting the pressures experienced as opposed to act on them. Thus, a separation between the new leader and the organisation can be ensured, and opportunities for the organisation to develop its own mind are possible.

The Stranger and the Establishment

The leader also brings with him his/her own personal anxieties. Bringing relevant skills poses a threat to the establishment, forcing the newcomer to hold to their identity, perceptions and ideas. Also to the inevitable disruptive possibilities with the organisation he/she is joining. In Bion's language (1961) the relationship is experienced as parasitic, which carries the risk of affecting (destroying) both parties. Envy has a major role in this aspect, if it is dominating in either the organisational or individual setting. In these cases the establishment loses the opportunity to contain and institutionalise any new ideas, since both sides are under threat of the projective relationship.

Projective processes, and in particular projective identification, are functions connected to objects. These processes, especially when intertwined with the subsequent introjective phase, serve to unite two individuals in a manner akin to Sartre's description. This union often results in an isolating experience of confusion and separateness, as both parties endeavour to establish a secure, conflict-free connection, or alternatively move toward separation as a necessary step to maintain their personal or organisational identities. At the core of both options lies the imperative to find a receptacle for the release of undesirable impulses, particularly those of an aggressive or socially unacceptable nature, such as envy.

Main's encounter with the large group (1975) prompted him to propose that envy plays a central role in understanding these phenomena. Envy, as he suggested, is the ailment associated with impoverishment through projective identification. This envy pertains to the real or phantasised abilities of others, particularly those who appear to retain their thinking capacity along with the positive qualities projected onto them. This leaves the rest of the group feeling depleted and even more envious.

In this light, established organisations, especially when uncertain about their own skills, may seek out the envied stranger among them. Initially, this stranger serves as a safe repository for the organisation's disowned yet fundamentally valuable abilities. Later, the outsider may become an envied rival, effectively becoming the scapegoat.

The concept that envy is deeply entwined with projective identification, involving an intrusion into another person to destroy their most admirable traits, was further developed by Bion (1959). He expanded this understanding from a pathological to a healthier form of the process. Without delving into the distinction between projective identification and projection, it can be said that the former implies projecting a part of the ego, involving a process of splitting. Once projected, these fragments distort the object's perception, as well as the object's perception of themselves.

Clinically, this results in the recipient feeling manipulated into playing a role, albeit one that is often challenging to recognise, in someone else's fantasy – a common experience for leaders and consultants. Both in clinical and organisational contexts, such projective experiences are best not rejected when encountered, nor acted upon or acted out. Instead, they can be used for understanding in the development of what Hinshelwood (1989) terms the "social container" – a structure formed from projective and introjective experiences.

Conclusion

Leadership and containment are not a dichotomy, but an inevitable partnership. The paradigm I offer is that of the maternal figure and infant, engaged first in the illusion of the infant's power to create his/her universe, followed by a gradual disillusion enabling the infant to learn his/her limitations and to survive safely in the environment, i.e. containment. To enable this, the leader needs the capacity for "maternal" reverie, which allows the infant, new employee, to project feelings of concern and to return them detoxified (Bion 1967, p. 116). If not understood and accepted, the infant feels he is dying, the employee feels his concerns have been stripped of meaning and is left with the feeling of nameless dread. This may seem too dramatic and absolute, but in practice it encourages a rejection of acceptance of leadership whether from CEO or consultant (Gold 2003, pp. 1–19).

Acknowledgement

I would like to thank James Krantz, not only for his highly pertinent references in the text, but also for his leadership and especially his containment.

References

Alford, C.F. (2001). Leadership by interpretation and holding. *Org. and Soc. Dynamics* 2: pp. 153–173.
Amado, G. & Elsner, O. (2007). *Leaders in Transition*. Karnac. London.
Bion, W.R. (1959). Attacks on linking. *Int. J. Psychoanal.* 40: p. 315.
Bion, W.R. (1961). *Experiences with Groups*. Tavistock. London.
Bion, W.R. (1962). *Learning from Experience*. Maresfield Reprints. London. p. 42.
Bion, W.R. (1967). A theory of thinking. In *Second Thoughts*. Jason Aronson. New York. p. 101.
Bion, W.R. (1970). The mystic and the group & container and contained. In *Attention and Interpretation*. Tavistock. London.
Bion, W.R. (1977). *The Grid and the Caesura*. Imago Editora. Rio de Janeiro. p. 60.
Bion, W.R. (1978). *Four Discussions with W.R. Bion* (M. Blanchard, ed.). Clunie Press. Edinburgh. pp. 12, 21–22.
Bion, W.R. (1981). Memorial meeting for Dr Wilfred Bion. *Int. J. Psycho-Anal.* 8: pp. 3–14.
Bion, W.R. (1990). *Brazilian Lectures*. Karnac. London.p. 5.
Bion, W.R. (2018) *Bion in New York and Sao Paolo*. The Harris Meltzer Trust. London.
Bion, W.R. (2013). *Los Angeles Seminars and Supervision* (J. Aguayo & B. Malin, eds). Karnac. London. p. 5.
Bridger, H. (2005). The discovery of the therapeutic community. In *The Transitional Approach in Action* (G. Amado & L. Vansina, eds). Karnac. London. pp. 15–39.

Brown, N. (1966). *Love's body*. Berkley, CA. University of California Press. pp. 146/147.

Fairbairn, W.V.R.D. (1943). The repression and the return of the bad objects. *British Journal of Medical Psychology*. XIX. In *Psychoanalytic Studies of the Personality*. Routledge and Kegan Paul. London. (1952). pp. 59–81.

Gold, S. (2003). Swimming with sharks: The politics of survival in the large group. *Org. and Soc. Dynamics* 6: pp. 1–19.

Gold, S. (2006). Are the basic assumptions basic? *Org. and Soc. Dynamics* 6(1): pp. 86–94.

Gold, S. (2014). The impossibility of trust. *Socio-Analysis* 16: pp. 51–64.

Gold, S. (2016). Self and non-self: The persecution of the imaginary scapegoat. *Org. and Soc. Dynamics* 16(2): pp. 198–214.

Grinberg, L. (1975). *Introduction to the Work of Bion*. Clunie Press. Edinburgh. pp. 17–20.

Grinberg, L. (1988). Bion's contribution to the understanding of the individual and the group. In Pines, M. (ed.) (2000) *Bion and Group Psychotherapy*. Routledge & Kegan Paul. London. p. 186.

Grotstein, J.S. (2003). *Building on Bion: Branches* (R. Lipgar & M. Pines, eds). International Library of Psychoanalysis. London. p. 11.

Hinshelwood, R.D. (1979). The community as analyst. In Hinshelwood, R.D. and Manning, N. (eds) (1979) *Therapeutic Communities: Reflections and Progress*. Routledge and Kegan Paul. London. pp. 103–112.

Hinshelwood, R.D. (1989). Projective identification. In *A Dictionary of Kleinian Thought*. Free Association Books. London. pp. 386/387.

Hinshelwood, R.D. (2003). Group mentality and "having a mind". Lipgar, R.M. and Pines, M. (eds) (2003) *Building on Bion – Roots: Origins and Context of Bion's Contributions to Theory and Practice*. Jessica Kingsley Publishers. London. p. 181.

Hirschorn, L. (1990). Leaders and followers in a post industrial age. *J. Applied Behavioural Science* 26(4): pp. 529–542.

Kernberg, O. (1976). *Object Relations Theory and Clinical Psychoanalysis*. Jason Aronson. New York.

Kernberg, O. (1979). Regression in organisational leadership. *Psychiatry* 42(1): pp. 89–107.

Klein, M. (1931). A contribution to a theory of intellectual inhibition. *Int. J. Psycho-Anal.* 12: pp. 206–218.

Klein, M. (1946). Notes on some schizoid mechanisms. In Klein, M. and Riviere, J. (eds) (1989) *Developments in Psycho-Analysis*. Karnac Books and the Institute of Psycho-Analysis. London. pp. 292–320.

Krantz, J. (1990). Lessons from the field: An essay on the crisis of leadership in contemporary organisations. *J. Applied Behavioural Science* 26(1): pp. 49–64.

Krantz, J. (2015) *The Century of the System – FETL, Leaders for Leadership*. https://fetl.org.uk/wp-content/uploads/2016/09/leaders-leadership.pdf. pp. 6–25.

Krantz, J. (2020). Personal communication.

Laing, R.D. (1970). *Knots*. Tavistock. London.

Lawrence, G. (2005).Thinking of the unconscious and the infinite, of society during dark times. *Org. & Soc. Dynamics* 5(1): p. 61.

Lawrence, G. & Armstrong, D. (1998). Destructiveness and creativity in organisational life. In P. Bion-Talmo et al. (eds) *Bion's Legacy to Groups*. Karnac. London. p. 62.

Main, T. (1975). Some psychodynamics of large groups. In L. Kreeger (ed.) *The Large Group*. Constable. London. pp. 57–86.

Meltzer, D. (1981). Memorial meeting. *Int. J. Psycho-Anal.* 8: pp. 3–14.

Menzies Lyth, E. (1970). *The Functioning of Social Systems as a Defence Against Anxiety*. Tavistock. London.

Miller, E. (1998). Are basic assumptions instinctive? In P. Bion-Talmo et al. (eds) *Bion's Legacy to Groups*. Karnac. London.

Rosenfeld, H. (1965). *Psychotic States*. Hogarth. London.

Sandler, P.C. (2003). Bion's War Memoirs. In Lipgar, R.M. and Pines, M. (eds) (2003) *Building on Bion – Roots: Origins and Context of Bion's Contributions to Theory and Practice*. Jessica Kingsley Publishers. London. p. 60.

Sartre, J.-P. and Barnes, H.E. (1956) *Being and Nothingness: An Essay on Phenomenological Ontology*. Philosophical Library. New York. pp. 471–558.

Segal, H. (1981). Memorial meeting. *Int. J. Psycho-Anal.* 8: pp. 3–14.

Simpson, P. & French, R. (2005). Thoughtful leadership. *Org. and Soc. Dynamics* 5(2): pp. 280–297.

Skolnik, M. (1998). Schizophrenia from a group perspective. In P. Bion-Talmo et al. (eds) *Bion's Legacy to Groups*. Karnac. London. p. 72.

Stein, H.F. & Allcorn, F. (2014). Good enough leadership: A model of leadership. *Org. and Soc. Dynamics* 14(2): pp. 342–366.

Winnicott, D. (1974). Fear of breakdown. *Int. Rev. Psychoanal* 1: pp. 103–107.

Winnicott, D. (1987). *The Child, the Family and the Outside World*. Cambridge. Perseus. p. 85.

Winnicott, D. (1989). On the use of an object. In C. Winnicott et al. (eds) *Psychoanalytic Explorations*. Boston, MA. Harvard University Press. pp. 217–227.

Chapter 13

Father, Mother and the Guinea Pig Children

John Diamond

Introduction

This paper explores the experience, meaning and management of an incident at a residential therapeutic community school for severely traumatised and emotionally troubled children. I will analyse this incident with relevant theory to argue my hypothesis that an 'external' social dynamic became 'present' and influenced the inner world of the organisation. I have found the concept of 'applied clinical sensibility' useful in this study:

> Applied clinical sensibility legitimately involves the discriminating use of emotional sensibilities and the analysis of counter-transference type experiences arising from direct contact with social situations.
>
> (Cooper and Lousada, 2005)

A Therapeutic School

The primary task of the school is the care, treatment and education of severely emotionally deprived children of primary school age. (Ward, 2003 p.13) identifies three core issues underpinning therapeutic community work:

- Group care for its account of the overall context and mode of practice.
- Psychodynamic thinking as an underpinning theory, with the concepts of the holding environment and of the therapeutic community as increasingly specific models of practice.
- Systems thinking as a way of holding the whole thing together.

The school operates in recognition of the containment provided through the systemic links between referring authorities, parents and carers of children and the whole (large group) community and its small group sub-systems.

Father, Mother and the Guinea Pig Children

In June 2001, I was appointed as director of the school, due to start in post after the half term holiday that month. My predecessor had resigned after ten years in post. We had worked together on the transition. This process had included informing

DOI: 10.4324/9781315146416-17

staff and children within a manageable time-frame, and providing space for discussion at all levels of the school. I was aware that we would need more opportunities in small and large groups to continue to talk and think about the feelings this change would bring.

During the half term holiday I followed the media coverage and national debate about the potential release of Robert Thompson and John Venables, the two young people involved in the murder of James Bulger in 1993. At the time of the murder both had been aged 10. The reporting ranged from thoughtful discussion about the rehabilitation of offenders, to sensationalism about revenge killings of the two of them.

Issues of care and control (central to the work of the school, where we aspire to consciously work to ensure they reflect and reinforce each other) were polarised and reflected in the national mood for either punishment or rehabilitation of the two boys. The media wondered whether 'such children' should be held in secure or open environments, and whether they were evil, mad, bad or all of these things. As a result of this perceived social climate of splitting between care and control a range of views were shared – "that they should remain locked up and the key thrown away" – but also thoughts about how our society might apply some understanding and compassion to the events – a nation more able to own its own murderous feelings.

And so, with these thoughts and connections having been considered, I returned to work a little apprehensively to start in my new role as director.

I cannot remember much about the first few weeks apart from being very preoccupied with the work and conscious of my newness in this role for staff and children. Despite the usual complexities things seemed to be going relatively smoothly…

At about 8 am on Sunday 17 June, 'Father's Day', I was phoned at home. A senior colleague who had been 'on call' overnight told me the following story. Early that morning, two boys from one of the residential houses, one aged 9, the other 9.5, had quietly dressed themselves, crept downstairs and forced open a window lock in the living room. They had then gone across the field to another of the households. They entered the garden and opened the pen containing three guinea pigs, a white mother and her two brown babies.

They said their original intention was to play with the animals. When the guinea pigs did not respond they killed all three by smashing their heads against the wall of the children's sandpit and hitting them with sticks. They also joked about hanging them from the washing line, but instead, they left the garden with all three bodies. They placed the two babies alongside the wooden fort in the adventure playground. They separated the mother and put her in a 'den' (their own words) among nettles on the other side of the hedge.

Over the next few hours, more news filtered in via the phone, and the implications of the act and the shock waves it created reverberated through myself and the whole school community. This news included the impact:

On those who went looking for the animals, and as the morning light increased and the mist lifted, found the bodies – one adult later remarked it was as though the scene was from a murder story:

Of hearing of adults and children crying together as the children were told the news in anticipation of them making the grisly discovery themselves;

On adults who wept as they attempted to clean the blood off the walls of the sandpit;

Of the symbolic and ritualistic disposal of the bodies, the mother discarded, the children left at the edge of the playground – as though in cynical mockery of the potential of a play space for children.

After discussion with senior staff I decided to maintain a 'reflective' distance from the events of the day, to be able to keep thinking about the implications of the act. I remember mulling over every detail again and again, and returning with each newly accepted piece of information to thinking 'I wish this hadn't happened'. My thoughts ranged from disbelief to fury and revengeful anger. I could no longer calmly and rationally reflect on the psychodynamic meanings of the nation's attitude to Robert Thompson and John Venables, or more thoughtful and measured connections between this current incident and what the two boys had experienced in their early lives, and the recent holiday.

I remembered reading Winnicott writing about children in the wartime evacuation hostels who would murder mice and bury them, so they had a place to mourn their own losses. Here then was an enactment for and on behalf of the whole group, to ensure we all had to think about the change we were part of, and to remind us that loss and change are painful.

Over the following days the two children were kept closely alongside adults, and their families and professional networks informed. After discussion it was decided to run a whole school large group meeting, which I convened, to allow the children and adults to talk about the impact and their feelings. A clear subtext of the meeting was that there were to be no revengeful actions or scapegoating of the boys. We decided to use the theme of the two boys acting out strong feelings which had gone beyond the usual manifestations of verbal and physical intimidation.

Nearly all members of the meeting were able to say something; one memory is of a child who angrily said "why didn't you just hit nettles?" In this respect the meeting allowed for the contained expression of strong feelings. It also allowed everyone to struggle with the tension of owning their own murderous feelings enacted through the desire to exclude the boys, thereby removing the pain of the action with them.

Both boys were able to change and grow significantly over the following years. The incident is a reminder of the importance of therapeutic environments where destructive feelings can be acted out and the resolution managed in a meaningful and contained way. The strong feelings expressed are a reminder of how easy it is to project and to blame. Ultimately, we are lucky that it was animals that were hurt. In the 'outside' world, or in another situation, the consequences of the murderous pairing could have been far more serious.

Commentary and Analysis

My first hypothesis is that the two boys in 'basic assumption pairing' (baP) (Bion, 1961), were acting out an 'undigested' (uncontained) experience of the Bulger murder. This is likely to have been as a result of their unregulated contact with the 'excitement' of the tabloid media story during the holiday. In this sense, the 'social function' of the action could be seen as a communication of their lack of emotional containment.

Bion (1961, p. 72) writes about baP:

> if this behaviour was to be accurately keyed to the emotions of that time and place, then the interpretation needed to be one that gave due weight to the social functions the individuals were performing. I… interpreted their behaviour as a manipulation of the group; they were trying to break up the fight-flight culture by establishing pairing relationships.

Perhaps it could be seen as an anticipative communication of their anxiety about whether I would let the community descend into anarchy and chaos (fight/flight). These inchoate feelings amplified by the recent change of leadership were a testing out, and an avoidance of communication about what this new "paternal - authority" would mean to them – how authoritarian and retributive would my response be:

> in the pairing group the basic assumption made it difficult for any individual to have a conversation with myself.
>
> (1961, p. 73)

The oedipal connotations of the action, killing the mother and siblings, ritualistically separating them (as their right to parenting had been severed) was a sobering reminder of their own circumstances, and heightened the symbolism of the act occurring on 'Father's Day' a commercialised societal expression of 'gratitude' for the perceived role of the father. In this sense the acting out might be seen as an envy of, and a desire for, a father to keep them 'safe' from their own murderous feelings.

The Circulation of Beta-Elements

In *Learning from Experience* (1962) Bion proposes that in early infancy the baby develops a process of 'digestion' of raw sense impressions and proto-mental pleasures and pains, he calls these beta elements. Through alpha function, beta elements are converted into alpha elements (digested experience) which are stored and form a contact barrier which retains and separates emergent conscious and unconscious thoughts and processes. The unwanted beta elements are 'evacuated' through the process of projective identification.

Watson (2002, p. 248) writes:

> what are the implications of Bion's suggestions for thinking about group systems? What would happen if we were to take the group as the unit of analysis? Instead of seeing individuals projecting out parts of themselves into others, we would see assemblages of bodies between which circulate a vast number of affective entities of the type which come under Bion's umbrella term beta-elements.

Following this, it is possible to hypothesise that as society could not digest and contain the experience of the Bulger murder, so its indigestible 'beta elements' were projected out, and 'found' the school as a container. Taking this hypothesis further, the two boys could be seen as carrying the appropriate valency for holding this 'discharge' of intolerable feeling. Why might a therapeutic community school be the container of such projections? Maxwell Jones wrote in 1968:

> The psychiatric hospital (therapeutic community) can be seen as a microcosm of society outside, and its social structure and culture can be changed with relative ease, compared to the world outside.
>
> (p. 12)

So we could interpret the action on two levels – as the boys finding a meaningful receptacle for their confusions about a lack of adult holding of the Bulger material, plus fear of their own murderous impulses, and the school as a social receptacle for society's inability to own, digest or think about its murderous feelings. Ironically, it was two children, who might suffer precisely those projections of being mad or bad who forced the debate and resolution through their action.

> the mentally ill person is seen as a member of an oppressed group, a group deprived of adequate social solutions to the problem of individual growth and development.
>
> (Gray, Duhl & Rizzo, 1969, p. 263)

In the following sections I will look at systems theory, focusing on how the concept of 'boundary' as a 'regulator' might influence the 'flow' or 'exchange' of material from the outside to the inside of individuals, groups and organisations.

Inside and Outside: The Function of 'Boundary' in the 'Open Systems' Model

Miller and Rice (1975) proposed that any 'open system' is defined by its ability to exchange materials with its environment. They applied this concept to understanding the functioning of organisations. This concept was based on a synthesis of the work of Kurt Lewin (1947) and that of von Bertalanffy (1950) who studied biological systems using the second law of thermodynamics as a theory base.

This theory implies that a system promotes a 'stable state' of 'equilibrium' for itself through the exchange of energy with its environment. If this exchange reduces, i.e. it gives off energy that cannot be retrieved, then 'entropy' ("the inverse measure of a system's capacity for change") (Wheatley 2002) resulting in death, is the ultimate outcome and the system is closed.

The open system therefore requires a process of input, conversion and output. In the biological system the "intake" may be food, the 'conversion' to energy, and the "output" waste matter. Analogously, in the school the 'intake' might be seen as anti-social children, the "conversion process" achieved through relationship based therapeutic care, treatment and education, and the 'output' a more integrated child with an improved sense of self, better able to make and sustain relationships.

In their analysis of such systems, Miller and Rice concluded that:

> in the analysis of systems of activities two types of regulatory activity can be identified: monitoring and boundary control.
>
> (1975)

and stated:

> thus a system has a boundary which separates it from its environment.
>
> (p. 46)

Miller and Rice explored this idea of boundary in relation to the mature individual personality, and suggest that the psychoanalytic idea of the ego is that which regulates, and therefore acts as such a boundary between the inner world and the external environment of the individual (pp. 53–54).

In my role as director, and by maintaining a reflective distance from the incident, I feel I was in a position to provide an appropriate or auxiliary ego function for the organisation.

Non-Linear Dynamics

However, the theoretical "orthodoxy" of this theory is currently under challenge. Several writers (Abadi 2003; Cooper and Dartington 2005; Hirschorn 2003) have argued that the bounded organisation is disappearing:

> As systems, organisations are less bounded than they were and the boundaries that exist more permeable. This is true of... their capacity to control exchange with their outside environment. Partnership, collaboration, outsourcing are all contemporary reflections of the trend towards 'networked organisational functioning'.
>
> (Cooper and Dartington 2005, pp. 128–129)

Both Wheatley (2002) and Stacey (2001) have explored Prigogine's (Prigogine 1996, Prigogine and Stengers 1984) "far from equilibrium" thermodynamics which challenges the second law of thermodynamics, by focusing on a system's self organising and emergent capacity. Prigogine demonstrated that disequilibrium is the necessary condition for a system's growth, and named these newly identified systems "dissipative structures". Stacey (2000) has termed these "complex responsive processes":

> only when networks operate in the phase transition – bounded instability – at the 'edge of chaos' that they are capable of evolving, that is producing new patterns of relationship.
>
> (Stacey 2001, p. 96)

This field is known as 'non-linear dynamics' and is increasingly applied to the study of organisations. Stacey argues that the analogue for this process in organisations is free-flowing conversation that is collectively owned, safely contained, and allows for diversity and deviance from the dominant power ideology to produce new forms of relating and creativity. 'Bounded instability' is a useful term, as it captures something of the essence of the incident described and of therapeutic community work generally. The incident might be seen as a catalytic action, which required me, and the community, to find a new way of relating and defining my directorship. However, the school does not operate internally as a networked organisation, it relies on the lived experience and presence of relationships and group work to achieve its primary task.

I will now explore how my role as director at the boundary of the organisation – the interface with the external world allows for a reflection on, and mirroring of, society. This position is analogous to the 'boundary function' of the individual and group described above.

Management at the Boundary

I see my role as director to be strategically positioned to provide 'management at the boundary' (Roberts, 1994, p. 37). The Janus position personifies this – attending to the system's internal and external dynamics whilst remaining at the boundary. I was aware of being conscious of the importance of not being pulled too far in or out, or not returning to the boundary which would imply a loss of effective management. That is why I decided to stay at home and maintain a reflective distance from the events. I was also conscious of helping the organisation to develop this reflective capacity, without dependence on my presence. This position also implies being the "gatekeeper", or "filtering" issues and dynamics from the outside that may influence the organisation's internal task.

One of the tasks, then, for the 'manager at the boundary', is to 'scan' the external environment for information relevant to the task, an emotional vigilance with one's receptive 'antennae' attuned to the links and connections between conscious and unconscious relational and social information, nuances, and details. During the holiday, in preparation for my new role, I applied this clinical sensibility to the debate created by the news of the Bulger case.

> The work of the group is situated on a number of boundaries-between social and individual experience, between conscious and unconscious apprehension of the dynamics of social life, between attention to what is outside of the group and what is unfolding within it, and so on. However it is the emergent preoccupations of the group that are the central object of interest and learning.
>
> (Cooper and Lousada, 2005)

This positioning at the boundary, and use of an applied clinical sensibility, has similarities with the working method of the OPUS (Organisation for Promoting Understanding of Society) "Listening Post" (LP) model.

Society as an Intelligible Field of Study

The proposition that society might be an "intelligible field of study" (Bion, 1961, p. 104) has been developed by OPUS and evidenced from participants' shared experiences and observations as reflective citizens through the medium of "LP" meetings. The aim of an LP is:

> to enable participants as individual citizens to reflect on their own relatedness to society and to try to develop an understanding of what is happening in society at this moment.
>
> (Stapley 2005)

The method of the LP is for a group of 8–15 people to be convened to work associatively in order to experience:

> that the dynamics of the group may be such that even a small group may nevertheless act as if it is a microcosm of the large group that is society... the themes that emerge through associative dialogue may legitimately be analysed for their societal content.
>
> (Stapley 2005)

My proposition is that by applying a clinical sensibility, and using associative dialogue to understand the societal content of the incident, we deepened our understanding of this process, ultimately allowing the incident to be managed and resolved.

Conclusion

I have explained how a convergence of events created a dynamic within the school which reflected an external social issue and preoccupation. I propose that this was because the thoughts, feelings, assumptions, attitudes and recent experiences of individuals were made present in the group, transported or input by membership on arrival from across the boundary. In this sense the organisation was not isolated from society and the boundaries were permeable. Thus any transaction across the boundary will have both a conscious and unconscious effect on the life of the group (or organisation). In this sense, and from the case material I have presented, we can hypothesise that through an understanding based on applied clinical sensibility, the significance of society as an "intelligible field of study" for organisations is understanding how at any time:

Society is present in the group; society and the group are present in the individual.

(Khaleelee and Miller 1985, p. 382)

References

Abadi, S. (2003) Between the frontier and the network: Notes for a metapsychology of freedom. *International Journal of Psychoanalysis*, 84(2): 221–234.

Bion, W. (1961) *Experiences in Groups*. London: Tavistock.

Bion, W. (1962) *Learning from Experience*. London: Karnac.

Cooper, A. & Lousada, J. (2005) *Methodological Reflections: Clinical Sensibility and the Study of the Social. Borderline Welfare: Feeling and Fear of Feeling in Modern Welfare*. London. Karnac

Cooper, A. & Dartington, T. (2005) *The Vanishing Organization: Organizational Containment in a Networked World. Working Below the Surface, the Emotional Life of Contemporary Organizations* (Huffington et al., eds). London: Karnac.

Diamond, J.(2003) Who's in charge here? Managing the mess. *Therapeutic Communities*, 24(1): 5–21.

Gray, W., Duhl, F. & Rizzo, N. (1969) *General Systems Theory and Psychiatry*. Boston, MA: Little Brown.

Hirschorn, L. (2003) *Reworking Authority*. Cambridge, MA, London: The MIT Press.

Jones, M. (1968) *Beyond the Therapeutic Community: Social Learning and Social Psychiatry*. New Haven, CT: Yale University Press.

Khaleelee, O. & Miller, E. (1985) Beyond the small group: Society as an intelligible field of study. In Pines, M. (ed.) *Bion and Group Psychotherapy*. London. Routledge.

Lewin, K. (1947) Frontiers in group dynamics: 1. Concept, method and reality in social sciences; social equilibria and social change. *Human Relations*, 1: 5–41.

Miller, E.J. & Rice, A.K. (1975) Selections from systems of organization. In Colman, A. & Bexton, W. (eds) *Group Relations Reader 1*. Washington, DC: A.K. Rice Institute.

Prigogine, I. (1996) *The End of Certainty*. New York: The Free Press.

Prigogine, I. & Stengers, I. (1984) *Order Out of Chaos; Man's New Dialogue with Nature*. New York: Bantam.

Roberts, V.Z. (1994) The organization of work. In Roberts, V.Z. & Obholzer, A. (eds) *The Unconscious at Work: Individual and Organizational Stress in the Human Services*. London: Routledge.

Stacey, R.D. (2000) *Strategic Management and Organizational Dynamics, the Challenge of Complexity*. 3rd edition. London: Prentice Hall.

Stacey, R.D. (2001) Complexity at the 'edge' of the basic-assumption group. In Gould, L.J. et al. (eds) *The Systems Psychodynamics of Organizations: Integrating the Group Relations Approach, Psychoanalytic and Open Systems Perspectives*. London. Karnac.

Stapley, L. (2005) Flier for a new year's listening post 'Britain and the world at the dawn of 2005', '(Country) and the world at the dawn of 2005'. Notes for convenors, www.opus.org.uk

von Bertalanffy, L. (1950) The theory of open systems in physics and biology. *Science*, 3, 27–29.

Ward, A. (2003) The core framework. In Ward, A., Kasinski, K., Pooley, J. & Worthington, A. (eds) *Therapeutic Communities for Children and Young People*. London: Jessica Kingsley.

Watson, S. (2002) Complexity and the transhuman. *Organisational and Social Dynamics*, 2(2): 245–263.

Wheatley, M.J. (2002) *Leadership and the New Science: Discovering Order in a Chaotic World*. 2nd edition. San Francisco, CA: Berrett-Koehler Publishers.

Chapter 14

The Challenge of Containment

A Psychoanalytic-Systemic Approach

Avi Nutkevitch

Let me begin with a short introduction to the notion of "containment" as I will use the term in this chapter, in the conceptual discussion of an organizational intervention I will be presenting. Originally a military and diplomatic meaning given, there is an interesting definition in Wikipedia where containment is related to as: "A structure or system designed to prevent the accidental release of radioactive materials from a reactor". I liked it since I thought that we can all connect to the idea that often when we are required or challenged as consultants or psychoanalysts or managers or parents to contend with strong and disturbing feelings that are stirred up in us in an interaction with others, we might experience then a centrifugal force inside us that strives to throw out these disturbing and painful feelings; we are in a way aware that "radioactive material" that is created by the storm inside us, might be released and harm the well-being of those whom we may deeply care about: a child, a patient, a partner or a friend. We try what we might to contain the release of radioactivity. We don't always succeed.

The psychoanalytic concept of containment was developed, as described in previous chapters, by Bion in the 50s and 60s. It is a process of psychic "digestion" of what has been projected by the other person via projective identification. To be able to "digest" it requires the capacity for *reverie*. Reverie can be described as being in a state of mental openness and receptivity, a "looseness of thinking", a state which is a "kind of dreaming", or day-dreaming. According to Bion, it is a factor or a necessary condition for the operation of alpha function. It offers the potential for transforming beta elements into alpha elements, a transformation which is crucial in the container–contained model. Reverie, projective identification, digestion, alpha function, transforming beta elements, all are part of the process of containment, and it is a challenge to try and describe them experientially, to try and bring them down from the height of theoretical concepts to the ground of describable experience. Having said that let me turn now to **the challenge I faced some years ago** when I worked as an organizational consultant in a governmental human service organization that dealt with baby and child adoption.

The newly appointed director of the service invited the consultation. Already at the early stages of the organizational diagnosis it turned out that the organization was in a bad state: splits, coalitions, hostile relations and distrust prevailed. The

DOI: 10.4324/9781315146416-18

board of the organization had not been convened for over a year due to the poor re-lations between its members. It felt to me that the underlying hostility and distrust were so fierce and deep that I couldn't see a group exploration of the dynamics that will do anything good. On the contrary, I sensed that such a discussion will explode and I – or rather the consultation that held some hope – will be the victim. Thus, during the first months of my work with the board, I tried mainly to help it formulate its primary task, to decide who belongs to the board and who doesn't, to think and decide about the frequency and length of its meetings, the structure of the meetings, as well as the process of making decisions. I also suggested that they hold a review period at the end of each meeting, with the task of reflecting on how they worked together during that meeting. Following that I helped the di-rector and the board to assimilate these changes, and also worked with the board on other important organizational issues. Whereas I developed a good working relationship with the director, being seen as an extension of her I felt at times a target of hostility, especially coming from two of the more senior members of the board. There were times I felt I had to clinch my teeth and swallow saliva when these board members spoke and behaved in a passive aggressive manner, or in an outright hostile and devaluing manner, especially towards the director but at times towards me too.

It was very clear that the poor interpersonal relationship among members of the board had a highly negative impact on everything taking place at all levels across the organization. Breaches of confidence, hostility and distrust were always pre-sent. I chose as I said not to devote a meeting to these fundamental issues, even though they were apparent and came out in the open from time to time. It was clear that nearly every discussion, no matter how task oriented, was suffused by these dynamics. Over a year passed before it was agreed with the director, at my initiative, that the board would discuss the topic of "trust at work". At that stage of the consultation my working arrangement with the board was such that every two weeks I would spend several hours with it working on a number of chosen topics, after which I would leave and the board would continue with its daily work.

Soon after the discussion on trust began it became difficult, acrimonious and stormy; and it was hard to see how the members of the board could continue to work together, and how they would continue the meeting after I left. I found my role difficult, and as the person responsible for running this part of the meeting, I decided to cancel the discussion on another topic planned for the same meeting. Time past and we approached the ending of this part of the meeting. As we were about 15–20 minutes before the 13:30 ending time there began to be a lot of pres-sure to continue and not to close this part of the meeting at the appointed time. "We just can't stop now, when such harsh things are being said", one of the members said to me in an attacking way. Another board member joined her. The director sat silently. Perhaps they are right, I thought to myself. How can I stop the meeting when the board seems to be in pieces? I felt that my competence and professional-ism were tested. Some board members wanted me to fail: my failure would be the director's failure. I made a big mistake by bringing this topic up for discussion I thought to myself with a somewhat painful feeling of regret. Not only that I skipped a planned topic, but I also skipped the scheduled short break; but it was clear to me that there were many things that hadn't been said, and that the problems in question would not be resolved during that discussion. Yet again I had a thought that to leave the board of these organization "in pieces" felt like a "big problem". For a second I felt like a dysfunctional parent, and had a fleeting thought about the issue of incapable parenting that is so much part of this organization dealing with adoption. I wondered fleetingly: Was this experience of mine projected into me via projective identification? Was I therefore experiencing/carrying an organizational dynamic? How can I end the meeting and leave two board members who were attacked and accused by their colleagues humiliated and/or furious? What should I do? Perhaps I should end on time, my Group Relations self came into action. But, am I being rigid not extending the meeting? I heard the voices inside me telling me that I can be rigid. Some shame for being rigid was creeping up in my mind. I was wondering in myself whether the fact that the two "hostile" board members were challenged by their colleagues – something I thought was important – would influence my decision. While having all those thoughts and feelings, my psychoanalytic-systemic training was raising its voice telling me I must "manage the time boundaries", namely I can't just let it go for more time without saying anything. **I have to make a decision and state it**. It was 13:35 when I said that we won't finish discussing the issues that were raised and that we have to stop the meeting now and continue some other time. There was no time for review. The review section at the end of a meeting that I heralded and with much effort instituted in their meetings didn't take place when **I led the meeting**. Was it a sign I didn't manage things well, that I didn't contain the storm? Everybody in the room seemed to understand that I kept more or less to time boundaries that had been planned, despite the intense hostility in the air.

I left the room disturbed and worried. Did I do the right thing? Is there a right thing? That evening the director called me up to tell me that the meeting the board had after I left was efficient and productive. I obviously felt a relief. Perhaps I did the right thing. Perhaps ending on time was an **act of containment** I thought to myself. Was it?

Here are the experiences I had at that consultation meeting that felt like a stormy whirlpool, can we however connect these experiences with the concepts related to containment?

Was I in a state of reverie? Given the intensity and hostility in that last part of the meeting was I in a state of reverie "under fire"? Isn't fire and reverie contradictory and mutually exclusive? Can they come together? Was I struggling to contain beta elements? Was the way I acted a testimony that beta elements were transformed into alpha elements? Can I say that what I described as my inner thoughts, fleeting feelings and associations are **the work of alpha function**?

Bion's theories and concepts are not easy to comprehend; many may be seen and experienced as abstract and elusive. Yet, the challenge we face is to "bring them to the ground of experience". I believe therefore that indeed my internal state at the meeting represented an attempt of reverie – that receptive, open, a dream-like state of being – even if "under fire". In a way **the challenge of containment is always under fire**. At times repressed or denied or dissociated fire. I want to believe that I got in touch with beta elements, that in my reverie I gave them names – such as shame, incompetence, anxiety – and that process transformed them to mental elements available for thinking, thus alpha elements, that enabled me to take action – ending the meeting more or less on time – that constituted, I believe, an act of containment. Perhaps then that the internal process I described is the work involved in alpha function.

I thought that perhaps one impact of my containment – which means I wasn't destroyed – of the difficult feelings projected into me on the board was that the aggression and intense hostility existing in the board were experienced by the board – unconsciously, I assume – not as destructive and unbearable, that can't be contained, so that it wouldn't be possible to continue the work together. Perhaps they – the board members – might have felt that they are not just destructive, but have also constructive parts that can cooperate and stay together to work.

As we can see **the work of alpha function entails pain**, and requires the capacity to stay in pain. In this respect it's important and interesting to refer to Bion in his *Attention and Interpretation* chapter "container and contained transformed" (Bion 1970, pp. 106–124), one of the two articles – only two – that have containment in their title.

First, he states that the configuration of container and contained – thus containment – is "perhaps the most important mechanism employed by the practicing psychoanalyst". As a psychoanalyst I fully agree with him. As an organizational consultant and director I think that containment is one of the greatest challenges and also principles in taking up these roles. I will develop this idea a bit later, but let me go to Bion who describes the way containment is being actually practiced and experienced in the analytic situation – which is basically the same in any other role.

He writes: "In every session the psycho-analyst should be able – especially with regard to the idea of no memory and no desire – to be aware of the aspects of the material that… is unknown to him… must resist clinging to what he knows… must be in a state of mind analogous to the paranoid-schizoid position". (p. 124) This state of affairs is referred by Bion as a state of "patience". He writes: "I mean this term – patience – to retain its association with suffering and tolerance of frustration" (p. 124). Interestingly to note that the word "patience" comes from the old French word "pacience" which stands also for suffering. I would like to suggest that the stage of "patience" could be seen as "absorbing", as holding things inside, as biting our lips, as is often referred to in daily life as "count to ten before you react". This stage – patience – is necessary but not enough, claims Bion, who continues on to say that: "Patience should be retained without 'irritable reaching after fact and reason' until a pattern evolves. This state is the analogue to what Melanie Klein has called the depressive position" (p. 124).

We can say that the "evolving pattern" is the result of reverie and the work of alpha function; and that **patience and security** are the essence of containment. Patience and the work of alpha function weaved together so that they lead to "security" are containment, or using Bion's words "the oscillation between 'patience' and 'security' are an indication of valuable work", and I would add that this oscillation entails containment.

We can thus say that patiently absorbing and holding what's being projected into us and the subjective parts stirred up in us **is a necessary condition for containment** to take place. **Necessary, but not sufficient**. Reverie and the work of alpha function weaved together with patience constitute containment. **Only patience without the transforming work of alpha function is bound to leak out as "radioactivity"**. In psychoanalysis we might see this leaking out in the form of an enactment by the psychoanalyst. In organizational work we might relate to enactments as "a critical event" that tells the story of non-containment.

Were the fleeting feelings I had of failed parenting, possible rigidity or lack of professionalism a result of the board's projective identification or an expression of sensitivities I brought "from home"? Or perhaps both projected and subjectively produced? Assuming the analyst or the consultant or the manager are not "empty containers", these projected parts into them via projective identification evoke threatening and anxiety-laden parts that belong to their own subjective world. That creates inside them a **complex beta element**: a weaving of the projected part and the subjective part. This complex element I term an **"intersubjective beta element"**. Like any beta element it exerts force to be expelled, to be excluded from one's psyche; hence creating for us – in our various roles – a challenge of containment; but this time in our internal "alpha function work" we can't just say that all unpleasant feelings are the result of projective identification, and may **need than to own** our subjective contribution to **what we experience as the challenge of containment**.

Let me go back to my consultation vignette: I believe I acted in a containing way but what helped me contain? Well, one could say that I was able to face, to stay with, to think about even if in a rudimentary way, feelings, mental elements, intersubjective beta elements. Thus, my psychological makeup and years of analysis enabled me – at least at that time – to contain. Yet, I want to claim that to a significant degree, the boundaries of time, the boundaries of my role and my authority, the boundary of the primary task were crucial for my ability to contain. My internalized Tavi or psychoanalytic-systemic "upbringing" forced me **not to ignore** those boundaries, to think about them, to manage them. I as a container was contained in a way by those boundaries. As I was protecting them they the boundaries protected me. I call it **"The container and its containment"**. There is never complete digestion of beta elements, never finishing the work of alpha function, so that the need to manage boundaries and make decisions accordingly forces us to take an active conscious move or intervention; hopefully what we do is "containing enough". The maximum we can be is "good enough containers".

Following the meeting I described, I said to myself that it wouldn't have been possible to hold such a discussion in the board a year or even six months earlier. It was clear to me that it was the fact that the board had been meeting regularly for about a year, had worked on defining its primary task, the frequency and length of board meetings, had come up with a general structure of meeting, of managing an agenda, of a decision-making process, of a short review at the end of meetings; all that and the fact that with my help the meeting took place regularly helped to create a framework – a container in the language of this paper – that could contain that stormy meeting without "falling apart" and regressing to its pre-consultation condition. Thus, the board was then better equipped to contain itself.

From the Individual to the Organization

So far I have mainly discussed containment in relation to an individual.

Much of Bion's discussions in his articles regarding containment revolve around group and societal processes and are associated with exclusion or inclusion of a threatening individual representing a threatening idea in a group or in society. Bion claims that an individual in a **group** or in society that is perceived as "a genius" or "a mystic", as one that presents unusual ideas, might be experienced as threatening to the group or society. The dilemma facing the group or the establishment in the society in relation to the "mystic" is **inclusion or exclusion**. This tension between inclusion and exclusion represents the main dynamic related to containment both by a group and an individual.

Let's raise our eyes from the individual to the group and the organization. We can thus state that to contain and **containment** are concepts that relate to the capacity of any entity – group, team, department, organization – to **keep within its boundaries and digest** parts that are threatening such as anxiety, shame, envy, competition, helplessness, etc. These parts are the product of projective identification emanating from outside the given entity or are internally produced. These organizational entities can either contain these parts or get rid of them by projecting into an external sub-group, sub-system or an individual. When that happens, the organization may become dysfunctional.

Anton Obholzer and Jon Stokes have written about containment in organizations and organizations as containers. What they stress is that in order for organizations to be "reliable containers" for projections coming from within as well as from the environment, there needs to be a good functioning of the board. For that to take place they recommend continuous work by the board to clarify its primary task, to define roles and authority structures. Many will justifiably claim that clarification of boundaries of task, time, role, authority and decision-making process are important for efficient functioning of the organization, yet what I propose is that clarification and management of these boundaries constitute a kind of a "safety net" for maintaining the containing function of both the person in authority and the group itself. This safety net is man-made, and as such needs to be woven by people, but the very fact of its existence helps the consultant, the psychoanalyst, the manager, maintain their containment ability, and hence the intactness of system/board/group/ any organizational entity that they manage.

However, creating these "safety nets" is looking only at one aspect of their use in organizational life. Organizational entities – and especially entities who have a managerial function – that are clear in terms of boundaries of primary task, time, boundaries of belonging, of roles, of authority, of structure etc., are better equipped to deal with internal and external dynamics, thus better equipped to contain intersubjective beta elements, hence better equipped to serve as organizational containers; something highly needed for the well-being of the organization. Moreover, such organizational containers if they are "good enough" enable people to realize their personal potential, make possible the existence and the inclusion of the "mystic" (see Bion, 1970); enable the expression of the "mystic"/"genius" that is in each one of us; and harness it to the task of that organizational container.

Thinking about the dynamic of creating "safety nets" I recall the Jewish saying that "more than the Jewish people preserve the Sabbath, the Sabbath preserves the Jewish people".

The dialectic that exists between "the preservation of the Sabbath" and the "preservation of the Jewish people" represents the dialectic that exists between measurable boundaries of task, territory, time, decision-making processes etc. – that's how the preservation of the Sabbath goes – where the unspoken and/or unconscious desires, yearnings, rebelliousness and other individual, group and societal unconscious dynamics often threaten these boundaries, hence necessitating the clear definition and adherence to these boundaries in order to preserve the group, thus the preservation of the Jewish people.

The dialectic between boundaries and slippery unconscious defensive processes touches respectively on the dialectic between open systems theory and psychoanalytic theory.

That brings me to the psychoanalytic-systemic approach which guides my discussion regarding containment and the challenge of containment.

The Psychoanalytic-Systemic Approach

The psychoanalytical-systemic approach is a scientific discipline that studies the interrelationships that exist between individual – group – organization and society (Nutkevich, work in progress). It is theoretically based on the weave created by psychoanalytic theory – especially that of Wilfred Bion and Melanie Klein – and by open systems theory in its application to organizations developed by Eric Miller and A.K. Rice (1967). The origin of the ideas underlying the approach in its conceptual and applied aspects were developed at the Tavistock Institute of Human Relations in London since its establishment in 1947, and later on since 1995 in the two-year program for Organizational Consultation and Development: A Psychoan-alytical-Systemic Approach, based in Israel.

Any organizational phenomenon relating to the individual holding a role, or a department or a team or the organization as a whole, is explored through two main prisms: 1) that which is based on concepts emanating from psychoanalytic theory such as projective identification, splitting, envy, jealousy, anxiety, defense against anxiety as well as valency and the pool of the anonymous contributions – two concepts taken from Bion's psychoanalytic group theory. 2) Concepts emanat-ing from open systems theory such as boundaries, role and primary task which accompanies open systems theory. However, these two prisms or theories weave together and create a "third entity" which is represented by the "hyphen" of the "psychoanalytic – hyphen – systemic approach". The hyphen is both a dividing line and a connecting line, and requires the binocular shifts between a psychoana-lytic point of view, an open systems point of view, and a combined psychoanalytic and systemic point of view.

In the background of the psychoanalytic-systemic approach is the more known approach developed at the Tavistock Institute by Eric Miller in the late 1980s named "systems psychodynamics". This approach is using psychoana-lytic theory, open systems theory and concepts associated with what's called Group Relations as the basis of the approach to study and understand organiza-tions as well for organizational consultation and training for leadership. The main emphasis, as the name "systems psychodynamics" seem to indicate, is on the role psychodynamic/psychoanalytic theory has in understanding systems and organizations. Whereas the "psychoanalytic-systemic approach" relates to the two "branches" – psychoanalytic and open systems theory – as two equal theories, as well as postulating a "conceptual third" represented by the "hyphen" in understanding organizational phenomena and in organizational consultancy and development.

In Figure 14.1 at the end of the chapter, one can see the various concepts associated with each branch as well as what can be on the hyphen. What we focused on in this chapter in relation to the hyphen is what's defined in the diagram as the "**container and its containment**" and "**the drama of taking a role**".

Some Thoughts Regarding the Role of the Organizational Consultant

We have discussed so far the process involved in containment both in relation to the individual and in relation to the organization. What does it mean in terms of organizational consultation?

An organizational consultant working with the aim – which is recommended – of assisting organizations and their managers in creating and managing "organiza-tional containers" is operating from a psychoanalytic perspective, from an open systems perspective as well as from a **psychoanalytic-hyphen-systemic perspective**. Helping the board of an organization in the process of formulating its tasks and roles, in establishing meeting procedures regarding time, frequency, agenda setting, decision-making processes etc., may seem to be focusing on "technical" and "practical" issues, on "open systems" concepts which are associated with traditional organizational consultation. However, dealing with these issues that are related to open systems theory, we are to a no lesser degree guided by and applying psychoanalytic understandings. The emphasis a consultant places on the structure and design of organizational entities constitutes a pivotal factor in organizational consultancy guided by a psychoanalytic-systemic perspective. This emphasis on primary task, boundaries, on structure and design in no way disregards the need for understanding, relating to and working on unconscious processes on the level of the individual, the group, the organization and the processes associated with society at large. Anxieties, defense mechanisms and defensive structures (Menzies, 1959) are extremely important conceptual prisms through which we gain understandings regarding what is happening, to decide upon a consultative intervention and to navigate through the complex and often difficult terrain of the consultative process.

Concluding Thoughts

A question that might be on people's minds is: what can help each one of us to be able to contain? Or rather, to contain more times?

I already said that one's personality is crucial in one's ability to contain, yet, I also talked about the "safety net" of boundaries that could also be crucial at times in our daily struggles to contain.

So, let me mention a few things that I believe can be helpful:

1 Training ourselves to be in a position of reverie, a position of internal openness and receptivity where there is "no memory, no desire and no understanding".
2 In any work related situation when relevant: define a primary task and establish time, space and other relevant boundaries.
3 Learning theoretically and experientially (Group Relations Conferences and other experiential events) the psychoanalytic-systemic perspective/discipline. The idea of the relatedness between the part and the whole can help us think about **our** experiences not only as personal but as "systemic". Ask yourself: whose is the painful shame that **I** experience?
4 Keep in mind that containment is not just absorbing painful feelings, but it involves digestion – alpha function – and a containing act can be that of setting a firm boundary.
5 Our reverie can bring us at times to decide to own our part in the dynamics that has evolved. Such owning can be an expression or actually an act of containment.

Psychoanalytic Theory	Hyphen	Open Systems Theory
In relation to: **The Individual** • The unconscious • Appearances of Uncs • Anxiety • Defenses • Projection • Splitting • Projective identification • Envy/competition • Containment • Transference • Counter transference • Uncs field/matrix • Enactment • Paranoid schizoid/ depressive position **The Group** • Valency • Group as a whole • Projective identification in groups • Basic assumptions • Relatedness **The Organization** • Extrapolation from group to organization • Organization in the mind • Container for societal anxieties • The "systemic" process • Relatedness **The Environment** • Societal phenomena associated with BA dynamics	**Primary Task** and its vicissitudes **Social Defenses** The **Container** and its **Containment** **BA Groups** vs **Work Groups** **Authority** and its **Sources** **Leadership** The **Drama** of taking a **Role**	• Primary task • Open system: Input/Conversion/Output • Boundaries (role, time, territory, responsibility etc.) • Role

Figure 14.1 Psychoanalytic-systemic approach/discipline
Source: © Avi Nutkevitch, PhD

References

Bion, W. (1970) *Attention and Interpretation*. London: Karnac Books.

Menzies, I.E.P. (1960). A case-study in the functioning of social systems as a defence against anxiety: A report on a study of the nursing service of a general hospital. *Human Relations*, *13*(2), 95–121.

Miller, E. and Rice, A.K. (1967) *Systems of Organisation: Task and Sentient Systems and Their Boundary Control*. London: Tavistock Publications.

Nutkevich, A. (work in progress) *The Historiography of the Psychoanalytic-Systemic Approach*.

End Note

By this point, you, the reader, will have concluded that there is a flourishing creativity in the thinking about how psychoanalysis shines insight onto organisations and their appropriate and inappropriate functioning. Arising from the experience of people who have drawn on either their experience of working in an organisation or of consulting to one, these chapters represent a variety of directions that an approach to applying psychoanalysis is taking. Whilst the original impetus was to explore the way containing human stress and suffering often fails, and is failed by the organisational culture, leading to socially organised forms of practice, the result in this book has been a wide-ranging survey of this thoughtful landscape. Even if it may seem to some that the complex of experiences and ideas is too varied to assimilate easily, it provides a stimulus to further clarify and develop the understanding of how the unconscious of human minds contributes and adds to, or subtracts from, the collaboration and achievement of working together.

Crucially the way that organisations and institutions inhibit their own work is a vitally important form of investigation. The hidden role of the unconscious mind cannot be emphasised too much as it puts obstacles in the way of human collaboration that we always need to recognise. At the same time, the intuitive creativity that so frequently bursts mysteriously from the unconscious when conditions are right needs to be maximised. As the recognition of institutionalisation from 70 or more years ago showed, the removal of so many mental capacities of so many people remains of critical importance in all organisations. The containing function of colleagues and of organisational cultures is a paramount priority for maximising the potential to work collaboratively. Failing containment, with a degeneration into social organised and imposed defences, needs to move up the list of priorities in all who lead and organise our collective working.

It is not easy to end a book. There were many questions answered, but those simply raise even more questions. It was possible to see the origins of the concept and address some of its applications. But it is also true that not all possibilities were explored. The book does not explore the always present problems regarding mental hospitals and prisons, and the roles they play for society. Containment of madness in locked institutions has certainly been a theme for practitioners work-ing in the field of mental health organisations. Prisons seem to play a similar dilemma.

It is also important to notice that we did not dive into the problem of group therapy, especially what makes for successful or unsuccessful containment in this respect, a problem that is at the core of the preoccupations of group therapists. All in all there is room for more work to be done in the field, and even for different perspectives to come to the fore.

As a final note, this book would not have been possible without the authors' understanding and their receptiveness to our comments and suggestions. We would also like to acknowledge Routledge in the process, and also their unwavering sup-port for the book. Finally, to the readers, we hope you find this book as enjoyable to read as it was to edit.

Index

Locators in *italic* indicate figures and in **bold** tables.

For Product Safety Concerns and Information please contact our EU
representative GPSR@taylorandfrancis.com
Taylor & Francis Verlag GmbH, Kaufingerstraße 24, 80331 München, Germany

www.ingramcontent.com/pod-product-compliance
Ingram Content Group UK Ltd.
Pitfield, Milton Keynes, MK11 3LW, UK
UKHW021842240425
457818UK00007B/263